W9-CEH-171

Closing the Literacy Gap

Thomas G. Gunning

Central Connecticut State University, Adjunct Professor

Southern Connecticut State University, Professor Emeritus

PEARSON

Boston • New York • San Francisco • Mexico City • Montreal • Toronto
• London • Madrid • Munich • Paris • Hong Kong • Singapore •
Tokyo • Cape Town • Sydney

To my wife, Joan Marie Gerben Gunning, who
kept me going when **Closing the Gap** *was more of*
a challenge than I bargained for.

Series Editor: Aurora Martínez Ramos
Series Editorial Assistant: Kevin Shannon
Senior Marketing Manager: Krista Clark
Editorial-Production Service: Helane M. Prottas/Posh Pictures
Electronic Composition: Silver Graphics/Dayle Silverman
Composition and Manufacturing Buyer: Andrew Turso
Cover Administrator: Kristina Mose-Libon

Copyright © 2006 by Pearson Education Inc.

All rights reserved. No part of the material protected by this copyright notice may be reproduced or utilized in any form or by any means, electronic or mechanical, including photocopying, recording, or by any information storage and retrieval system, without the written permission of the copyright owner.

Library of Congress Cataloging-in-Publication Data
Gunning, Thomas G.
  Closing the literacy gap/Thomas G. Gunning.
    p. cm.
  Includes bibliographical references and index.
  ISBN 0-205-45626-X
    1. Reading—Remedial teaching.   2. Literacy programs.
    3. School improvement programs
  I. Title.

LB1050.5.G848 2005
372.43—dc22

2005047513

Printed in the United States of America
10 9 8 7 6 5 4 3 2 1   05 04 03 02 01 00

Contents

5   *Building Higher-Level Thinking Skills and Comprehension*   **57**

8   *Phonological Awareness and Word Analysis*   **117**

11   *Organizing to Close the Gap*   175

Preface

This text is written for anyone interested in closing the literacy gap between those who achieve and those who don't. You might be a classroom teacher, the reading/language arts coordinator, the reading specialist, the learning disabilities teacher, or the superintendent of schools. The suggestions in this text will work better if a whole school or, better yet, if an entire district implements them. But they will also work if they are implemented by just one teacher in a school. Many of the suggestions are expressed in such a way that they involve the whole school. However, most can be applied by the classroom teacher at the classroom level. Even if you are going it alone, you can improve the program in your classroom and the literacy of your students. If you are going it alone, ideally you will be able to persuade others to join you. In unity, there is additional learning.

The text begins by highlighting the nature and causes of the gap. Chapter 2 features descriptions of programs in which schools with high levels of poverty had high levels of proficiency. Based on the characteristics of these schools and the research in this area, key elements for an effective program are explored. Chapter 3 discusses the concept that a literacy improvement program is built upon assessment. Because language is the foundation of literacy, Chapter 4 highlights the importance of building language, especially vocabulary. Chapter 5 discusses ways in which higher-level thinking and comprehension skills are built. Chapter 6 focuses on building background, which leads into Chapter 7. Chapter 7 emphasizes using wide reading to build both background and skills. Chapter 8 lays out the building blocks for a systematic program of word analysis. With its emphasis on affective factors, Chapter 9 is the heart of the program. Chapter 10 talks about ways in which resources, such as tutoring, summer school, after-school programs, preschool, and kindergarten, might help close the gap. Chapter 11 discusses organizational factors that might be optimized. The last chapter, Chapter 12, draws on all the previously introduced elements to put together a program of literacy improvement.

Throughout the book, checklists are provided so that you can assess and plan a program that helps underachieving students close the gap. The underlying philosophy of the book is that closing the gap is possible, but that it requires optimizing every aspect of the literacy program. The degree that the gap can be closed depends upon the degree to which the best possible literacy program has been created and implemented.

Acknowledgments

My sincere gratitude to Aurora Martínez Ramos, series editor, and Kevin Shannon, editorial assistant, for their invaluable assistance. Special thanks, too, to the following reviewers for their insightful suggestions: Stephanie Kirby, Metro Nashville School System; Susanne Lapp, Florida Atlantic University; and Maureen F. Ruby, Red Gem Educational Services.

1

The Literacy Gap

The literacy gap is a persistent, pervasive, and significant disparity in educational achievement and attainment among groups of students. A gap exists between middle and lower class students, racial and ethnic majority and minority students, and disabled and nondisabled pupils (Closing the Achievement Gap Section, 2004). According to National Assessment of Educational Progress (NAEP) data, the gap between black and white children's reading achievement scores was reduced by at least 30 percent between 1971 and 1989 (Jencks et al., 1998). Unfortunately, since that time, the gap has remained virtually unchanged (Donahue, Daane, & Grigg, 2003). A gender gap also exists. Girls outscore boys in reading and writing, and the gap grows wider as boys and girls move up through the grades.

Dimensions of the Gap

The gap starts early. At eighteen months, all children have an equal vocabulary, regardless of the educational or economic status of their families (Hart & Risley, 1995). However, after that, vocabulary growth starts to diverge. By age three, the gap is noticeable. Other indicators of the literacy gap include the following.

- By the time children enter kindergarten, 66 percent of students can recognize the letters of the alphabet. However, only 41 percent of children whose caregivers are receiving welfare can recognize the letters of the alphabet (West, Denton, & Germino-Hausken, 2000).

- According to the Early Childhood Longitudinal Study, students who enter kindergarten with one or more risk factors start out behind children with no risk factors and gain less through third grade in reading than do students who have no risk factors (Wirt et al., 2004). Family risk factors include household income below poverty level, non-English primary home language, mother's highest education less than a high school diploma/GED, and single-parent household. Children with two or more risk factors have lower reading achievement scores than children with just one risk factor. Boys start out slightly behind girls and stay behind. African American children perform below other groups. The gap between those with no risk factors and those with two or more risk factors at the end of third grade is estimated to be about six months in reading.
- According to the 2003 NAEP report, by the end of grade 4, African American, Latino, and poor students of all races are already two years behind other students in reading (Donahue, Daane, & Grigg, 2003).
- By the end of grade 8, African American, Latino, and poor students are more than two years behind other students in reading.
- Fourth-grade students who are identified as having physical or mental disabilities are about three years behind in reading. Eighth-grade students with disabilities are about four years behind.
- Fourth-grade Limited English Proficient (LEP) students are about three years behind other fourth-grade students in reading. Eighth-grade LEP students are about four years behind. (LEP students are English language learners (ELLs) whose English is so limited that they cannot participate effectively in the regular curriculum.)
- In grade 4, NAEP reading scores between boys and girls differ by nearly one year. By grade 8, the difference grows to a full year.
- Boys have a more negative attitude toward recreational and academic reading (McKenna, Kear, & Ellsworth, 1995). For recreational reading, the gap widens with age.
- More girls than boys complete high school, and females make up almost 60 percent of college students.

Beyond Test Scores

Although test scores, such as those from NAEP, highlight the gap, they do not give a complete picture. As Ceci and Williams (Jencks et al., 1998) explain,

> While we do want equity in test scores, what we want even more is equity in individuals' abilities to use their minds well. Because test scores are only an indirect and partial proxy for true mental muscle, policies aimed at boosting scores do not always overlap with policies for building minds. For example, in recent years several states and many school districts have renewed their efforts to retain students whose test scores are inadequate. Yet as research has demonstrated, retention

undermines achievement and dramatically increases the chance of dropping out. Given existing differences in blacks' and whites' achievement scores, this politically popular policy will perpetuate the gap rather than close it.

Schools That Fail to Make AYP

Another indicator of the literacy gap is the number of schools that do not make adequate yearly progress (AYP). According to NCLB, 100 percent of all students are expected to reach a proficient level in math and reading/language arts, as determined by state tests, by school year 2013–2014. The starting date was 2001–2002. This gives schools twelve years to meet the goal of 100 percent. Each state sets its own initial standards. In most instances, the initial standard is the percentage of students at the proficient level who are in the school at the 20th percentile in the state. In other words, the state ranks all the schools by percentage of proficiency. It then counts upward until it reaches 20 percent of total enrollment. The percentage of students proficient in that school is the starting point. Because the 20th percentile was chosen as a starting point, approximately 20 percent of the schools will have to improve to meet the starting standard.

Schools are required to make AYP toward meeting the goal. If underperforming schools fail to meet AYP for two years in a row, they are subject to corrective action. Not only must the student body as a whole make AYP, but each subgroup must also make AYP. Subgroups include economically disadvantaged students, major ethnic and racial groups, students with disabilities, and LEP students. Some schools with overall high achievement might be cited because their ELL or economically disadvantaged students are not making adequate progress. However, there is a safe harbor provision. Schools will not be cited if the percentage of nonproficient students in the group (subgroup or entire school) is reduced by 10 percent from the previous year, and the group also meets the requirement for an additional indicator of progress, such as an increase in writing scores. About 13 percent of all Title I Schools (6,000) have been identified as being in need of improvement. These are schools that have failed to make AYP for at least two years in a row (Center on Education Policy, 2005). To reach the goal of 100 percent proficiency by 2013–2014 , schools will be required to have a higher percentage of students reaching the proficiency level on state tests. The required percentage rose in 2005–2006 and will continue to rise every two or three years until it reaches 100 percent.

Causes of the Gap

Major causes of the literacy gap fall into two categories: society-related and school-related. A key society-related cause is poverty. Associated with poverty is poor health care, high mobility, limited literacy resources in the home, limited resources for building skills, and fewer background experiences needed for school (Educational Research Service, 2004). Children living in families that fall below the poverty level are less likely to participate in preschool education than children in families living at or above the poverty level. The difference in rates of participation between children from poor and nonpoor families was 12 percentage points in 2001 (47 versus 59 percent) (Wirt et al., 2004). Parents living in poverty often have limited educations and so may be less able to foster academic development. Unfortunately, schools that have large numbers of economically disadvantaged students are often educationally disadvantaged. They tend to have less qualified teachers, fewer materials, inadequate funding, and lowered expectations (Educational Research Service, 2004).

Student versus Teacher Perceptions of Causes of the Gap

In an article entitled "Helping All Students Achieve: Closing the Achievement Gap," Kati Haycock (2001) of the Education Trust contrasted the attitudes of teachers with those of students as they viewed the causes of the gap. Teachers made comments such as "They're too poor." "Their parents don't care enough." "They come to school without an adequate breakfast." "They don't have enough books in the homes" (p. 8). However, students had a different response.

> They talk about teachers who often do not know the subjects they are teaching. They talk about counselors who consistently underestimate their potential and place them in lower-level courses. And they talk about principals who dismiss their concerns. And

BOX 1.1 *NCLB: Personal Perspective*

The impact of NCLB can be quite dramatic. Before receiving a Reading First grant, Urban Public had a reading program that consisted of an out-of-date basal. (Urban Public is the fictitious name of a composite of several elementary and middle urban schools where the author was a consultant or observer.) Although there was some differentiation, much of the instruction at Urban Public was whole-class. Apart from standardized tests and state competency tests administered yearly, there was no systematic program of assessment and no reading consultant or reading specialist. Classroom libraries were limited, and there was no school library. Reading First and some generous donors bought Urban Public a new library. Reading First funds purchased a new scientifically based literacy program, intervention programs, tutors, two literacy coaches, a carefully designed assessment system, and, most important of all, extensive professional development. Needless to say, reading and writing skills improved dramatically.

they talk about a curriculum and a set of expectations that feel so miserably low-level that they literally bore the students right out of their minds. (p. 8)

The students admit that poverty makes learning harder. "But," they say, "what hurts us more is that you teach us less" (p. 8). As Haycock concludes, "It's not that issues like poverty and parental education don't matter. Clearly they do. But we take the students who have less to begin with and then systematically give them less in school" (p. 8).

Role of NCLB in Closing the Gap

NCLB was designed to close the achievement gap. NCLB mandates that states have a set of standards and accountability systems that measure students' progress toward meeting those goals. Most states agree with the goals of the law and also agree that setting high standards and having an accountability system in place that measures progress toward meeting those goals will result in higher achievement and will help close the achievement gap (Center on Education Policy, 2005). States are working hard to meet the provisions of the law. They are taking steps to improve assessment and instruction and to increase the qualifications of teachers and paraprofessionals. Efforts to improve instruction through curriculum revision, new materials and techniques, and professional development had been initiated before the passage of NCLB. However, NCLB has intensified these efforts and has also focused on the most disabled readers and writers. Although most states were optimistic that their efforts would increase the achievement of all groups of students, some believed that the gains would be only temporary or, because of an overemphasis on test preparation, would exist only on paper. Some feared that an increase in test scores would not mean that students had actually increased their levels of achievement (Center for Education Policy, 2005).

Despite its stringent requirements, NCLB is having a positive effect. Schools identified as needing improvement are taking steps to help students. There is an increased use of assessment to help plan instruction, curriculum and assessment are being aligned with standards, and more schools are offering after-school, Saturday, and summer sessions. Increasingly, research is being used to determine decisions about improvement strategies. More than half the schools have a research-based program (Center on Education Policy, 2005).

Composition of Your Class or School

What is the composition of your class, school, or district? How many students do you have who might fall into one of the major at-risk categories? Fill in Table 1.1 to get an overview of how many at-risk students you might be working with.

TABLE 1.1 *Analysis of Students by Category*

Student Categories	Number of Students	Number Making at Least a Year's Growth in Reading	Number Achieving Proficiency in Reading	Number Making at Least a Year's Growth in Writing	Number Achieving Proficiency in Writing	Number Being Given Extra Help in Classroom	Number in Special Programs
Racial/Ethnic Group							
American Indian							
Asian American							
Black							
Latino							
White							
Other Race							
Other Categories							
Disabled							
Nondisabled							
Limited English Proficient							
English Proficient							
Economically Disadvantaged							
Economically Nondisadvantaged							

2

Programs That Close the Gap

Schools That Beat the Odds

There is no shortage of schools that beat the odds. About 4,500 schools have been classified as being high-poverty and/or high-minority schools but have high performance. In these schools that beat the odds, students' reading and/or math performance was in the top third among all schools in the state at the same grade (Education Trust, 2004). The schools also met either one or both of the following: the percentage of low-income students in the school was at least 50 percent and ranked in the top third of schools at that grade level; and/or the percentage of African American and Latino students in the school was at least 50 percent and ranked in the top third of schools at that grade level. Based on these criteria, the Education Trust identified

3,592 high-performing, high-poverty schools;
2,305 high-performing, high-minority schools; and
1,320 high-performing, high-poverty-and-minority schools.

Altogether, these schools educate approximately 2,070,000 public school students, including about 1,280,000 low-income students; about 564,000 African American students; and about 660,000 Latino students.

90/90/90 Schools

In 90/90/90 schools, 90 percent or more of the students are eligible for free or reduced-price lunches and are members of ethnic minority groups, but also meet academic standards in reading or another area (Reeves, 2000). These schools have the following features.

- Focus on academic achievement
- Clear curriculum choices
- Emphasis on nonfiction writing
- Collaborative scoring of student work by teachers
- Frequent assessment of student progress and multiple opportunities for improvement

Assessment works best when it is tied into instruction and the attitude that all students can learn if given adequate instruction and whatever assistance they need. Assessment becomes a blueprint for instruction rather than a judgment. In 90/90/90 schools, there was frequent assessment of student progress with multiple opportunities for improvement. In many instances, assessments were weekly and were constructed by classroom teachers. Since many of the students in these schools were struggling readers and writers, they often did poorly on assessments. However, the consequence of a poor performance was not a low grade or a sense of failure but additional instruction and practice. Students were provided with instruction and practice until they achieved proficiency. As a result, not only did they master skills, they also began to see themselves as competent learners.

Characteristics of Schools That Beat the Odds

In their study of successful schools, Mosenthal, Lipson, Sortino, Russ, and Mikkelsoen (2002) found commonalities in diversity. The schools differed in location, nature of student body, and approach used. Some schools were located in upscale areas, others were in poor rural areas, and some were in urban areas. Approaches also differed. Some used a literature approach; other used basals. Others used a combination of approaches. What mattered more than the specific approach was how well the approach was implemented. Regardless of the program adopted, successful schools had a balanced approach in which all major areas of literacy received intensive attention.

Effective Teachers

The foundation of successful schools is the teacher. "In our research sites, success is a function of teachers' commitment, knowledge, and expertise across the grades within a school" (Lipson, Mosenthal, Mekkelsen, & Russ, 2004, p. 537). Effective teachers had effective classroom management. In addition to maintaining an orderly room, teachers were able to orchestrate a variety of activities so that students were engaged in worthwhile reading and writing tasks. Grouping and instruction were multifaceted and included whole-class instruction, small-group instruction, and independent work at centers or with reading buddies (Lipson et al., 2004).

In schools that beat the odds, teachers have a sense of shared mission and responsibility. They work together and do whatever it takes to help all children learn. A teacher at T. W. Ogg Elementary School, which was honored as a National Title 1 School, explains:

> Very few people, if you ask them to do something in this school, balk at doing it. . . . They are more than willing to do it if they possibly can and that includes coming early, staying late, whatever it takes. Because, like we say, children come first. . . . They're willing to come and give that extra time and extra effort if it'll pull these kids up where they need to be. (Council of Chief State School Officers, 2002, p. 10)

Principles of Successful Teaching

Both effective and ineffective teachers teach skills explicitly. However, effective teachers follow up the group teaching of skills with individual help for students who need it and with on-the-spot lessons (Pressley, Wharton-McDonald, Raphael, Bogner, & Roehrig, 2002). Effective teachers probe students' responses instead of simply calling on a second student when the first student fails to respond satisfactorily. One set of researchers found that teachers' careful probing helped students in economically disadvantaged classes to answer questions successfully 80 percent of the time (Taylor, Pearson, Clark, & Walpole, 2002). The most effective teachers also coach students in the use of strategies, such as looking for familiar parts in an unknown word (Taylor, Pearson, Clark, & Walpole, 2002).

Not only do students in the most effective classes spend more time on task, they spend the greatest proportion of time on the tasks that have the highest payoff. For example, when writing and illustrating a piece about eggs hatching, students guided by a highly effective teacher spend more time on the writing than they do on the drawing of the illustrations (Pressley et al., 2002).

The most effective teachers integrate reading and writing with content (Pressley et al., 2002). There is also a greater buildup of interest in the most effective classrooms. In a highly effective classroom, for example, students might watch as eggs hatched and then read, discuss, and write about what they had seen. In a less effective class, the students might only answer questions about a chart that displays the hatching process.

The most effective teachers build students' independence. They encourage them to take charge of the learning: to take steps to decode unfamiliar words, to be aware when text doesn't make sense and to take corrective action, and to check over pieces of writing (Pressley et al., 2002; Taylor, Pearson, Clark, & Walpole, 2002).

Successful teachers also foster extensive reading. On average, teachers in successful schools have classroom libraries of five hundred or more books. More importantly, the teachers make the books readily available to students so that actual reading becomes a focus (Lipson et al., 2004). Students in effective schools spend 50 percent more time reading independently (Taylor, Pearson, Clark, & Walpole, 2002).

Developing Expertise in All Teachers

Although schools vary in the amount of progress their students make, variability within a school is often greater than the variability between schools. One way of closing the literacy gap is taking steps to improve the quality of instruction so that the weakest teachers start getting the same type of results as the best teachers (Hill

& Crévola, 2000). For a school to be highly effective, it is not necessary that every teacher have a high level of expertise (although, of course, this would be helpful). In one set of schools judged to be highly effective, only about half the faculty was listed as being highly effective (Taylor, Pearson, Clark, & Walpole, 2002).

Effective Administrators

Effective teachers are supported by effective administrators. The administrators at T. W. Ogg Elementary School encourage a sense of shared mission and responsibility (Council of Chief State School Officers, 2002). Teachers at that school are also encouraged to suggest and implement new ideas. The fourth-grade teachers instituted a highly successful team-taught writing program. The administrators also built teacher capacity. Another example occurred at Loma Terrace, which was named as a National Title 1 School. Recognizing that the special education teachers had specialized skills and knowledge, the principal of Loma Terrace arranged for the special education teachers to attend training sessions and to share what they had learned with the rest of the staff.

> We're lucky enough to have [a principal] that will let you try an idea. He'll always say, "We'll try it your way, but if it doesn't work we're going to go back and try another way." Well, that was all he could do. We only had 75 percent of our kids passing writing, . . . so he let us try it and our scores went from 75 passing to 90 passing the first year, so that was a pretty good indication we could do something. He's worked with us ever since. He gave us our common planning time where we could plan together and work together, and it changes every year. We change it every year. It will never be set in stone because you get a different group of kids every year. (Council of Chief State School Officers, 2002, p. 64)

Speaking of the school's cooperative spirit, teachers at Loma Terrace explain:

> If we don't have enough strategies to reach this child, then we talk with a team member who we feel is successful, and we try some of [that teacher's] strategies. Then if the team member doesn't have [a strategy that works] we throw it out on the table and say, "What do you have that worked in the past for a child with this type of behavior or this kind of learning problem?" (Council of Chief State School Officers, 2002, p. 78)

Children-First Philosophy

All of the highly effective schools use a children-first philosophy. They emphasize meeting the needs of each child. Teachers and support staff are quick to note learning difficulties that crop up and to provide needed assistance. These types of schools have student support teams that meet to discuss ways of helping students who aren't succeeding. However, teachers at Baskin go the extra mile. Baskin, which was cited for beating the odds, has an Adopt-a-Student program in which staff members agree to look after students who continue to struggle despite having been provided with extra help. They check the students daily to see how they are doing and offer encouragement and support (Council of Chief State School Officers, 2002).

Sense of Common Purpose

Many schools succeed despite being in high-poverty areas and having limited resources. To determine the characteristics of such schools, the Department of Education commissioned a study of nine high-performing urban public elementary schools (Johnson, 2002). Not only did these schools perform better than similar urban schools, they surpassed many affluent suburban schools.

Although they differed in location and approach, the nine successful schools had a number of factors in common. Chief among these was creating a sense of common purpose. Faculty were described as families or teams. Their focus was on helping children learn. Prior to improvement efforts, much of the teachers' energies had been devoted to settling conflicts. Through examples, discussions, meetings, and constant reminders, the schools' leaders led teachers, paraprofessionals, parents, and community members to rise above their personal concerns and focus on helping children succeed. The refocusing fostered improved working relationships. Feeling more valued and appreciated, the staff began treating students in a more caring fashion. As Johnson (2002) comments, "Visitors to these schools quickly sense that teachers and other staff members genuinely love and care for students" (p. 101). Needless to say, discipline also improved.

But it wasn't just words or a sense of caring that created a sense of common purpose; at each of the schools teachers helped plan and implement the school's program. Their input was sought and utilized. A "we're all working together" spirit was created. All staff members were involved in working to solve the school's problems, seeking solutions, and implementing a schoolwide improvement program.

Part of the building of a common sense of purpose was providing opportunities for teachers to work together. Time was set aside for teachers to meet. In some schools, this occurred during the school day. In others, it occurred before school or after school. Principals juggled schedules to create convenient times for meetings.

Key components of bringing about significant improvement in students' learning include selecting elements that are substantial enough to make a difference in key areas of students' learning, effective staff development, adequate implementation, and goal setting and monitoring (Joyce & Showers, 2002). Significant change in a reading program might be implementing a voluntary reading initiative, a new system of assessment, new materials, or a new approach to teaching comprehension, such as reciprocal teaching.

Small-Group Instruction

Small-group instruction is emphasized in the most effective schools. In one study, students in the most effective schools spent nearly twice as much time in small groups as did students in less effective schools (Taylor, Pearson, Clark, & Walpole, 2002). Explaining the significance of small groups, one teacher states, "Small groups are crucial. Children are more likely to succeed when they are in small groups of six with two teachers than when there are 12 children with one teacher" (Taylor, Pearson, Clark, & Walpole, 2002, p. 42). Effective schools use various techniques for differentiating instruction. In many schools, aids, volunteers, or specialists come into classrooms during reading time to guide small groups (Taylor, Pearson, Clark, & Walpole, 2002).

Higher-Level Thinking Skills

Teachers in the most effective schools are firmly committed to instructional grouping so that students are given materials and instruction on the appropriate level. However, even the lowest achieving groups are provided higher-level thinking skills. In fact, they spend as much time with higher-level activities as do achieving students (Taylor, Pearson, Clark, & Walpole, 2002). Teachers in highly effective schools ask a greater number of higher-level questions, although they still overemphasize literal questions (Taylor, Pearson, Clark, & Walpole, 2002).

Coaching Style

Highly effective teachers are also more likely to use a coaching rather than a telling style in which they help students work out difficult words or use evidence to draw conclusions rather than simply supplying the unfamiliar word or the conclusion (Taylor, Pearson, Clark, & Walpole, 2002). Effective teachers make skillful use of scaffolding, in general, and prompts, in particular, to foster higher levels of engagement and independence. Through scaffolding, teachers provide support so that students can perform at higher levels than they could have if they had been working strictly on their own. For instance, when a student is stumped by a difficult word, instead of simply telling the student the word, a highly effective teacher prompts the student to seek out a known part of the word, such as a prefix or a root, and to use that to figure out the meaning of the word.

Collaborative Approach

In highly effective schools, teachers use a collaborative approach in which classroom teachers and specialists work together for the common good of the students. Often this means that the reading specialist or special education teacher guides groups of students in the classroom, giving students most in need, for example, two blocks of small-group instruction instead of the one typically offered (Taylor, Pearson, Clark, & Walpole, 2002).

Flexibility and Determination

The best teachers are flexible. As one group of researchers observes, "Our very best teachers expressed commitment to the principle that they would do whatever it took to meet the wide array of individual student, needs encountered every day in their classrooms" (Taylor, Pearson, Clark, & Walpole, 2002, p. 62).

Effective Teaching

As is seen in this brief review of characteristics of schools that beat the odds, the key characteristic is the staff. Schools that beat the odds require teachers and administrators who beat the odds. In one study of effective teachers, it was found that students who had effective teachers for three years in a row outscored students who had ineffective teachers for three years in a row by 50 percentile points (Sanders & Rivers, 1996). The authors concluded that teacher effectiveness is the single biggest factor influencing achievement gains. It is, as Carey (2004) notes, an "influence bigger than race, poverty, parent's education, or any of the other factors that are often thought to doom children to failure" (p. 4). Based on their research on teacher effectiveness involving hundreds of teachers and thousands of students, Rivkin, Hanushek, and Kain (1998) conclude that "there can be little doubt that teacher quality is an important determinant of achievement" (p. 20). The difference is such that students could achieve 40 percent more with an above-average teacher than with a below-average teacher. The difference between having a superb teacher and a poor teacher could be more than 70 percent added learning.

A key characteristic of effective teachers is their focus on what is important and what each student needs. Focused teaching is based on a thorough understanding of how children learn to read and write. It is practiced by teachers who are adept at organizing and differentiating instruction (Taylor, Pearson, Clark, & Walpole, 2002).

External Support

Many successful schools have external support that helps strengthen their program. For some, it is a connection with the literacy or language arts department of a university. For others, it is membership in a Reading Recovery consortium. The schools use expert guidance to help them achieve success (Lipson et al., 2004).

Complexity of School Improvement

Improving a school's literacy program is complex. There are no simple answers or formulas that are guaranteed to work. Each school has unique characteristics that must be taken into consideration (Lipson et al., 2004). Mindlessly applying research-based characteristics of effective schools may result in shallow gains. We need to dig deeper and see what is behind the characteristic (Duffy & Hoffman, 2002). For instance, time on task is a characteristic of effective instruction. However, it isn't just the time that matters; it matters more how that time is spent. If that time is spent on high-quality activities that address the students' needs and are at the students' instructional level, then the instruction will most likely be effective.

As Duffy and Hoffman (2002) note, "Literacy instruction is most effective when embedded in thematic units, play activity, simulations, and other forms of engaging, worthwhile literacy activity" (p. 378).

Summarizing the research on effective literacy instruction, Hill and Crévola (2000) found that the following three factors result in high performance: high expectations of student achievement, engaged learning time, and focused teaching that maximizes learning within each student's "zone of proximal development" (p. 1). The difference between what a child can do on his own and what the child can do with the assistance of an adult or more knowledgeable peer is known as the zone of proximal development. Hill and Crévola (2002) discovered that many of the characteristics of high-performing schools are found in most schools. However, in only a few schools are all of the characteristics found. In addition, although many teachers include these elements in their classrooms, often they are not implemented in the most effective fashion (Hill & Crévola, 2000).

Creating a Program That Beats the Odds

Closing the gap demands creating an optimal program. According to Marie Clay (2003), the creator of Reading Recovery, an early intervention program that revolutionized the teaching of reading in much of the English-speaking world, the key to intervention is to optimize students' progress. When someone suggested to Clay (2003) that Reading Recovery represents instruction that is as good as it gets, she replied that it wasn't. An optimal program is one that is in a continual quest for further improvement. It's never as good as it gets because it is always getting better. The concept of continuous optimization is the foundation of closing the gap. The best way to close the gap is to optimize, keeping in mind that your program is never truly optimal because you are always making it better. All aspects of the program need to be optimized from professional development to availability of materials to home-school cooperation.

Closing the literacy gap is a daunting challenge. It also represents a dramatic change in the way that public schools operate. The underachievement of poor or minority students, English language learners (ELLs), and special education students is amply documented. In the past, some literacy educators accepted the fact that some students will fail to achieve adequate literacy. With the passage of the No Child Left Behind (NCLB) Act, we are saying that we are no longer satisfied that significant segments of our population are not learning to read and write adequately. Our goal now is to truly educate all children.

In a sense, we will close the gap one child at a time. Reporting on the progress of two Reading Recovery students, Jason and Antonio, Mallette (2003) gives an example of this principle. Both students were chosen for intervention because they weren't making sufficient progress. At the start, Jason was slightly ahead of Antonio. For the first five weeks of the program, both boys made encouraging progress. After the fifth week, Antonio began to lag behind. By the end of fifteen weeks of lessons, Jason was at level fourteen, which is near the end of first grade. Antonio was at level three, which is a beginning reading level. Dissatisfied with Antonio's progress, the teacher analyzed his program and compared it with Jason's. As it turned out, Jason had spent most of his time in books that were relatively easy. Antonio's books had been difficult. In addition, Antonio had spent much of his time in pattern books. Pattern books incorporate predictable sentences together with pictures that illustrate key words. For instance, a pattern book might feature the sentence frame "I can ____" with each page showing something that the character in the selection can do, such as running or jumping or singing. Although such books provide children with a sense of what reading is and provide practice with high-frequency words, they don't do a very good job of reinforcing basic decoding skills and, in fact, may lead to an overreliance on picture clues. Antonio's program needed optimizing. Easier books and a more systematic approach to decoding were called for. As Clay (2003) notes, there is no program that will work for all children. Just when we think we have such a program, "children's individual differences will prove us wrong."

Creating a Vision

In creating an optimal program, you are asking, "What can we do better?" (Pane, Mulligan, Ginsburg, & Lauland, 1999). Before you can decide what you can do better, you need a vision of where you want to be. What do you see for your program? Make your vision inclusive. Talk to students. What aspects of the literacy program are important to them? What reading/writing skills would they like or need to learn? Maybe they need to learn study skills so they can do better on content-area tests. Or maybe they need to learn how to select books that are not too hard for them. Or maybe they would like to learn how to write letters, so they can correspond with their grandparents who live across the country. Talk to parents. Ask them what they would like for their children. Also talk to staff. Being inclusive doesn't mean that you will reach 100 percent consensus. But do try to get a buy-in from everyone. Your vision statement should include the following.

- Mission: What is the purpose of our program?
- Values: What do we believe in?
- Future: What do we want to look like in the future? (Pane, Mulligan, Ginsburg, & Lauland, 1999)

Here is a sample vision statement for a literacy program.

The literacy program will develop students' literacy skills to their fullest. It is our belief that given the right kind of instruction, effort and motivation on the students' part, and home and community support, virtually all children can become competent readers and writers. In cooperation with students, parents, and the community, we see all our students as being competent readers and writers who not only can read and write but also see these as valuable activities and so read and write on their own.

Vision statements should reflect the dreams and desires of those involved and so will vary from school to school.

Optimizing a program is hard work. Staff members need a vision statement to inspire and guide them. Reporting on the successful turnaround of an elementary school in Florida, King and Torgesen (2000) observe:

> Many of our earlier changes were infrastructure type changes. These included an emphasis on uninterrupted classroom instruction, increased instructional time resulting from master schedule changes, elimination of pull-out programs and other measures outlined earlier. The point here is that these types of changes can be degraded and undermined if teachers and staff are not continuously reminded of the vision statements that guided these changes in the first place.

Setting Goals and Objectives

Growing out of the vision statement are the program's goals. The goals reflect the vision by stating in broad terms what students should know and be able to do. A vision statement translated into goals is the foundation of a program designed to close the literacy gap.

In setting goals, consider the school's and school district's curriculum framework, and state and national standards. Setting goals should be a collaborative activity among the staff in a school. Teachers need to agree on what they want their literacy program to do and what shape it will take. After goals have been stated, objectives are created. Objectives, which are sometimes known as benchmark standards, are a more specific restatement of goals.

Objectives should be measurable. Objectives should also be challenging but realistic. While it's important to aim high, it's discouraging if the objectives can't be met. In a literacy program, objectives should include indicators of progress in reading and writing and also some indicator that students are reading on their own. Often objectives are stated in terms of standards: All students will read on grade level. Objectives that are stated in terms of a cutoff score or a benchmark to be reached, such as being able to read on grade level, may hide progress. Many students who failed to reach grade level might nevertheless have made substantial progress. That progress should be noted. It is disheartening to students, teachers, and parents when schools are cited as needing improvement because a certain percentage are reading below grade level, even though many of the students might have made dramatic progress. In their long-term study of schools in Baltimore, sociologists Alexander, Entwistle, and Olson (1997) found that students in impoverished areas were making just as much as progress as students in more affluent areas, but weren't given credit for this. Instead, they were downgraded because students in impoverished areas were reading below grade level. Students were reading below grade level because they started out behind and lost ground during the summer months. However, during the school year they made just as much progress as their more privileged counterparts.

As MacIver (1991) asserts, "Traditional evaluation systems often do not adequately recognize the progress that educationally disadvantaged students make, because even dramatic progress may still leave them near the bottom of the class in comparative terms or far from the percent-correct standard needed for a good grade" (p. 4). To rectify this situation, the Incentives for Improvement program implemented such an evaluation and incentive system in four Baltimore public schools. Teachers helped students develop "specific, individualized, short-range goals that are challenging but doable based on the students' past performance" (MacIver, 1991, p. 5). Students received recognition for improvement as well as for high levels of achievement. Students participating in the program received higher grades and were more likely to pass. Incentives for Improvement students also worked harder and showed a greater intrinsic interest in the subject matter they were being taught.

Involving Students in the Goal Setting Process

What happens when you set goals as opposed to not setting goals? For most of us, setting goals is the first step to action. Not setting goals generally results in inaction. This same principle applies to students. After determining students' overall literacy needs, help them set goals. After setting long-term goals, they should set short-term objectives. The more concrete the goals the better. The goal of learning new words is more likely to be achieved if it is broken down to learning 200 new words by year's end. Once concrete objectives have been set, determine how the objectives might be met: through reading 30 minutes a night and recording difficult words, through completing one vocabulary building exercise each day, through joining a study group that is exploring the meanings of words.

Monitoring progress and providing feedback are essential. A student needs to know how she is doing. If the student has skipped her independent reading for a week or has noted no new words, you need to supply direction. Or if she is looking up the new words in the dictionary but getting the wrong meanings, you need to review the skill of locating appropriate definitions. Also built into the process is an outcome assessment. How will the student and you determine whether she has learned 200 new words? This might be a survey test on the 200 words studied.

Conducting a Needs Assessment

The next step in creating an optimal program is to take a close look at the current program and note its strengths and weaknesses. This needs assessment is based on the school's objectives. Include indicators as to what extent objectives are being met. Use formal test data as well as informal assessment, observations, and interviews. Obtain information from staff, parents, community, and, most important of all, from students. Information should include national, state, and local test scores; teacher assessments such as informal reading inventories (IRIs) or Developmental Reading Assessment (DRA) results (which gauge students' progress by having them read selections that gradually increase in difficulty); number of books read or average minutes spent reading each night; results of writing assessments; achievement in content areas; and performance on end-of-theme or end-of-unit literacy tests, writing samples, and portfolios. Talk to staff, students, and community about what they see as the major strengths and weaknesses of the program. Use the needs assessment as a basis for planning a program of improvement, including professional development. Using the sample needs assessment of a K–6 school shown in Table 2.1 as a starting point, create your own needs assessment checklist and conduct a needs assessment for your class, department, school, or district.

After conducting a needs assessment, discuss results with the school's literacy committee. In fact, the school's literacy committee should decide what the needs assessment should include, how it might be conducted, and what timeline to set. The sample needs assessment in Table 2.1 was conducted over a two-month period. The assessment turned up a number of significant needs. Plans were then discussed for addressing the students' needs. How to meet a school's needs in its efforts to close the literacy gap is the subject of the rest of this text.

BOX 2.1

Needs Assessment: Personal Perspective

The needs assessment in Table 2.1 is based on the performance of students at Urban Public. Surprisingly, the most valuable data for the needs assessment came from the unit end-of-theme tests that accompanied the students' basal series. These tests, which were similar to the state's high-stakes test that the students were scheduled to take beginning in grade 3, revealed significant difficulties in responding in writing to higher-level questions. A careful analysis of students' responses revealed a general need for a more intensive reading program and specific needs for instruction in responding to higher-level comprehension questions. The tests were supplemented in grade 1 by a listing of pattern words taught in each of the ten themes or units. These word pattern tests indicated whether students had mastered the phonic patterns taught in a particular theme. Results of the theme word pattern tests were used to locate students who hadn't learned the patterns. These students were given added instruction so they would have a solid foundation for the next theme's phonic patterns.

An analysis of additional assessment data from a variety of formal and informal measures indicated other needs. Because the needs highlighted by the assessments were many and varied, priorities were established. A systematic literacy program was initiated, followed first by enhanced vocabulary development and intervention programs. As teachers grew accustomed to these core elements, refinements were implemented and reciprocal teaching, independent reading, literature circles, content-area reading, and process writing were integrated into the program. Special attention was directed to higher-level comprehension skills and composing responses to comprehension questions. Program changes were carefully monitored, and adjustments were made as called for. For instance, when an examination of reading logs revealed that only 50 percent of students were reading at home, measures were put in place that fostered home reading by virtually all students.

TABLE 2.1   *Literacy Needs Assessment*

Objectives	Performance	Evidence	Needs
Overall			
Read at grade level	1/2 in K–2 at level 1/3 3–6 at level	Terra Nova Modified DIBELS IRI	Bring up to grade level
Write at grade level	1/3 satisfactory	State tests Sample pieces Observation	Develop writing skills
Emergent Literacy			
Recognize the letters of the alphabet	85% end of K	Observation Emergent Literacy Survey	Learn all letters
Identify rhyme and beginning sounds	80% end of K	Observation Emergent Literacy Survey	Learn rhyme & beginning sounds
Learn beginning consonants correspondences	75% end of K	Phonics Survey Basal test	Learn initial consonants
Learn easy short-vowel patterns	60% end of K	Phonics Survey Basal test	Learn short-vowel patterns
Read 20 high-frequency words	60% end of K	Word Survey	Learn added high-frequency words
Write their names	100% end of K	Observation	Instruction in alphabet & name writing
Word Analysis			
Learn consonants, consonant digraphs, clusters, short vowels, long vowels	70% end of 1 90% end of 2 100% end of 3	Phonics Survey Developmenal Reading Assessment (DRA) IRI Basal test	Learn clusters, advanced short-vowel patterns, and long-vowel patterns
Learn long vowels, other vowels, *r* vowels, and vowel patterns	70% end of 2 90% end of 3	Phonics Survey DRA IRI Basal test	Learn advanced vowel digraphs, *r* vowels
Read with accuracy, fluency, and expression at the appropriate rate	75% overall	DIBELS Timed IRI Observation	Increase reading rate
Use syllabic analysis skills at appropriate level	60% end of 2 70% end of 3 80% end of 4 90% end of 5	IRI analysis Syllable Survey	Learn syllable patterns Apply syllabic analysis
Use predictionaries and simplified glossaries	75% end of 2	Observation	Look up hard words

(continued)

TABLE 2.1 *Literacy Needs Assessment (continued)*

Objectives	Performance	Evidence	Needs
Use dictionaries at appropriate level	75% 3 80% 4–6	Observation	Pick correct definitions
Use context at appropriate level	80% 2–6	IRI analysis Observation	Make better use of clues
Use morphemic analysis	75% 4 80% 5–6	Observation	Learn advanced elements Learn to note elements in words
Use a vocabulary that is grade appropriate	30% K 40% 2–6	Peabody Picture Vocabulary Test End-of-unit tests	Acquire more vocabulary words
Comprehension			
Comprehend grade-level materials with 70% accuracy	50% 1–2 40% 3–6	DRA IRI Basal tests	Learn higher-level skills, especially inferences
Use a range of comprehension strategies	60%	DRA IRI Observation Basal test	Use questioning, imaging, & summarizing Integrate strategy use
Content/Study			
Read content-area texts with 70% accuracy	60% 3–6	Quizzes Unit tests	Learn to cope with technical vocabulary
Apply study strategies	60% 3–6	Quizzes Unit tests	Learn effective study habits Learn to apply SQ3R
Wide Reading			
Read a variety of books and periodicals and Web materials	75%	Reading logs Observation	Read periodicals & more nonfiction
Read a total of two hours a day	50%	Reading logs Observation	Read more at home
Writing			
Write a variety of texts at the appropriate grade level	30–40%	State test Sample pieces	Develop pieces more fully Focus on a few ideas
Compose an adequate response to on-demand writing tasks	1/3 able to compose an adequate response 3–6	State test End-of-unit tests	Respond to questions & prompts more fully & accurately
Use grade-level spelling	35% 2–6	Spelling inventory Sample pieces Observation	Learn spelling strategies
Use grade-level mechanics	30–40% 1–6	Sample pieces Observation	Learn to use end & internal punctuation & avoid run-ons Show verb tenses

3

The Role of Assessment in Closing the Gap

Evaluation is an essential element in closing the literacy gap (Good, Simmons, Kame'enui, Kaminski, & Wallin, 2002). Your program needs to be data- or assessment-based. An assessment-based system is crucial for the following reasons.

- What gets assessed gets taught. (Assessment results provide the data for needs assessment.)
- If you don't assess results, you can't tell success from failure.
- If you can't recognize failure, you can't correct it.
- If you can't see success, you can't reward it. — *enhance strengths (2-3)*
- If you can't see success, you can't learn from it. (Pane, Mulligan, Ginsburg, & Lauland, 1999).

(2-3 areas of concern)

The first step in evaluation is to set challenging but realistic goals for all students and translate these into specific objectives or benchmarks as noted in the previous chapter. For kindergarten, this might be the ability to identify the twenty-six letters of the alphabet, provide sounds for twenty consonants, read easy short-vowel patterns, and read twenty high-frequency words. For third grade, it might be the ability to read third-grade passages with 70 percent comprehension and to read at a rate of 100 words per minute. Once objectives and benchmarks have been established, conduct an initial assessment to find out where students are. As part of the initial assessment, you will make the match.

Making the Match

Just about the most important instructional decision that schools make is making the match (Fry, 1977). Making the match means that you match students with appropriate level materials. Although turnaround programs vary in their approaches, one of their foundational principles is making sure that students are given materials on the appropriate level (Gill, 2004; Schefelebein, 2004). Students work best and learn the most when they are successful. In reading, they are most successful when they know at least 95 percent of the words and have 70 percent or greater comprehension. The 95 percent–70 percent standard is known as their instructional level, which means that students can get by with knowing only 95 words out of a 100 because they will be getting instructional help, such as being taught difficult vocabulary or unfamiliar concepts or background before they read. If students are going to read on their own, they should know at least 98 percent of the words and have 80 percent comprehension. This is known as their independent level. Students read at their instructional level during guided reading. When reading on their own, they should be reading materials that are on their independent level. Reading on the independent level helps build fluency. Reading on the instructional level helps build vocabulary and other skills (Carver, 1994; Nation, 2001).

Reading Recovery and a number of other systems set their levels at lower percentages. For Reading Recovery, 90 to 94 percent is considered the instructional level. The independent level is 95 percent and above. However, Reading Recovery consists of one-to-one tutoring so that a trained teacher is available to help each student with words that pose problems. In addition, Reading Recovery is set up in such a way that students are presented selections that contain words that they do not know. These are known as problems to solve. Instruction occurs when the teacher guides the child in solving the problems.

Research dating back to the 1940s (Betts, 1946; Killgallon, 1942) strongly suggests that the more conservative figures of 95 percent word recognition and 70 percent comprehension are more valid. As percentage of words known dips below 95 percent, students' achievement falls (Enz, 1989) and attention suffers (Anderson, 1990).

Obtaining Placement Information

To make the match, it is necessary to determine the level of materials that students can handle. Ascertaining students' reading levels has been compared to the process of trying on shoes. Students try on representative series of reading passages of increasing difficulty until they reach their instructional and independent levels. Most instructional materials are accompanied by placement tests. In addition, a number of commercially produced informal reading inventories (IRIs) are available (see Table 3.1), or benchmark books can be used. Most IRIs consist of a series of graded word lists and test selections. Test selections are designed to be given orally and silently. Word recognition in context, comprehension, and oral reading rate can be checked with the oral selections. Comprehension and reading rate can be checked with the silent selections. To save time, select an inventory that has shorter passages. Beyond the first-grade level, the selections in the Basic Reading Inventory (Johns, 2001) consist of just 100 words. Also administer just the oral passages.

Reading Recovery has an IRI procedure known as running records, in which only oral passages are administered. The Developmental Reading Assessment (DRA) (Celebration Press) is a commercial version of a running record.

TABLE 3.1 *Commercial Reading Inventories*

Name	Publisher	Grades	Added Skill Areas
Analytic Reading Inventory	Prentice Hall	1–9	Contains science and social studies passages
Bader Reading and Language Inventory	Merrill	K–12	Phonics, language, emergent literacy
Basic Reading Inventory	Kendall/Hunt	K–8	Emergent literacy (has a Spanish version)
Burns and Roe Informal Inventory	Houghton Mifflin	1–12	
Classroom Reading Inventory	McGraw-Hill	1–8	Spelling
Critical Reading Inventory	Prentice Hall	1–12	Critical thinking
Developmental Reading Assessment	Celebration Press	K–3	
DRA 4–8	Celebration Press	4–8	
Ekwall/Shanker Reading Inventory	Allyn & Bacon	K–12	Emergent literacy, word analysis
English-Espanol Reading Inventory for the Classroom	Prentice Hall	K–12	Emergent literacy (has an English-only version)
Informal Reading Thinking Inventory	Harcourt	1–11	
PALS	University of Virginia	K–3	Emergent literacy, IRI, word reading, spelling
Qualitative Reading Inventory IV	Longman	1–12	Has rereadings and, for grades 5-12, think-alouds
Steiglitz Informal Reading Inventory	Allyn & Bacon	K–8	Emergent literacy
Texas Primary Reading Inventory	Texas Education Agency	K–3	Emergent literacy, phonics (has a Spanish version)

Making the Match at the Upper Levels

At the upper levels, where teachers meet with one hundred or more students each day, administering individual placement can be prohibitive in terms of time. Teacher-created group inventories can be administered (see Johnson, Kress, & Pikulski, 1987, for instructions). There are also two commercially produced tests that function as group inventories: Scholastic Inventory and Touchstone's Degrees of Reading Power. Both use modified cloze, also known as maze (fill-in-the-blanks), by selecting the word that best completes the sentence. A third inventory, STAR Reading (Renaissance Learning), which is designed to be used with Accelerated Reading but can be used with any program, is administered via computer. STAR Reading combines brief, in-context vocabulary items with modified cloze passages. Testing time is only about 10 minutes. Assessments range from K–8. One

1	2	3	4	5	6	7	8	9–12
I	please	branch	reason	escaped	absence	continuously	calculator	administrative
the	never	middle	distant	business	instinct	application	agriculture	spontaneous
we	hour	stronger	lonesome	continue	responsible	incredible	prohibited	molecule
go	climb	picture	silent	obedient	evaporate	maximum	legislation	ritual
hat	field	hunger	wrecked	entrance	convenience	environmental	translucent	recipient
help	spend	several	decided	applause	commercial	accumulate	astronomical	conscientious
coat	side	empty	certainly	government	necessary	geographical	optimistic	infectious
are	believe	since	favorite	celebration	recognition	triangular	narrate	beneficiary
how	happen	impossible	realized	microscope	vertical	pollutant	persuasive	affiliation
work	suddenly	straight	solution	navigate	starvation	currency	obnoxious	paralysis

FIGURE 3.1 *Word Reading Survey*

From *Building Literacy in the Content Areas* by T. Gunning, 2003. Boston: Allyn & Bacon. Reprinted by permission of Allyn & Bacon.

way to compile a group inventory fairly easily is to administer reading passages from the Qualitative Reading Inventory IV (QRI), the Basic, or another inventory and have the students compose a written retelling of the passages and/or answer in writing the questions that accompany the inventory selections. The instructional level would be the highest point at which students scored 70 to 80 percent. To obtain students' reading levels, Schefelebein (2004), the literacy specialist at Carpentersville Middle School in Illinois, adapted the QRI so that students read passages silently and constructed a written retelling and answered a series of questions. The QRI was administered three times a year as a check on placement and to monitor progress.

The major shortcoming of group inventories is that they assess only comprehension. They don't assess students' ability to read words. To obtain this information, you might use an oral words reading test such as the Slosson Oral Reading Test (norm-referenced) or the Word Reading Survey (informal) in Figure 3.1. Taking only about 5 minutes to administer, these tests give a quick estimate of the students' reading abilities. Because comprehension is not assessed, results have to be interpreted with care. Word list tests, group inventories, and all other placement inventories should be validated by noting students' actual performance on classroom and outside reading materials.

Screening Students

In addition to helping determine the appropriate level of material that students should be given, placement tests can also be used as screening devices. Screening devices are assessments used to identify students who need additional assessment because they appear to be at risk. Students who score very low on placement tests should be provided with additional assessment and/or an intervention program. For emergent readers, tests of alphabet knowledge or phonological awareness might function as screening tests. Word list tests composed of words that gradually increase in difficulty might also be used as screening tests. Students are usually screened at the beginning of the school years or, if they are transfer students, when they enter the school. Data from this initial assessment can also be used to provide evidence for the needs assessment.

Continuous Progress Monitoring

Based on students' current status, target objectives, and needs assessment, plan a program. To make your planning concrete and realistic, plan backwards. Instead of deciding how you will start off, decide what it is that students should know and be able to do at the end of the year. If you are planning for a first-grade class, picture in your mind what you want your first-graders to know and to be able to do when they enter second grade. This, of course, should include school and district standards or objectives, but also should include your vision for your students. In backwards planning, you start with the end-of-the-year target goal and then plan whatever activities and instruction might be needed to reach the objectives. Make provision for students who might need additional support or even intensive help. Students entering first grade who lack awareness of beginning sounds would need more help than those who have mastered initial consonant correspondences. Create a time chart showing where students should be at various points of the year, perhaps quarterly. You mark the end point and the beginning point and then decide about how much progress each student has to make to reach the end point or the objective. Reading level, reading rate, acquisition of phonics elements, and similar indicators of progress could be charted. The chart in Figure 3.2 shows the

Name _____ Grade _____ Date _____

Level	Sept.	Oct.	Nov.	Dec.	Jan.	Feb.	Mar.	Apr.	May	June
2b-L										
2a-K										target
2a-J										√
1-I								√	√	
1-H						√	√			
1-G					√					
P-F				√						
PP3-E		√	√							
PP2-D	√									
PP1-C										
Early PP-B										
Emergent-A										

FIGURE 3.2 *Continuous Progress Monitoring Chart*

Note: PP stands for preprimer; P stands for primer. Numbers stand for grade levels. Letters are guided reading levels.

targeted progress in reading levels for a struggling second-grader. Since he is behind, more than a year's growth has been plotted out. Note that he missed his target by just one level.

Struggling readers are monitored more frequently than achieving readers. Struggling readers should be monitored at least once a month. With frequent monitoring, you are quicker to note when students are lagging behind and so need additional instruction, more review, or better materials. In addition to having a solid core curriculum and high-quality instruction, an effective program has procedures to identify students who need additional intervention and a mechanism to deliver additional intervention and to increase that intervention if needed (Good et al., 2002).

Monitoring Program Progress

Monitoring should take two forms. You should monitor the overall progress of classes and you should monitor the individual progress of each student. Just as monitoring progress should be ongoing, so, too, should measures to improve the program. As monitoring reveals weaknesses in the program, changes should be made to strengthen the program. For instance, you might note that some students are not reading the required 20 minutes per night. On closer examination, you find that these are reluctant readers who are turned off by print-filled books. You seek out books that are of high interest and well illustrated or you obtain magazines such as *Sports Illustrated for Kids,* which is highly motivating. To optimize your program, you need to be continuously seeking out ways to make it better. Along with planning instructional improvements based on assessed needs, you need to monitor progress toward achieving objectives and make adjustments as needed.

Simply monitoring progress improves performance by a month or two. When teachers gear instruction based on the results of monitoring, gains can be quite dramatic and may be a year or more (Black & Williams, 1998). Results are magnified if the whole school is engaged in the monitoring process and grade-level meetings are held to discuss students' progress and ways of improving the program.

Using Informal Assessment

When monitoring students' progress, don't rely on just one source of information or overlook informal measures. An economical but effective way to track students' progress is to assess key skills. For emergent and very early readers, that might be alphabet knowledge or phonological awareness. For developing readers, it might be phonics or the ability to read words that become increasingly difficult. For more advanced readers, it might be comprehension of increasingly difficult passages. Charts of books read also enable you to track student progress. If students are lagging behind in their book reading, you can intervene. Weekly quizzes, unit tests, work samples, checklists, and observations should also be used to shed light on students' performance and track students' progress. End-of-unit tests that accompany basals or that you construct yourself can be used to monitor students' progress. An especially rich source of cumulative information is the portfolio.

BOX
3.1 *Model Program: Beating the Odds with Monthly Portfolio Meetings*

At the Simpson-Waverly School in Hartford, Connecticut, portfolios are used to make sure that every child is making adequate progress. Although 95 percent of its students live in poverty, Simpson-Waverly's scores on the demanding Connecticut Mastery Test are equal to those of suburban schools. Strong leadership, a dedicated staff, a push for excellence, and help from community institutions, such as lectures provided by Trinity College professors to students in grades 4 through 6, help account for the school's success. However, a key factor is the school's monthly portfolio review process. Once a month the school's review team meets with each teacher. The review team consists of the principal, reading specialist, curriculum specialists, and other staff members. Team members examine test scores, quizzes, writing samples, logs of books read, and any other artifacts or work samples from the portfolio that might shed light on students' progress. The team plans program improvements and makes suggestions for teachers, with special attention being paid to students who are not making progress. Although individual folders are analyzed, sometimes common needs are noted so suggestions are made for techniques or materials that might be used with a group or the whole class. Cumulatively, the review process reveals schoolwide needs, and so the review sessions are used to plan professional development (Gottlieb, 2004).

Continuous Progress Monitoring Tests on the Web

Several continuous progress monitoring (CPM) tests are available on the Web. The best known of these is the Dynamic Indicators of Basic Early Literacy Skills (DIBELS), which has been used by more than a million students and is free. The DIBELS (http://dibels.uoregon.edu) and most other CPM assessments are designed to be quick probes. The DIBELS assesses alphabet knowledge, phonological awareness, vocabulary, fluency, and, to a very limited extent, comprehension. The tests are timed. Students read as many letters, nonsense syllables, or words in a passage as they can within 1 minute. The DIBELS is designed to be given three times a year. However, it has many forms and could be given monthly. If students are having serious difficulty with their reading, you could administer the CPM more frequently, perhaps even once every two weeks. That way you could make necessary adjustments more quickly.

The emphasis in the DIBELS is on lower-level processes such as speed of pronouncing printed words. Higher-level comprehension skills are neglected. However, in the Oral Reading Fluency assessment, the system does offer a number of passages at each level (end-of-first to sixth) that might be used to track growth. These might be given as directed or modified, and administered in the same fashion as an IRI or running record. You might also implement a traditional retelling. In both an IRI and running record, students' miscues or errors are recorded and analyzed. If given in both standard and modified fashion, the passages will yield scores for reading rates, reading levels, and retelling. By analyzing miscues, you could also determine word recognition needs. If adapted, the DIBELS will yield more valuable data.

Another CPM system is AIMSWeb. AIMSWeb features periodic assessment probes for reading fluency, comprehension, spelling, and early literacy (phonological awareness and phonics). Comprehension is assessed through mazes. In mazes, students select from three possible choices the one that correctly restores a word that has been deleted from the test passage: The dog lapped water from its (bell, bowl, bed). Assessments range from K–8. AIMSWeb is a fee-based system.

Reservations about the Use of Nonsense Words

The DIBELS and a number of other tests use nonsense words to assess decoding skills. Using nonsense words is problematical. The rationale for using nonsense words is that students will not have seen these items before and therefore will not be responding to them as words that they have memorized. However, when students decode a word, there is a feedback step in which they note whether the item they have decoded is a real word. In a well-planned word recognition program, students are taught that if the item being decoded is a nonword, then they should try again. Because the feedback step is not present when dealing with pseudo-words, decoding nonsense words is apparently more difficult than decoding real words (Cunningham et al., 1999). Waslmley (1978–1979) also found that pseudo-words and rare words were more difficult to read than real words and words in common use. Moustafa (1995) noted a tendency for students to misread pseudo-words as real words. In all three studies, nonsense words were harder to read than real words. Using nonsense words provides some information about students' ability to decode words. However, because the test task is more difficult than the task students actually face when reading, tests using nonsense words underestimate students' ability to decode words and may indicate a problem where there is none.

Distinguished literacy educator Jiménez (2003) recounts being informed that his first-grade son was flagged as being at risk for having difficulty learning to read. Jiménez was surprised since he and his wife had spent a great deal of time reading to their son and playing word games with him. In addition, their son was interested in bats and was able to read words that describe them, including the word *echolocation*. Jiménez obtained a copy of the DIBELS and discussed it with his son. Used to creating meaning when he decoded words, Jiménez's son commented that the words were weird. On closer examination of the nonsense words, Jiménez discovered that three of the nonsense words were actually real words in Spanish. Jiménez wondered how many Spanish-speaking ELLs might have been marked wrong because they gave the words a Spanish pronunciation.

Adapting the DIBELS

If you avoid giving nonsense words and make adjustments, the DIBELS can be a useful CPM measure. Progress on the DIBELS can be charted and can be an indicator as to whether students are on track for reaching the goals you have set. You can create your own charts or have the DIBELS create them for you. The charge for tracking progress is just $1 per student.

Diagnosis

In addition to being used to screen and place students and monitor progress, assessment devices are also used for diagnosis and outcome measures. If students fail to make progress despite careful teaching and placement in intervention programs, an in-depth diagnosis might be required. Diagnosis is typically conducted by a team of professionals and might include assessment by the school psychologist, learning disabilities specialist, reading specialist, and other professionals.

Outcome Measures

You also need to collect and examine outcome data. Outcome data is examined to see if objectives have been achieved and also to note the strengths and weaknesses of the program and to plan for ways to improve the program. Outcome measures are typically given at the end of a quarter, semester, or year. Outcome measures include standardized tests given by the school, school district, or state. However, in addition to these formal measures, data collected from portfolios, IRIs, or running records given at the end of the period of instruction; completed checklists; tallies of number of books read; end-of-book tests or end-of-theme tests; and portfolios should also be used to assesses the overall progress of students and effectiveness of the program. Although there is a temptation to focus on the results of high-stakes tests because that's what gets reported in the newspapers, schools should consider other indicators of progress. Staff should look at the outcome measures in terms of the school's objectives. Which objectives were met? Which weren't? What are the strengths and weaknesses of the program? What improvements might be made?

How Effective Schools Use Assessment Data

At JFK Middle School, a high-poverty turnaround school, the principal asked teachers on a weekly basis to document all the services they made available for students who were experiencing difficulties and to document how far students had progressed (Picucci, Brownson, Kahlert, & Sobel, 2002). Effective schools not only examine current data, but also look at longitudinal data. Tonasket Middle School and Pocomoke Middle School, two other turnaround schools, for example, obtained the elementary school test data for entering sixth-graders. Teachers used this information to analyze the skill level of each incoming student. They were then able to emphasize certain areas and to lay a strong foundation on which students could build as they moved through the grades.

Data can also be used to address nonacademic issues that affect student performance. At Inman Middle School, a Texas turnaround school, teachers discovered that several students who lacked basic school supplies and were scoring poorly on assessments shared the same address in a government housing complex (Picucci et al., 2002). The staff contacted the Boys and Girls Club serving those stu-

BOX
3.2 *Model Program: Using Data to Make Improvements*

When scores of students at Baskin Elementary School began to slip, teachers at first blamed changes in the population (Council of Chief State School Officers, 2002). But after careful analysis, they put the blame on themselves and attacked the problem. They made several improvements that stopped the decline and started scores climbing upwards once more. At these and other high-performing schools, teachers use test data to assess themselves. If students don't do well, the teachers analyze the data and look for ways to beef up instruction. As the principal of the Loma Terrace School explains:

> Our teachers, they don't give excuses. We're in a culture of success and we don't accept excuses. Children can learn. All children can. You might have to work a little harder, you might have to overcome a few obstacles, because we realize that our kids statistically are underdogs, but we won't accept that and the people won't accept that. If the student is here, we've got to teach [him]. We've got to work on those obstacles. (Picucci, et al., 2002, p. 9)

dents and enlisted its help in providing the students and their families with basic social services and school supplies.

Since the emphasis is on closing the gap for each child, assessment data should be examined in the light of each child's progress as well as the progress of the school. Staff need to feel a concern not just for the progress of the students they teach but also for the progress of the school. That way they are more willing to work together and help each other out.

Although the public focuses on outcome results, especially high-stakes tests, schools should stress the assessment that teachers use on an ongoing basis to monitor progress and make informed instructional decisions. Teachers and administrators should work together to forge an assessment plan that places emphasis on ongoing monitoring. Parents and the community at large should be aware of the function of these assessments and their importance in providing useful information about student progress (Paris, Paris, & Carpenter, 2002). In addition, each assessment should serve a purpose. When new assessments are adopted, take a look at current assessments to make sure there is no duplication. Sometimes mandated assessments are simply added to current assessments. If the mandated tests cover the same ground as the current assessments, some of the current assessments might be eliminated.

Assessing Materials

Estimating students' reading levels is essential but not sufficient. It is only half of the instructional match. The other half of the match is estimating the difficulty level of the materials that students will be reading. Publishers of school materials generally provide readability levels, as do some trade book publishers. Renaissance Learning (http://www.renlearn.com/) provides readabilities for about fifty thousand trade books. The Lexile Framework for Reading (http://www.lexile.com/) provides readabilities for more than forty thousand books. Touchstone Applied Science Associates (http://tasaliteracy.com) offers readability estimates for more than six thousand textbooks in current use. TASA also has easy-to-use software that contains the readabilities of about twenty thousand books.

Unfortunately, readability sources don't all speak the same language. Renaissance Learning uses grade equivalents, as do most formulas. However, Lexile readabilities are expressed in a scale of numbers known as Lexile units, and Degrees of Reading Power scores are expressed in DRP units. Leveling systems are sometimes used instead of formulas to assess the difficulty level of materials. Leveling systems use subjective factors to estimate readability levels. Two of the best known leveling systems are the Reading Recovery system and the Fountas and Pinnell (1996) guided reading leveling system. Reading Recovery uses the numbers 1 to 20 to indicate finely graded levels that range from very beginning reading to mid-second grade. Guided reading uses the letters A to Z to indicate levels ranging from beginning reading to eighth grade. Table 3.2 provides a comparison of key ways of indicating difficulty levels. An extensive listing of books that have been leveled using either the Reading Recovery or guided reading methodologies

TABLE 3.2 *Comparison of Readability Levels*

Grade Equivalent	DRP	Lexile	Guided Reading	Reading Recovery
Emergent			A	1–2
Preprimer 1			B–C	3–4
Preprimer 2			D	5–6
Preprimer 3	34–36		E	7–8
Primer	37–39	200–300	F	9–10
First	40–43	300–400	G–I	11–17
2–1	44–45	400–500	J–K	18–20
2–2	46–47	400–500	L–M	
3	48–49	500–700	N–P	
4	50–51	700–800	Q–S	
5	52–53	800–900	T–V	
6	54–55	900–1000	W–X	
7	56–57	950–1050	Y	
8	58–59	1000–1100	Z	
9	60	1050–1150		
10		1100–1200		
11		1100–1200		
12		1200–1300		

BOX 3.3

Leveling Books: Personal Perspective

At Urban Public, we held an after-school leveling party. The principal supplied pizza and soda. Teachers were given instruction sheets for leveling books and several practice runs. We found that the readability levels provided by Renaissance Learning (http://renlearn.com) were a good starting point. Subjective factors were then used to adjust the levels up or down. Renlearn worked well except for first-grade level books. Renlearn was able to indicate fairly reliably that books were on a first-grade level, but was not able to say with sufficient precision where on the first-grade continuum of difficulty first-grade books lay. Because the first-grade students were using a series that emphasized decodable text, the texts were subleveled according to the difficulty level of the phonic items needed to read them. For instance, the easiest books required only short *a* and short *i* words and a few high-frequency words. The most difficult books required knowledge of basic single-syllable phonics, including short vowels, long vowels, *r* vowels, and other vowels, as well as an increasing range of high-frequency words. A listing of key elements for each level is presented in Table 3.4. The sequence is fairly universal so it can be easily adapted to most programs. Since the first-grade program has five books, with each book subdivided into two themes for a total of ten levels, first-grade books were designated on a 1 to 10 scale.

It should be noted that the program used by Urban Public was based on the premise that students should be taught a sequence of phonics skills and that skills needed to read a text should be introduced before that text is read. A corollary of this premise is that the books novice readers use should reinforce the phonics elements they have been taught. All basal programs and most intervention programs follow this same premise. However, some nonbasal programs are based on a natural language premise. Their early materials consist primarily of high-frequency words and predictable rather than decodable language. Leveling based on phonics doesn't work quite as well with predictable materials. For books beyond first grade for which there were no levels provided by Renlearn, a combined objective-subjective system was used (Gunning, 2005).

is found in Fountas and Pinnell (1996, 2005) and Pinnell and Fountas (2002). Levels for more than fourteen thousand books are available at http://www.fountasandpinnellleveledbooks.com for a fee. Two free sources for book levels are the Leveled Books Database (http://registration.beavton.k12.or.us/lbdb/), which was created by the Beaverton (Oregon) Public Schools, and Leveled Books (http://www.leveledbooks. com/index.htm).

Of course, if the text that you are planning on using does not have a difficulty level noted or is not listed in an available source, you might want to use a readability formula or leveling system to estimate the level of challenge. Another way of gauging the difficulty level of materials is to compare the material being assessed with a series of benchmark passages to see at what level the passages are similar. Benchmark passages and procedures for using them are found in the following sources: Carver, 1975–1976; Chall, Bissex, Conard, & Harris-Sharples, 1996; Gunning, 2005; or Singer, 1975.

TABLE 3.3 *Subjective Readability Factors*

Background required to read text	Familiar	Limited amount	Considerable
Difficulty and density of concepts	Easy	Average	Challenging
Difficulty of vocabulary	Easy	Average	Challenging
Complexity of language	Easy	Average	Challenging
Degree of interest of content	High	Average	Low
Use of graphics and other aids	High	Average	Low

TABLE 3.4 *First-Grade Levels as Determined by Presence of Phonic Elements*

Level	Key Elements
1	Short *a*, short *i* patterns
2	All short vowels patterns
3	Short vowels with *r* clusters
4	Short vowels with *s* & *l* clusters
5	Long vowels: *a* & *i*
6	Long vowels: *o, e, u, ai/ay*
7	Long and other vowels: *oa, oo, ew, igh*
8	Other vowels: *ou, ow,* compound words
9	Other vowels: *oi, oy, au, aw*
10	*r* vowels

Because readability formulas typically consist of some measure of vocabulary and sentence length, but don't consider factors such as background needed to read the selection or the interest level of the material, the use of a readability formula should be complemented by the use of subjective factors, as noted in Table 3.3. On the other side of the coin, use of a subjective leveling system should be buttressed by the use of objective data such as that yielded by a readability formula. The best estimates use both objective and subjective measures. For more information about assessing materials, see Gunning (2003).

Assessing the Assessment Component of Your Program

Assessment is the foundation for a program that helps beat the odds. Use the checklist in Table 3.5 to determine strengths and weaknesses of the assessment component of your program.

TABLE 3.5 *Assessment Checklist*

Action	Fully	Partially	Limited	Suggestions
Objectives, assessment, and instruction are aligned.				
Assessment is used to plan programs and professional development.				
A variety of outcome measures are used.				
Informal as well as formal measures are used to assess students' progress.				
Students are given screening tests in key areas.				
Students are given IRIs or other placement tests.				
Students are assessed in terms of how much progress they made and whether they have reached proficiency.				
Rubrics are used to assess writing assignments.				
Students are involved in creating rubrics for writing.				
Portfolios are maintained.				
Continuous monitoring is used to evaluate instruction and to make changes as needed.				
Students who fail to make progress despite intervention are given a diagnostic assessment.				
Readability levels of texts are obtained.				
Texts are leveled.				
Students are provided with books and other materials that are on the appropriate reading levels.				
Grade-level meetings are held to discuss assessment results, to provide suggestions for improving program, and to assist students not making adequate progress.				
Professional development sessions are held to discuss interpretation of assessment devices.				
Assessment results are shared with parents and students.				

4

Building Language

Language is the basis of reading and writing. To close the literacy gap, you must close the gap in language. According to research by Hart and Risley (1995), different children have vastly different experiences with language. In a landmark study, Hart and Risley (1995) observed forty-two families for an hour each month to discover how parents interacted with their young children as the children learned to talk. The researchers wanted to find out what caused the great differences in children's language development. Although Hart and Risley (1995) found that all of the families studied were caring and loving and wanted the best for their children, they found incredible differences in the amounts of language to which children were exposed. Within the first four years of life, children from welfare families would have heard about 13 million words, children from working-class families would have heard about 26 million words, and children from professional families would have heard about 45 million words. In addition, children from the most privileged families would have received more of the kind of feedback that would encourage them to learn and explore. Children from welfare families were more likely to receive negative feedback in the form of corrections or prohibitions. The quality of the interactions also differed. As the authors state:

> In our intensive examination of a small sample of American families we saw virtually all the professional families preparing their children for symbolic problem solving from the very beginning of their children's lives.
>
> We saw them devoting time and effort to giving their children experience with the language diversity and symbolic emphasis needed for manipulating symbols; we saw them using responsiveness and gentle guidance to encourage problem solving; we saw them providing frequent affirmative feedback to build the confidence and motivation required for sustained independent effort. We saw how strongly related the amount of such experience was to the accomplishment of working-class families. But we saw only one third of the working-class families and none of the welfare families similarly preparing their families. (pp. 203–204)

The key to developing young children's language was in the amount of talk. All parents used talk to regulate their children. It was the extra talk that resulted in the greater gains. As Hart and Risley (2002) comment:

> The data showed that when parents engaged children in more talk than was necessary to take care of business, the content changed automatically. When parents began to discuss feelings, plans, present activities, and past events, the vocabulary became more varied and the descriptions richer in nuances. Their talk also became more positive and responsive to their children's talk. (p. xx)

Although children from more privileged backgrounds are more likely to be provided with the skills necessary for success in school, social class is not the deciding factor. As Hart and Risley (1995) comment:

> Our data showed that the magnitude of children's accomplishments depend less on the material and educational advantages available in the home and more on the amount of experience children accumulate with parenting that provides language diversity, affirmative feedback, symbolic emphasis, gentle guidance, and responsiveness. (p. 210)

The implications for schooling are clear. While it is important for the school to stress language development, higher-level thinking skills, and an affirming and encouraging atmosphere, it is also important that the school work with parents. Parents can be shown ways to listen to and talk with their children and to encourage them. Schools can emphasize students' positive achievements and encourage parents to build on them. In addition, programs that coach parents of infants and toddlers to talk to and encourage their children should result in children who have a richer vocabulary and more advanced language development, which is the foundation for literacy (Gunning, 2005).

Developing Language in the Classroom

The secret of the development of language and thinking skills is talk and lots of it. In their study of exemplary fourth-grade teachers, researchers discovered that although the teachers were a diverse group, the characteristic that stood out most was the nature of their classroom talk (Allington, Johnston, & Day, 2002). Teachers talked to their students on a personal level to find out about their interests, their activities, and their concerns. In their instructional talk, they encouraged students to go beyond the surface and to think deeply about topics. Not surprisingly, the students of exemplary teachers did well on standardized reading and writing tests. More importantly, the thoughtful, high-quality literacy instruction offered by exemplary teachers "produced students who demonstrated dramatic improvements in the literate conversations, evidence of internalizing the thinking that was routinely demonstrated" (Allington, Johnston, & Day, 2002, p. 465). "Much, if not most, of the learning was fostered by the routine engagement in powerful class-room conversations" (p. 466).

Clay (2003) fostered language development by increasing students' opportunities to have conversations. She advised making activities in school so exciting that students want to talk about them. She suggested setting up activities in such a way that conversations are maximized.

Building Vocabulary

In addition to building language skills in general, it is also important to emphasize vocabulary development. Children enter school with widely varying vocabulary levels. Children at the 25th percentile are about one year below average whereas children at the 75th percentile are about a year above average (Biemiller, 2001; Biemiller & Slonin, 2001). Average students come to school knowing about 5,000 words. The lowest 25 percent of students have acquired just 3,000 words; the highest have acquired 8,000 words. Instead of closing the gap, traditional schooling seems to widen it. One reason is that children who have larger vocabularies can make better use of context and so can learn words at a faster pace than children with a more restricted vocabulary (Hart & Risley, 1995). Another factor is that much instruction in the primary grades is limited to words that children already know. By third or fourth grade, when the language of school texts becomes significantly more advanced, students with limited vocabularies experience difficulty with comprehension, even though they may have adequate decoding skills. As Biemiller (1999) comments:

> Early delays in oral language come to be reflected in low levels of reading comprehension, leading to low levels of academic success. If we are to increase children's ability to profit from education, we will have to enrich their oral language development during the early years of schooling. Although not all differences in language are due to differences in opportunity and learning, schools could do much more than they do now to foster the language development of less-advantaged children and children for whom English is a second language. (p. 2)

At age seven, students experience an increase in working memory capacity (Case, 1992). With increased working memory, students are able to both analyze new words and keep story context in mind (Biemiller & Slonin, 2001). They are also becoming capable of asking about words that they do not know. This fosters word learning ability. Before that age, children seldom ask questions about words, although they may ask lots of questions about objects. When asked how they learned some recently acquired words, children report that they learn words by asking about them or by having them explained by others (Biemiller, 1999).

For each year in school students gain approximately 1,000 word families (Nation, 2001). A word family consists of its headword, its inflected forms, and its closely related derived forms. A ten-year-old knows about 10,000 word families.

Educated speakers know about 20,000 word families. To catch up, low-vocabulary students would need to acquire about 1,500 word families a year.

Changing Nature of Reading

Schools do a relatively good job of teaching phonics and other beginning literacy skills. However, as students progress through the grades, vocabulary plays an increasingly prominent role. Students encounter an increasing number of technical and lower-frequency words. At about third or fourth grade, some students whose reading was satisfactory begin to experience difficulty. Lack of adequate vocabulary begins to hamper their progress. Chall, Jacobs, and Baldwin (1990) refer to this as the fourth-grade slump. Preventing or overcoming the fourth-grade slump requires a program of vocabulary instruction.

At-risk children enter school knowing fewer words than their more privileged counterparts. That gap remains or grows wider during the primary school years. In the primary grades, schools focus on what children know. In reading, they are taught the skills they need to sound out familiar words. The stories they read are mostly nonfiction and use familiar words. Discussions are about familiar topics: home, family, neighborhood, pets, and so forth. What is needed is a program that systematically helps narrow the vocabulary gap. Vocabulary is the foundation of reading and writing. Students can't read and write words that they don't know, no matter how well practiced their phonics and spelling skills are. Language limits how well they will be able to read and write. To improve their reading and writing, it is necessary to build their language. The vocabulary program should be deliberate and systematic, and it should focus on the most essential words.

The Words Students Need to Know

In one study, it was estimated that texts that students use in school contain more than 50,000 words (Nagy & Anderson, 1984). English as a second language (ELL) and at-risk children would seem to be hopelessly behind. However, not all words are of equal importance. Some of those 50,000 words, such as *the*, *of*, and *are*, occur in almost anything that students read. Others, such as *converge* and *decibel*, occur only once in 1 million words (Zeno, Ivens, Millard, & Duvvuri, 1995), which means that if students read 1 million words, they will encounter the word only once. And some words, such as *acclimate* and *orthogonal*, occur less than once every 10 million words. Given the frequency of occurrence of some words and the rarity of appearance of others, it makes sense to focus on the words that students are most likely to meet in their reading and listening. It also makes sense to group related words into families. Once a student has learned the word *encourage*, learning *encourages*, *encouraging*, *encouraged*, *encouragement*, and *discourage* is relatively easy.

Nation (2001) recommends grouping words into families. Nation also recommends dividing words into four categories: high-frequency words, academic

TABLE 4.1 *Alphabetical Listing of 500 High-Frequency Words*

a	bell	could	farmer	grandmother	hurt	lion
about	best	couldn't	fast	grandpa	I	listen
across	better	cow	father	grass	I'll	little
afraid	big	cried	feel	great	I'm	live
after	bike	cry	feet	green	I've	long
again	bird	cut	fell	ground	if	look
air	birthday	dad	felt	grow	in	lost
all	black	dark	few	guess	inside	lot
alone	blue	day	find	had	into	love
along	boat	did	fine	hair	is	lunch
always	book	didn't	fire	hand	isn't	made
am	both	different	first	happen	it	make
an	box	do	fish	happy	it's	man
and	boy	doctor	fix	hard	its	many
animal	bring	does	floor	has	jeep	mark
another	brother	dog	flower	hat	job	may
answer	brown	don't	fly	have	jump	maybe
any	bus	door	follow	he	just	me
anybody	but	down	food	head	keep	mean
anything	by	drink	for	hear	kept	men
are	cake	drop	found	heard	kid	might
arm	call	duck	four	held	kind	minute
around	came	each	fox	hello	king	mom
as	can	ear	friend	help	kitten	money
ask	can't	earth	frog	hen	knew	moon
at	cannot	eat	from	her	know	more
away	car	egg	front	here	lake	morning
baby	care	end	fun	high	last	mother
back	cat	enough	funny	hill	late	mouse
bad	catch	even	game	him	laugh	move
bag	change	ever	gave	himself	learn	much
ball	children	every	get	his	leave	must
be	city	everyone	girl	hit	left	my
bear	clean	everything	give	hold	leg	name
because	climb	eye	go	hole	let	near
bed	close	face	gone	home	let's	need
been	cloud	fall	good	horse	letter	never
before	cold	family	got	hot	light	new
began	come	far	grandfather	house	like	next
behind	cook	farm	grandma	how	line	nice

(continued)

TABLE 4.1 *Alphabetical Listing of 500 High-Frequency Words (continued)*

night	pig	same	so	that	turn	which
no	place	sat	some	that's	turtle	while
noise	plant	saw	someone	the	two	white
not	play	say	something	their	uncle	who
nothing	please	school	sometime	them	under	why
now	pond	sea	soon	then	until	wife
of	pretty	see	sound	there	up	will
off	pull	seed	spot	these	us	wind
oh	push	seem	stand	they	use	window
old	put	seen	star	thing	very	wish
on	quick	set	start	think	voice	with
once	quiet	she	stay	this	wait	without
one	rabbit	sheep	step	those	walk	wolf
only	race	ship	stick	thought	want	woman
open	rain	shoe	still	three	warm	won't
or	ran	shop	stood	through	was	wood
other	reach	short	stop	time	wasn't	word
our	read	should	store	tired	watch	work
out	ready	shout	story	to	water	would
outside	real	show	street	toad	way	write
over	really	sick	sun	today	we	year
own	red	side	sure	together	we'll	yell
paint	rest	sign	surprise	told	week	yellow
paper	ride	sing	swim	too	well	yes
park	right	sister	table	took	went	you
part	river	sit	take	top	were	you'll
party	road	sky	talk	town	wet	your
people	rock	sleep	tall	train	what	you're
pet	room	slow	tell	tree	what's	
pick	run	small	ten	tried	wheel	
picture	sad	smile	than	truck	when	
piece	said	snow	thank	try	where	

From *Creating Literacy Instruction for All Students* (5th ed.) by T. Gunning, 2005. Boston: Allyn & Bacon. Reprinted by permission of Allyn & Bacon.

words, technical words, and low-frequency words. High-frequency words are those that occur in the top 2,000 words. Academic words include terms such as *accurate, circumstances,* and *locate.* Coxhead (1998) created a list of 570 academic words. Technical words are the subject-related words, such as *villi* and *bile,* that are used to discuss a particular topic. Low-frequency words are words such as *menda-*

cious and *obsequious* that occur rarely. In an academic textbook, about 80 percent of the words are high-frequency words, 10 percent academic words, 5 percent technical words, and 5 percent low-frequency words (Nation, 2001).

Nonacademic texts have a higher proportion of high-frequency words. If you know the top 1,000 words, you will know 82 percent of the words used in popular fiction (Nation, 2001). If you know 2,000 words, you will know 87 percent of the words used in popular fiction. Knowing 3,000 word families gives students the ability to read about 95 percent of the typical reading passage with 60 percent comprehension. Knowing 5,000 word families results in 70 percent comprehension. These figures exclude proper names, compound words, abbreviations, and foreign words.

Focus on High-Frequency Words

The most efficient way to assist at-risk students and ELLs is to first develop the high-frequency words and then the academic vocabulary. Beginning readers and early reading books naturally reinforce the highest frequency words, and many teachers focus on the 200 words contained in the Dolch or Fry list. However, beyond the first 200 words, there is no systematic attempt to develop the highest frequency words. This works out just fine for achieving readers, but ELLs and struggling readers need a systematic approach. They need a program that introduces and reinforces the words they are most likely to need to know. A listing of the 500 most frequently occurring words is presented in Table 4.1.

Assessing Students' Word Knowledge

By matching learners to appropriate word study activities, teachers encourage students to join the stream of literacy learning and not get swept under in a "whirlpool" of mismatches between what is taught and what they are able to learn (Bear & Helman, 2004). Keeping in mind the principle of starting where students are, assess their word knowledge. Use the results from any vocabulary tests that students have taken. Keep in mind that if students had to read the vocabulary tests, their listening vocabularies might be underestimated, especially if they are struggling readers. There might be words that are in their listening vocabularies but that they didn't recognize in print. Also use informal methods to assess students' word knowledge. Note the range of words used in their writing and speaking. Note, also, the level of words that they understand but might not use. Students, especially ELLs, might have recognition vocabularies that far exceed their spoken or written vocabularies.

If you are working with students at the beginning reading levels or ELLs, you might find out how many of the high-frequency words in Table 4.1 students know. To determine whether students have the skills needed to decode the words, have students read them. If you want to see whether the words are in students' listening vocabularies, read the words to them and have them tell what the words mean.

You might also administer a test such as the Word Meaning subtest from the Diagnostic Assessment of Reading (DAR). The Word Meaning subtest is administered individually and requires students to define a series of words that increase in difficulty. The Word Meaning subtest is an expressive vocabulary test. It involves having students define words. A measure of receptive vocabulary is the Peabody Picture Vocabulary Test (PPVT). For this test, students are required only to point out the illustration that depicts the word spoken by the examiner. The PPVT is typically administered by a speech and language specialist.

Embedded and Systematic Programs

Vocabulary programs should be both embedded and systematic. Embedded vocabulary instruction entails learning the words that crop up in literacy selections, science, and social studies. Embedded instruction is teaching as needed. Systematic instruction means setting aside periods of time for the study of vocabulary. Targeted instruction in vocabulary works better than general instruction. Instructing students in words that they will be meeting in their reading is three times as effective as providing them with general lists of words to be learned (Stahl & Fairbanks, 1986). Whether instruction is embedded or systematic, it is important to select words that students will be meeting in their reading.

In the past, pronouncements on vocabulary instruction were pessimistic. There was a belief that students needed to learn so many words that a program of direct instruction would be virtually useless. However, research by Nation (2001) and Biemiller (2004) indicates that although there are a large number of words in the English language, most are relatively rare and occur less than once in a million times. The number of words to be learned is not overwhelming if instruction focuses on the most useful words. Beck and McKeown (2001; McKeown & Beck, 2004) recommend a program of direct instruction and maintain that it is possible to teach 400 words a year. According to Biemiller's (2001) research, students in the primary grades were able to learn 12 words a week through instruction and retained them when tested a month later. Biemiller (2001) also found that students, regardless of background, acquired vocabulary in approximately the same order. Thus, it is feasible to construct a program of vocabulary acquisition. A key element in such a program is the selection of the words. The words need to be developmentally appropriate but also of high frequency.

A Four-Part Program

To close the vocabulary gap, a four-part program is recommended. The four major components include the following.

- *Instruction in words as needed.* Each group will study the words it needs, before reading a selection in language arts class or in connection with content-area study, for instance. You might choose to have the most useful of these words recorded in vocabulary notebooks.

- *Planned introduction of words.* Five to ten words will be introduced each week. Emphasis will be on studying highly useful words in depth. Instruction can be whole group or small group. These words can be introduced during read-alouds or through other activities. Students record these words in vocabulary notebooks.
- *Individual word study.* Students will choose five words to study from their outside reading or other sources. Words will be recorded in vocabulary notebooks.
- *Learning to learn words.* An essential element in a program of vocabulary development will be learning how to learn words. Needed word identification skills will be introduced or reviewed: phonics and syllabic analysis, morphemic analysis (roots and affixes), context clues, glossary and dictionary skills. Instruction will be mostly small group. Instruction should be held daily for about 10 to 15 minutes and could be conducted in preparation for reading a selection. The element chosen for study is one that appears in the selection to be read and is one that students need to learn.

Using Read-Alouds to Build Vocabulary

An easy-to-implement, efficient way to build vocabulary is to read to students. Students will acquire vocabulary if you do nothing else but read to them. They will acquire more vocabulary if you read the same story two or three times. And they will acquire even more words if you take the time to explain and discuss some key words. Out of every 10 words that you introduce, children will learn 2 or 3 words. They learn only 2 or 3 words because in every class there is a wide range of word knowledge. Some of the students will already know some of the words that you present (Biemiller, 2004). And some will find that the more difficult words are too advanced for them.

Students will further increase their word knowledge if you review the newly introduced words. If children learn 3 words a day just about every school day, they will learn 500 words a year in this way. If these words are in addition to words that they learn at home or during other times during the school day, then this will be a powerful tool for closing the literacy gap.

To make reading aloud an effective approach for building vocabulary, you need to take certain steps. First, you have to choose books that lend themselves to vocabulary building. Select books that present a modest challenge to students. If the book has too many unknown words or concepts or requires specialized background that students lack, they will have a difficult time learning new words because the overall context of the selection will not lend them sufficient support.

When choosing words to present, select those that you believe will be challenging to students but not overly so. To gain insight into children's word knowledge, say prospective words and place on the board if you think students are able to read them. As you point to and say a word, ask students to raise their hands if they know the word.

Read-aloud books are better sources of new words for students in the early grades than are the books they read. Up until about grade 3, the books that students read are composed primarily of known words. Teachers frequently read books to students that would be too hard for them to read on their own. Carefully chosen read-alouds can be effective for building word knowledge. Whereas it is best to introduce words beforehand when students are reading on their own, it is better to discuss vocabulary words after a selection has been read aloud to students. If words are needed for an understanding of a selection, then they can be explained briefly as the selection is being read. This will enable students to use their knowledge of the new words to comprehend the selection.

Text Talk

Beck, McKeown, and Kucan (2002) created an approach known as Text Talk in which a portion of the read-aloud is devoted to developing vocabulary. From a series of well-respected children's book, two to four words were selected. The words selected were unknown to students, but they labeled known concepts. These included words such as *reluctant, immense, miserable,* and *searched*. The words were presented in the context of the story, discussed, and later used by students. Text Talk has six steps.

1. Presenting the word in story context
2. Providing an understandable definition of the words
3. Providing examples of the use of the word in other contexts, so that the word generalizes
4. Having children relate the word to their own lives
5. Reviewing the word
6. Encouraging students to use the word in their speaking and writing and also to note examples of hearing or seeing the words

Here is how the word *reluctant* from the classic tale, *A Pocket for Corduroy* (Freeman, 1978), was introduced.

Step 1: The teacher introduces the word *reluctant* to label Lisa's feeling. "In the story, Lisa was reluctant to leave the Laundromat without Corduroy."
Step 2: The teacher gives an understandable definition of *reluctant* and also has students say the word so that they can use the spoken representation to help store the word in memory. "*Reluctant* means you are not sure you want to do something. Say the word with me."
Step 3: The teacher provides examples of the word. "Someone might be reluctant to eat a food that he or she never had before, or someone might be reluctant to ride a roller coaster because it looks scary."
Step 4: The teacher invites students to relate the word to their lives. To assist the children, the teacher provides a frame. "Tell about something you would be reluctant to do. Try to use *reluctant* when you tell about it. You could start by saying something like 'I would be reluctant to _____.'"
Step 5: The teacher reviews the word. As appropriate, the teacher uses the word in other contexts. "I am reluctant to go outside because it is so hot."

Step 6: One key to vocabulary development is to note other contexts in which new words are used. Students are urged to be on the lookout for examples of new words in the reading that they do or on TV shows that they watch or in conversations or discussions that they hear. In an activity known as Word Wizard, new words are posted on the wall. Underneath the words, the students' names are listed. Students are given a check when they report an instance of hearing the word spoken or using the word in their writing or speaking. Students with the most checks are given awards.

As part of your read-aloud program be sure to include informational text. The read-alouds might be conducted as part of the science or social studies instruction.

Wide Reading

Once students are able to read challenging texts on their own, the best source of new words is through wide reading. If reading materials are on the appropriate level, students have about a 15 percent chance of deriving the meanings of unfamiliar words from context (Swanborn & de Glopper, 1999). Out of 100 hard words, readers would be able to derive a suitable meaning for 15 of those words. If students read a million words at 98 percent word recognition, they would encounter

BOX 4.1

Text Talk: Personal Perspective

Teachers are more likely to adopt a new technique or approach if they see a need for it, it fits into their program, and it doesn't add to an already overflowing workload. Because the students at Urban Public had limited vocabularies, which, left uncorrected, would limit their growth, vocabulary development was emphasized as an essential strand in the program. In addition to having their students acquire vocabulary from reading, subject-matter study, classroom discussions, and selection of words that students wished to learn, teachers were asked to use the Text Talk concept (Beck & McKeown, 2001). The basal program that they were using started each week's work with a read-aloud selection. Most of the selections contained a number of difficult but useful words. Along with reading the basal's read-aloud selection to their students, the teachers were asked to develop four or five vocabulary words. Since they were reading the selections to the students anyway, all that would be involved would be taking a few minutes at the conclusion of the reading to develop the vocabulary and planning some related activities such as having students make personal connections to the new words or to be the lookout for the words in their reading or other sources. For a time, teachers were given Vocabulary Planners in which the planning was done for them (see Figure 4.1). Using Text Talk with the read-alouds over a year's time, teachers were able to present between 100 and 150 additional words to students. Scores on end-of-year tests showed encouraging gains.

Selection: *Daddy, Could I Have an Elephant?*

Word	Context	Easy Definition	Personal Connection	Decoding
herds	Elephants live in herds.	Groups or bunches of horses, cows, or elephants	Tell about a time when you saw a herd of animals, either in person or on TV.	Have students note the *her* in *herds*.
flock	A flock of woolly sheep would be nice.	Group or bunch of sheep or birds	Tell about a time when you saw a flock of birds.	Note that *flock* is formed by adding *f* to *lock*.
definite	We could give them a definite bedtime.	For sure, will not change, no question about it, exact	What are some definite times that you have? Do you have a definite bedtime or a definite time to get up?	Note the *def* and the *it* in *definite*.
decided	What if they decided to climb in somebody else's window?	Made up your mind	Tell about something that you decided to do last week.	Note that *c* has an *s* sound so that *cided* sounds like *sided*.
screech	Parrots screech.	A loud, high sound	What kind of screeches have you heard? Can you screech?	Note the *ee* in the middle. Add *scr* and *ch*.

FIGURE 4.1 *Vocabulary Planner*

20,000 unknown words. Learning 15 percent of them means that they would pick up 3,000 words through their reading. Of course, if they read more and learned to make better use of context clues, they would acquire more words.

Another reason why wide reading is necessary for word learning is because readers might need to meet a word a number of times before deriving a meaning for it (Rapaport, 2004). Jenkins, Stein, and Wysocki (1984) estimate that it might require as many as six meetings before students accurately derive the meaning from context and also have sufficient exposure to the word so that they remember it. One way of looking at word learning is the concept of layers of meaning. When first encountering an unfamiliar word, we might get a general impression of its meaning. With subsequent meetings of the word, we add to that general meaning and acquire a greater depth and breadth of knowledge of the word. In a sense, we learn a word bit by bit.

For free reading, students should be reading on or close to their independent levels (98 percent). Otherwise, they will be meeting too many unknown words and so won't be able to use context clues. For vocabulary development, reading informational text is especially important. After learning the 2,000 most frequent words, students should start reading informational texts because these are the primary sources of an academic vocabulary (Nation, 2001).

Nation (2001) recommends that students reading at about a second-grade or third-grade level should read at least about 10,000 words a week. This assumes that newly learned words will be forgotten unless encountered within a week. Based on the frequency with which words at that level occur, students are most likely to meet them again if they read 10,000 words a week. Words at the 10,000 frequency level and slightly beyond occur about once every 10,000 words. If students read 100 words a minute, then they would need to read for 20 minutes a day for five days. This means reading 50 pages containing 200 words each. At the fourth- and fifth-grade levels, students would need to read almost twice as many words because they would be encountering lower-frequency words. But at that level, reading speed increases so chances are that little or no additional time would be required.

Vocabulary Notebooks

Word study or vocabulary notebooks foster the study of words. Separate sections might be used to list words that are studied in school and personal words that students add from their reading, conversations, or other sources. For older students, entries might include the word, its definition, the context in which it was used (this can be abbreviated), related words, and its etymology or history (Bear, Invernizzi, Templeton, & Johnston, 2004). Younger students might simply record the word, a simplified definition supplied by the teacher, and an example of the word's use.

Fostering an Interest in Words

Spurring student interest in words also bolsters vocabulary growth. This can be done by highlighting interesting or unusual words, exploring the history of words, having fun with words, playing word games, solving riddles, and completing crossword puzzles. Students should also be encouraged to become collectors of words. An especially effective technique for engendering an interest in words is the vocabulary selection strategy (VSS). VSS helps students personalize their learning (Ruddell, 1992). In VSS, each student chooses one word to learn. The word chosen is one that the student believes is important enough for the whole class to learn. The teacher also chooses a word. Students record the printed sentence or oral context in which they heard or saw the word, write down what they think the word means in the context in which it is found, and explain why they think the word is a good candidate for the whole class to learn.

With the whole class or in small groups, words and possible meanings are discussed; dictionaries and glossaries may be checked to make sure that the correct pronunciation and definition have been obtained. As the words and their possible meanings are discussed by the whole class, the teacher might model the use of context clues and the dictionary. Each small group might vote on one word to be studied, or in a whole-class discussion, students might select five or so of the words to be nominated. The teacher also submits a word, and then the complete list is reviewed. Words selected are recorded in vocabulary notebooks or study sheets. Realizing that they are responsible for selecting a word for the whole class, students suddenly become word aware and begin considering words as possible candidates for selection. As students become more conscious of words, they naturally acquire new vocabulary words at an increased rate (Shearer, 1999). VSS is initiated after the text has been read because being familiar with the text helps students select words that are important.

Vocabulary Activities

Word study lends itself to a variety of interesting reinforcement activities. Some possibilities, which are drawn from Beck, McKeown, & Kucan, 2002; Beers, 2003; Curtis & Longo, 2001; Nation, 2001, include the following.

- Matching words and definitions
- Answering questions and giving reasons
  Why might you be reluctant to wear your new shoes on a rainy day?
  Give three examples of things you are reluctant to do.
  Which of these things might a dog be reluctant to do?
  ____ go outside on a very cold day
  ____ chew on a bone
  ____ chase a cat
  ____ share its food with another dog
  ____ take a nice warm bath
- Making choices
  Which of these are delicious?
  ____ apple pie
  ____ chocolate ice cream
  ____ spinach
  ____ broccoli
  ____ chocolate cake
  ____ strawberries and cream
- Sorting
  Words are sorted or classified according to common features or shared meanings. They could be sorted according to whether they are nouns or verbs, are positive or negative, are reptiles or mammals, are large or small, and so on.
- Supplying examples
  List five condiments.
  List three natural disasters.
- Filling in blanks with the new words
- Matching sentence halves
- Matching words and illustrations that depict their meanings
- Collocations
  Collocations are words that frequently occur together: an opportune moment, a moment in time, in a few moments, a moment of silence (Nation, 2001). Knowing collocations helps students to use words correctly and speeds their reading. Collocations are processed as single units rather than as

separate words. Where possible, provide students with examples of phrases in which new vocabulary words appear.

- Completing unfinished sentences by supplying cause or effects
  I was anxious to go to school because_____.
  Because of the drought, the farmers had to _____.
  The building was demolished because _____ .
- Answering questions about words
  If you were adrift in a raft, would you rather see a beacon or a beggar?
  Give the name of a popular athlete.
  Can astronauts be in an audience?
  Tell about a time when you were famished.
- Noting examples
  Which of these are used to communicate?
  _____ newspaper
  _____ house
  _____ e-mail
  _____ tree
  _____ cell phone
- Substitution
  Students substitute a new vocabulary for a word or phrase that has the same meaning.
  Our efforts <u>were</u> <u>blocked</u> by a lack of supplies.
  A tall crane was <u>needed</u> to lift the steel beams.
- Cloze
  Students fill in the blanks of a passage with vocabulary words.
- Maze
  Students pick from three to five possible words the one that correctly fits in the blank.
- Words across contexts
  To broaden students' knowledge of multiple meanings of words, engage in Words Across Contexts (Beers, 2003). What would the word *stock* mean to banker, a cattleman, a chef, a store owner?
- Logographs
  Have students create logographs or illustrations for their words (Beers, 2003). In a logograph, students use a symbol or drawing to illustrate the meaning of a word.
- Chart of word forms
  Students fill out a form similar to the following (Nation, 2001):

Noun	Verb	Adjective	Adverb
accuracy		accurate	accurately
immensity		immense	immensely
conqueror	conquer, conquered, conquering		

- Composing the correct form
Because I had not done my homework, I went to school _____. (reluctant)
Because the dog would not follow commands, it was taken to _____ school.
(obey)

Using Imaging to Learn Words

Linguistic modality is not the only way of representing a word. Words can and
should be represented as images (Marzano, 2004). In one study, students learned
words twice as well when they created images of them as opposed to just learning
a definition (Powell, 1980). Graphic organizers can also be helpful. Graphic organizers
are semantic maps, pictorial maps, webs, and other devices that allow students
to view and construct relationships among words. Because they are visual
displays, they allow students to picture and remember word relationships. Having
visual ways of learning words can be especially helpful to ELLs or native speakers
who have a limited vocabulary.

Labeled Illustrations

Labeling illustrations can be used to reinforce vocabulary. Objects can range
from the names of common farm animals to the parts of a cell or the parts of computer.
A wide range of Label Me! printouts are available from Enchanted Learning
(http://www.enchantedlearning.com).

Setting Goals for Vocabulary Learning

Students should have vocabulary goals. What words do they want to learn and
why? It could be in preparation for an upcoming high-stakes test or to learn science
words or to expand one's vocabulary generally. Composing goals and selecting
vocabulary to achieve those goals is a characteristic of effective learners (Gu &
Johnson, 1996). Learners need a strategy for deciding which words to study and
finding sources for those words (Nation, 2001). For instance, they might decide on
a workbook program or focusing on the new words in a science text. Students also
need to be aware of strategies for learning and retaining words. Using context
might be followed by checking the words in the dictionary and recording words
on cards for study.

FAME: An Intensive Vocabulary Development Program

FAME is a sixteen-week vocabulary course in which struggling readers typically
gain a year's growth (Curtis & Longo, 2001). Curtis and Longo (2001) found that

limited vocabularies were causing comprehension problems and poor comprehension was limiting vocabulary development. In their intensive program, they spent 45 minutes day, five days a week, for sixteen weeks on vocabulary. Each unit consisted of 10 words. About half the words would be new. Students probably had some knowledge of the other half of the words.

The program was intensive. A key goal was to provide many opportunities for students to encounter the new words. Emphasis was on having students process the words so that both understanding and retention would be fostered. During the introduction of a new word, the teacher made sure the word was presented in a variety of contexts. In the presentation of the word *persistent,* notice the varied contexts and note, too, how the teacher draws out from students contexts in which the word might be used.

> A persistent person is someone who hangs in there despite difficulties. We often hear or read about people like this—people who overcame a bunch of obstacles to succeed. Like an athlete who was persistent even though he or she had injuries— they refused to give up. Can anyone think of someone they know or have heard about who was persistent, who refused to give up?. . . Could persistence ever be a negative thing? Can anybody think of a situation when someone's refusal to give up or let go might be harmful?. . . We had at least one word in an earlier unit that is related to *persistence*—can anyone think of one? The one I thought of was *endurance.* What connections do you see between *endurance* and *persistence*? (Curtis & Longo, 2001)

After the words have been introduced, students work together on an activity in which they complete unfinished sentences by providing examples of the words' meanings. They tell about a time when they were persistent. During discussions of the completed sentences, students use the new words and learn from each other. Listening to the discussions, the teacher can assess students' grasp of the words and provide clarification as needed.

Students then complete sentence and paragraph cloze activities. This provides additional opportunities to use the words in context. Students also complete analogies and respond to yes-no questions that include a pair of the words studied: Could something *persistent* ever *be extinguished*? Opportunities to use the words in conversation and writing are provided. In the conversations, the teacher starts talking about a topic, and students are encouraged to join in by using in their response one or more of the vocabulary words. Topics are chosen for conversations and for writing that lend themselves to the use of the new words.

To strengthen the relationship between word knowledge and reading, students read selections containing the new words. If selections cannot be found that contain the new words, they can be incorporated into questions about the reading selection. After reading about Goodyear, for instance, students might respond to the question: "What incidents from the article indicate that Goodyear was persistent?"

A key feature of FAME is ongoing monitoring of progress. For each unit students are given a multiple-choice pretest and a post-test. The pretest helps the teacher determine the extent of students' word knowledge. Words that most students had difficulty with can be given more emphasis. A post-test is given at the end of each unit. The post-test consists of the words introduced and five words from previous units. However, students are not assessed just on their scores on the post-tests; assessment also includes students' recognition of the new words in their reading and the use of the words in their speaking and writing. Teachers also hold conferences with students to talk over their progress and determine steps that they might take to improve. "Of particular importance is helping students understand that their grade on the post-test is only one aspect of their performance in the course. Being able to deal with words in listening, speaking, reading, and writing are all of equal significance in demonstrating vocabulary growth" (Curtis & Longo, 2001). A grade sheet is used to summarize students' performance. The grade sheet includes test scores as well as a rubric indicating performance on an activity sheet and the use of words in speaking and writing, as in the following sample:

Use of Words in Writing

_____ You did a great job in using your vocabulary words in your writing.
_____ You used some of your vocabulary words in your writing.
_____ Your writing assignments were incomplete or not handed in at all.

Standardized tests are also administered. Students typically gain a year in both vocabulary and comprehension (Curtis & Longo, 2001).

Commercial Programs

For the most part, words to be studied should be derived from materials that students are reading or words they need to know in the content areas. However, when students' vocabularies are lagging to such an extent that they are hindering progress, then, as suggested earlier, you might initiate a program of direct instruction in key words. A list of common root words is found in the appendix of _Language and Reading Success_ (Biemiller, 1999) or you might compose your own list. The best list is composed of words that students will be meeting in their reading and content-area texts. Also available are a number of commercially produced vocabulary programs. Information on FAME is available from Girls and Boys Town (https://www.girlsand boystown.org/pros/training/education/FAME_program.asp). A sampling of other commercial vocabulary programs is listed below.

- Connecting Reading and Writing with Vocabulary (Curriculum Associates). Combines vocabulary instruction with instruction in reading and writing. Introduces from 120 words (Book 1) to 192 words (Book 8).
- Elements of Reading: Vocabulary (Harcourt Achieve). Created by Beck and McKeown and designed for grades K–3, it implements many of the strategies in their Text Talk procedure in which new words are introduced in the context of selections read orally and are then discussed and used in a variety of contexts.

- Vocabulary Works (Modern Curriculum Press). Designed for grades 1–6, this program uses reading selections, writing, riddles, puzzles, and a variety of activities to reinforce words.
- Wordly Wise (Educators Publishing Service). Wordly Wise 3000 Books A, B, C (grades 2–4) presents 300 new vocabulary words. Provides variety of application exercises. Wordly Wise 3000 Books 1–9 (grades 4–12) presents 3,000 words from literature and provides a variety of exercises.

Helping English Language Learners

Ultimately, what hinders ELLs most is a lack of a large vocabulary. Young children enter first grade knowing about 5,000 words. Once in school, children learn about 1,000 word families a year (Nation, 2001). Although most ELLs learn words at the same rate as native speakers of English, they start off knowing fewer words. An ELLs entering first grade may be as much as 5,000 words behind.

Because many ESL and bilingual programs have been curtailed or eliminated, ELLs find themselves in situations where language is a barrier to their learning. To optimize instruction for ELLs, teachers will need to develop English language skills along with content. One focus of the literacy program should be on helping ELLs acquire a basic reading vocabulary. As noted earlier, with a vocabulary of just 2,000 words, students would be able to recognize nearly 90 percent of the words in popular novels and 80 percent of the words in newspapers (Nation, 2001). Even with a vocabulary of just 1,000 words, students would know more than 90 percent of the words in third-grade level texts.

Although wide reading is an excellent source of learning new words, ELLs have more difficulty using context to derive the meanings of unknown words. Being less familiar with English, ELLs are less able to use linguistic cues that are readily used by native speakers (Grabe & Stoller, 2001). With their limited vocabularies, ELLs are likely to meet a greater proportion of unknown words in reading selections. For that reason, do more vocabulary preparation before ELLs read a selection. ELLs may know a number of words that represent concepts or items, but they may lack the English labels. Selecting books that are heavily illustrated is especially helpful.

Many English words are cognates of words from the Romance languages (which include Spanish, French, Italian, and Portuguese). A cognate is a word that has the same root or origin as a word in another language: *autor* (Spanish) and *author*. About one-third of the words in English have cognates in Spanish. In her text on cognates, Nash (1993) lists 20,000 English and Spanish cognates. High-frequency Spanish cognates are shown in Table 4.2 (see Nash for a lengthy listing of cognates). Spanish-speaking students don't always recognize or use cognates. Helping them use cognates will make English texts more accessible and will help them build an English vocabulary.

To build vocabulary, a program of direct instruction of useful words is recommended. Also recommended is instruction in the use of word learning clues such as morphemic analysis, syllabic analysis, and dictionary skills. Such a program can be offered to classes in which there is a mixture of native English speakers and ELLs. In an extensive study of vocabulary development, both native speakers and ELLs benefited from instruction in vocabulary that featured introduction of about 12 new words a week and instruction in word recognition skills (Carlo et al., 2004). One helpful feature of the program was that the words chosen for instruction were defined in Spanish as well as in English. ELLs might find a definition provided in their native language to be of help when learning new English words.

Another way to assist English language writers is to respect their bilingualism by allowing them to use it. If students are better able to formulate a response in their native language, allow them to do so. If composing a written piece in their native tongue first and then translating that into English allows them to formulate a more elaborate piece, encourage them to do so.

Closing the Gap for ELLs

The gap between ELLs and English-speaking students is approximately 25 normal curve equivalents (NCEs) (Thomas & Collier, 2002). A NCE is a rank on a scale that goes from 1 to 100. An average NCE is 50. It is possible to make up the gap with either a bilingual program or an English immersion program, if well implemented. The most effective bilingual programs reduce the gap by about 5 NCE points per year. In other words, it takes approximately five years to catch up with the English-speaking population. The most effective English immersion programs reduce the gap by about 3 NCE points per year. In other words, it takes approximately 8 years to catch up.

The implications of the research are clear. ELLs should receive language support for a substantial period of time. Most students need five years or more. Class-

TABLE 4.2 *High-Frequency Spanish Cognates*

artista	elefante	insecto	papá
autor	enciclopedia	jirafa	perfecta
bebé	familia	mágico	rápido
biografía	famoso	mamá	teléfono
carácter	favorito	mayo	tigre
carro	foto	minuto	tomate
causa	fruta	música	uniforme
contento	gigante	necesita	vegetales
describir	gorila	nota	zoológico
diferente	grado	número	
difícil	hipopótamo	oficina	
eléctrica	importante	página	

room teachers need to continue to foster ELLs' language growth. In a sense, every teacher needs to become a teacher of English. Some steps that the classroom teacher might take to foster language development include the following.

- Speak slowly but distinctly and use gestures freely. Pantomime actions and demonstrate processes.
- Make directions as clear as possible. Show students what to do in addition to telling them. If possible, model the process for them.
- Whenever possible, use the visual to reinforce the verbal. When introducing a new word, show a picture of it if possible, and write it on the board. When mentioning a place, write its name on the board and show it on a map.
- Use audiovisual aids whenever possible. Use timelines, graphs, videos, and film clips on CD-ROM.
- Use realia such as nutrition labels, menus, job applications, and bank deposit slips.
- Use demonstrations and skits to make the language as meaningful as possible.
- Modify use of text. If necessary, read portions of the text with students or do a picture walk. In a picture walk, you go through a chapter or section that students are about to read and use the illustrations as a basis for discussing the text. For instance, before students read a trade book, such as *Mrs. Brown Went to Town* (Yee, 1996), explain that the first picture shows Mrs. Brown on her farm; the second picture shows a cow, two pigs, three ducks, and a yak, and it shows Mrs. Brown riding her bike to town. The next picture shows a terrier, tasting Mrs. Brown's feet. You might discuss what the expression "tasting feet" means. The picture walk continues through the rest of the text so that students become familiar with the plot and the language of the story. To provide some suspense to the story, you might stop toward the end of the story, encourage students to predict what might happen, and then have them read the text on their own to see how their predictions play out.
- Arrange for opportunities for students to talk over ideas. This could be in whole-class discussions, in pairs, or in small groups.
- Check students' understanding of the material frequently by asking questions about the material covered. Ask students to retell what they have learned or explain the significance of what they have learned.
- If possible, have a word wall of key items in which the words are written in English and also in the students' native language.
- Before students write, brainstorm possible words they might use. You might also add words to the list. Encourage students to use the words in their writing.
- Have available lots of dictionaries that define words both in English and in the students' native language.
- Label objects in the room and discuss the labels. If possible, the labels should be in the students' native language and in English.
- Use dialogue journals. In dialogue journals, students respond to a selection they are reading or they simply communicate with you about the selection or

a concern that they have about the selection. You collect the journals and respond to students. In your responses, you model questions and other structures, which students can then imitate.

Assessing the Language Development Component of Your Program

Both reading and writing are based on language. Use the language development checklist in Table 4.3 to determine strengths and weaknesses of the language development component of your program.

TABLE 4.3 *Language Development Checklist*

	Fully	Partially	Limited	Suggestions
Students' listening vocabulary is assessed with formal or informal measures.				
Students' reading vocabulary is assessed with formal or informal measures.				
Read-aloud program is designed, in part, to develop language.				
Teachers engage students in conversation and discussion individually and in groups.				
Teachers use prompts, probes, and wait time to foster expanded language.				
Key vocabulary is taught in every subject area.				
A segment of time is set aside each day for language and vocabulary development.				
Students are given opportunities to discuss in pairs and small groups.				
Adjustments are made for ELLs.				
For all students, but especially for ELLs, teachers develop language as they develop content.				
Students who have language difficulties are referred for assessment and special services.				
Parents are encouraged to talk more extensively to their children.				

5

Building Higher-Level Thinking Skills and Comprehension

One of the most effective things you can do to improve students' achievement is to foster higher-level thinking skills. Minority and low-income students are more likely to be taught basic skills rather than higher-level thinking processes. Students in programs that emphasize basic skills fall further and further behind as they progress through the grades and there is more of a demand for more advanced thinking. Reading scores drop off beginning in third grade when the emphasis shifts from decoding and asking low-level questions to dealing with more complex text and using higher-level comprehension skills. A survey of three hundred high-performing, high-poverty schools revealed that they spend more time providing instruction in reading and writing (Education Trust and the Council of Chief State School Officers, 1999). They also reported a decrease in such low-level activities as completing practice activities and increased use of such higher-level activities as discussing selections read. As they stated, "If we want to reduce the test score gap and the skills gap, we will have to organize classrooms to emphasize teaching and learning models that blend mastery of basic skills and higher order thinking for all students"(p. 4).

Most programs designed to close the literacy gap emphasize basic skills. Although emphasis on basic skills does result in test gains, it might limit students' acquisition of advanced skills. Researchers have found that programs that stress meaning and understanding are just as effective as basic skills programs in promoting basic skills and are more effective in fostering advanced skills. In reading, this entailed increasing the amount of reading students do; in writing, it meant having students write more extensive reports or longer stories (Knapp, Shields, & Turnbull, 1992). Means and Knapp (1991) concluded that programs that are restricted to basic skills have the following flaws:

> underestimate what students are capable of doing; postpone more challenging and more interesting work for too long—in many cases forever; and deprive students of meaningful or motivating context for learning or for employing the skills that are taught. (pp. 283-284)

BOX
5.1

Model Program: Fostering Thinking by Using a Scenario Approach

When teaching literature, Johannessen (2004) uses a scenario approach. Scenarios enable students to connect what they are reading and writing with their own lives and also engenders interest in what they are doing. To initiate a unit on heroes and heroism, Johannessen (2004) presents students with a list of ten scenarios in which deeds of varying degrees of heroism and/or danger are described. Students gather in small groups and rank the ten acts according to the degree of heroism they embody. Based on these rankings, students then compose a definition of what it means to be a hero. Analyzing and discussing the scenarios leads them to do some careful thinking about the qualities that make up heroism. The class regroups and then composes a set of criteria for heroism. These criteria are used to judge the heroes in the selections that they read. As Johannessen (2004) states, the reading becomes more purposeful, and students "have something to look for—the attitudes, behavior, motivation, and actions of characters presented in literature" (p. 645). Working with scenarios has enabled struggling students to become more analytical and to internalize the kinds of questions that achieving readers employ.

To foster higher-level thinking skills, Johannessen (2004) recommends implementing the following eight principles when working with struggling learners.

- Stress higher-level questions and problems.
- Embed basic skills instruction in the context of higher-level activities, so that needed reading and writing skills are taught as students compare two literacy pieces or compose a report, for example, on the effect of drought on disease.
- Make connections with students' experiences and cultures.
- Model effective thinking strategies—evaluating and summarizing a difficult passage or comparing conflicting information derived from multiple sources.
- Encourage students to describe strategies that they used to construct meaning from difficult text or to compose complex pieces.
- Scaffold tasks as necessary, by providing prompts or frames, for instance.
- Emphasize discussion and mutual construction of meaning. (Questioning the Author, accountable talk, reciprocal teaching, and similar approaches are designed to do this.)
- Use teaching approaches that help students internalize the kinds of strategies that effective readers and writers use.

Teaching Specific Thinking Skills

To be effective, programs designed to foster higher-level thinking should include the most useful strategies. In a review of learning strategies, Marzano and associates (2000) concluded that teaching students to compare and classify was the most effective strategy of all. Students who were taught these skills gained an average of

45 percentile points, which translates into a gain of about one and one-half years. Comparing and classifying and other essential thinking skills are described below.

Comparing

In a comparison task, students note essential similarities and differences. In general, it is easier for students to note differences, especially if the similarities are subtle. Differences seem to stand out more than similarities. To teach comparing, have students compare items in which the similarities are fairly obvious and concrete. To make the task easier, give them the dimensions for making the comparison: the experiences and the challenges faced by Sam from *My Side of the Mountain* (George, 1988) and Brian from *Hatchet* (Paulsen, 1987). As students become more adept at making comparisons, have them choose the areas for comparison (Marzano, Gaddy, & Dean, 2000). When discussing students' comparisons, be sure to have them explain their responses and back up choices by citing supporting text or explaining their reasoning.

Use comparing and contrasting as part of your everyday questioning and classroom discussions. Some possible comparisons include the following.

- Characters with other characters and characters with real people
- Settings with other settings and with real places
- Events, themes, and plots

Informational text offers unlimited comparisons, as the following examples show.
- Historical figures, events, and eras
- Political parties
- Ideas

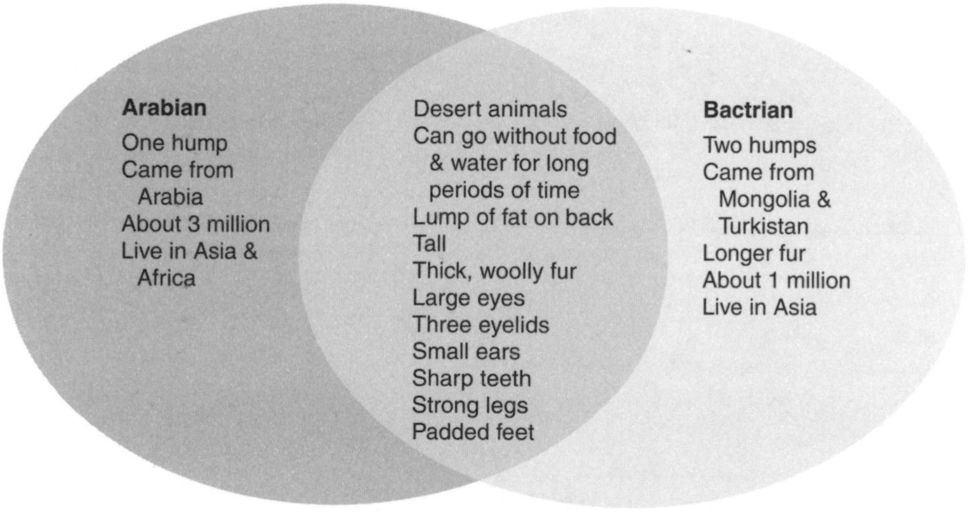

Arabian

One hump
Came from
   Arabia
About 3 million
Live in Asia &
   Africa

Desert animals
Can go without food
   & water for long
   periods of time
Lump of fat on back
Tall
Thick, woolly fur
Large eyes
Three eyelids
Small ears
Sharp teeth
Strong legs
Padded feet

Bactrian

Two humps
Came from
   Mongolia &
   Turkistan
Longer fur
About 1 million
Live in Asia

FIGURE 5.1 *Venn Diagram* Camels

- Inventions
- Cities, states, countries, continents
- Animals, insects, habitats, clouds, storms, discoveries, processes

Be sure to introduce and develop the meaning of comparison words: *compare, contrast, same, different, similar.* Also arrange for students to compose comparison/contrast pieces.

To foster making comparisons, introduce the use of graphic organizers. Venn diagrams, as shown in Figure 5.1, are an excellent device for displaying similarities and differences. Initially, provide students with partially completed Venn diagrams. Frame matrices (Figure 5.2) are also valuable for making comparisons. Frames make it possible to compare several items among a number of features. Semantic feature analysis (Figure 5.3) is also used to make comparisons. A semantic feature analysis is designed for making comparisons on the basis of whether particular features are present or absent. Students mark a feature as being present (+), absent (−), or not sure (?).

Classifying

Classifying is one of our most basic cognitive processes. Young children classify when they decide that a toy goes in the toy chest but a fork goes in the silverware drawer. Classifying skills should be fostered at all levels of education. To foster classifying, make sure that young students have a firm grasp of *same* and *different.* Ask students of all ages to tell how items are the same or different. Discuss similarities of sound and spellings, similarities and differences in characters and events

FIGURE 5.2 *Frame Matrix: Central America*

Country	Population	Size	Language	Per capita income (U.S. dollars)	Government
Belize	273,000	8.867 sq mi	English, Creole, Spanish	$5,000	Parliamentary democracy
Costa Rica	4,000,000	19,730 sq mi	Spanish	$8,300	Democratic republic
El Salvador	6,600,000	8,124 sq mi	Spanish	$4,600	Republic
Guatemala	14,300,000	42,000 sq mi	Spanish, Indian languages	$3,900	Democratic republic
Honduras	7,000,000	43,278 sq mi	Spanish	$2,500	Democratic republic
Nicaragua	5,400,000	49,998 sq mi	Spanish	$2,200	Republic
Panama	3,500,000	30,193 sq mi	Spanish	$6,200	Constitutional democracy

Source: Infoplease available online at http://www.infoplease.com/almanacs.html

Figure 5.3 *Semantic Feature Analysis: Cats*

Cats	Wild	Domestic	Large	Small	Can Purr	Can Roar	Eats Meat	Comes from Western Hemisphere	Comes from Eastern Hemisphere	Has Spots	Has Stripes
Persian		+		+	+		+		+		
Caracal	+			+	+		+		+	+	
Cheetah	+		?			?	+		+	+	
Jaguar	+		+			+	+	+		+	
Jaguarundi	+			+	+		+	+			
Leopard	+		+			+	+		+	+	
Lion	+		+			+	+		+		
Ocelot	+			+	+		+	+			
Puma	+		?		?	?	+		+		
Tiger	+		+			+	+		+		+

that they have read about, similarities and differences in books on the same subject, similarities and differences of objects that they see, people they know or read about, and topics that they explore.

Bear and associates (2004) have an extensive program for teaching spelling through classifying, which they refer to as sorting. Sorts can be open or closed. In open sorts, the teacher provides the categories. In closed sorts, students determine the categories. In a closed sort, you provide a sorting sheet in which the categories are listed, as in Figure 5.4. In an open sort, you provide a sorting sheet but don't identify the categories. The essential element in developing the ability to classify is not getting the sort "right" but in discussing why items were sorted in a particular way. In other words, what was the basis of the sorting? How were categories chosen and/or how did you decide to put items in particular categories? Therefore, it is essential to discuss students' sorts with them, asking such questions as "Why did you put yams in the root vegetable category?" Webs, as in Figure 5.5, are also a way of sorting items into categories.

FIGURE 5.4 *Closed Sort: Kinds of Vegetables*

Leaves Are Eaten	Roots/Tubers Are Eaten	Stems Are Eaten	Flower Clusters Are Eaten	Seeds Are Eaten (Fruits)
cabbage lettuce spinach kale	potatoes yams carrots onions	celery asparagus rhubarb	broccoli cauliflower	peas lima beans green beans tomatoes squash eggplant

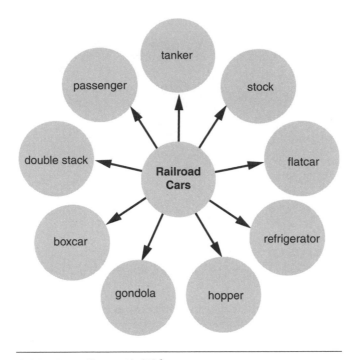

FIGURE 5.5 *Semantic Web*

Determining Main Ideas

Classifying is an essential part of determining or inferring a main idea. To compose a main idea, the reader must compare details and determine what those details have in common. The commonality is the main idea. If the main idea is stated, the readers use this statement to identify supporting or explanatory details. To prepare students for studying the main idea, have them classify words. They might tell which of the following words tells about all the others. For younger students, you might use words such as *red, yellow, green, colors, blue*. For older students, you might use somewhat more difficult items, such as *tornado, hurricane, storm, blizzard, typhoon*. Once they have caught onto the idea of classifying words, have students classify sentences by giving them a series of sentences and telling them to pick the sentence that tells about all the others. For older students, this might be sentences such as the following: We missed easy layups. Our foul shooting percentage was a miserable 25 percent. Our team played badly. The team had ten turnovers.

Making Inferences

Students have the cognitive ability to draw inferences and do so continuously in their everyday lives. They infer, for instance, when the people around them are happy or sad. They make their inferences based on facial expressions, actions, and language. However, students do not always make expected inferences as they read. They may lack the necessary background information, they may not put together the information necessary to make inferences, or they might not realize that inferences are called for. They might believe that only literal comprehension is called for (Westby, 1999). Building background and teaching specific strategies for making inferences should foster students' inference making.

In reading, students make both schema-based and text-based inferences (Winne, Graham, & Prock, 1993). Schema-based inferences depend on prior knowledge. For instance, reading the sentence, "The truck kicked up a cloud of dust," and inferring that the driver was on a dirt road, the road was dry, and the driver was going fast are schema-based. The reader is using her schema for travel on dirt roads and dry conditions. A text-based inference requires that the reader combine two or more pieces of information from the text. Reading that peanuts have more food energy than sugar and that a pound of peanut butter has more protein than thirty-two eggs but more fat than ice cream, the reader might put all this information together to infer that peanuts are nutritious but fattening.

To foster inference making, build and activate prior knowledge. Also ask the kinds of questions that require students to make inferences. Gordon (1985) mapped out a step-by-step process for making inferences.

Step 1. The teacher explains what the skill is, why it is important, and when and how it is used. This explanation might be illustrated with examples.
Step 2. The teacher models the process of making inferences. While modeling the process, the teacher demonstrates her thinking processes.
Step 3. Students and teacher share in the process of making inferences. The teacher asks an inferential question about a brief sample paragraph and then answers it. The students supply supporting evidence for the inference from the selection itself and from their background knowledge. The process is then reversed. The teacher asks an inferential question, and the students supply the inference. The teacher provides the evidence. As an alternative, the teacher might supply the evidence and have the students draw an inference based on it. Either way, a discussion of reasoning processes follows.
Step 4. The teacher just asks the inferential question. The students both make the inference and supply the evidence. Eventually students create their own inferential questions and then supply the answers and evidence. The students apply the process to texts and trade books.

Difficulties in Making Inferences

Some students' responses to inference questions are too limited (Gunning, 2005). In addition to knowing that they can use both text and background knowledge as sources of information, students need to learn to gather all the information that is pertinent (McCormick, 1992). They may need to base their inferences on several pieces of textual or background information. Some students choose the wrong information on which to base their inferences, and others do not use the text at all.

They overrely on prior knowledge or do not recall or use sufficient pertinent text to make valid inferences (McCormick, 1992). This is especially true of struggling readers. To counteract these difficulties, require justification for inferences and show students how to go back over the text to locate supporting facts or details.

Drawing Logical Conclusions

Drawing a conclusion is a type of inference. It entails examining several facts or details and coming to a conclusion based on the information. Drawing conclusions that are logical, have sufficient support, and consider all the evidence should be emphasized. In many instances, different conclusions can be drawn from the same set of facts. Students should be shown that they should reach the most likely conclusion while keeping an open mind because other conclusions are possible.

To introduce drawing conclusions, model the process and provide guided practice. Show students how you would consider the details in a story and come to a conclusion. For guided practice, supply evidence and have them draw a conclusion. Then supply a conclusion and have them find supporting evidence in the selection. As a last step have them both draw a conclusion and cite supporting evidence. You might have students use a chart such as the one in Figure 5.6. Have students apply the skill to all content areas, drawing conclusions about the main character in a piece of fiction, about experiments in science, and about historical events and figures in social studies. Stress the importance of basing conclusions on facts or details from the story and considering the evidence very carefully. Whenever students draw a conclusion, ask them to support it with evidence from the selection.

Predicting

Predicting is a form of inferencing. Based on experience or information garnered from illustrations, headings, introduction, or other sources, the reader makes a prediction. However, predicting is more difficult than inferring or drawing a conclusion. For inferring or drawing a conclusion, the reader uses what has already happened or been explained as a basis for drawing an inference. For a prediction, the readers must speculate as to what is about to happen or be explained.

A highly useful strategy, predicting can and should be taught even before children can read on their own. Before reading a storybook aloud, the teacher should read its title, show the students one or more illustrations, and have them predict what they think the story might be about or what they think will happen. Consensus is not necessary. Each student should feel free to make his own predic-

Drawing a Conclusion

Conclusion	Proof

FIGURE 5.6 *Drawing a Conclusion Chart*

tion. However, to foster thinking, you should guide students to make thoughtful use of titles, illustrations, headings, story introductions, and their own prior knowledge and background of experience to make predictions. Model the process and accompany it with a think-aloud so that students see how an expert reader goes about making inferences. Stress the need to base predictions on all the available information. When discussing students' predictions, ask them to justify them so that they acquire the habit of making information-based predictions. For example, for a prediction for Zion's *Harry the Dirty Dog* (1956), you might ask, "What makes you think that Harry will be given a bath?"

For setting up predictions, Nessel (1987) suggested two questions that could be asked at the beginning or at crucial points in the story:

1. What do you think will happen? (For example, What do you think X will do? How do you think this problem will be resolved?)
2. What makes you think so? (What have you experienced and what did you read in the story that leads you to make that prediction?) (p. 604)

The first question elicits the prediction; the second asks students to explain it to ensure that it is thoughtful and plausible. Students also must learn to be flexible so that they can alter a prediction if it proves to be off the mark.

In addition to teaching students what kinds of questions to ask, the teacher should show them the best sources of predictions: title, illustrations, introductory note, and first paragraph. Gradually, students can create their own predictions as they read.

Part of being an effective user of strategies is knowing when and where to use a particular strategy. Making predictions requires prior knowledge. Students beginning to read about a topic for which they have little background information will have difficulty making reasonable predictions and so should use another strategy.

Evaluating

In addition to understanding what they read, students should make judgments about what they read. Making judgments improves comprehension because the reader is actively engaged with the text. Because much of the information that we encounter in an information-rich society is of doubtful validity, evaluating what one reads is an essential skill. Students need to be able to judge sources of information, especially the Internet because it lacks the safeguards that traditional publishing has built in. Three main criteria are used to judge a source: whether it has expert knowledge about the subject, whether the information is up to date, and whether the source is unbiased.

Biased writing uses emotionally toned words and specially chosen details to create an unfairly favorable or unfavorable impression about a person, place, object, or idea. Show and discuss with students how words and details can be selected in such a way as to shape readers' opinions. Show, too, how you evaluate as you read: how, for example, you note inflammatory language, question the author's conclusions, or note that important facts have been left out.

Focus on Comprehension

Fostering comprehension is a natural way to teach thinking skills. Higher-level comprehension skills require organizing, manipulating, and evaluating information. To close the literacy gap, more time needs to be devoted to teaching comprehension, especially in the primary grades (Taylor et al., 2002). With the focus in the early grades on learning to read, all too often teachers' main goal is for students to become proficient decoders. However, during these years, the foundation for the kinds of thinking that comprehension requires should be set. Students should be predicting, inferring, categorizing, comparing and contrasting, organizing, and evaluating. They should be building their language skills and background. For example, Taylor and colleagues (2002) found that only 16 percent of primary teachers observed in schools that beat the odds emphasized comprehension. However, as a group, effective teachers place more emphasis on comprehension and ask a greater proportion of higher-level questions, especially questions that require drawing inferences (RAND Reading Study Group, 2004). Effective teachers also help students make connections between what they read and their personal lives and make greater use of small-group instruction.

Effective strategy instruction requires a depth of instruction. Strategies also need to be connected to content. Students need to see that strategies are a means of learning. As the RAND report (2004) states:

> Unless the strategies are closely linked with knowledge and understanding in a content area, students are unlikely to learn the strategies fully, may not perceive the strategies as valuable tools, and are less likely to use them in new learning situations with new text. (p. 730)

A checklist for assessing a comprehension lesson is presented in Table 5.1. You can use the checklist to evaluate your own lessons or, if you are assisting others, to evaluate their comprehension lessons.

In turn, an effective way to foster comprehension instruction is to combine strategy instruction with discussion of the text. The discussion should be collaborative. It might be guided by the teacher, but both teacher and students should work together to construct meaning. Techniques that foster this collaboration include ReQuest, reciprocal teaching, Questioning the Author, and accountable talk.

ReQuest

Because it actively involves them, ReQuest (reciprocal questioning) (Manzo, 1969; Manzo, Manzo, & Albee, 2004) has the potential to work wonders with students who fail to understand what they are reading because they are not focused. In ReQuest, the teacher and students take turns asking questions. ReQuest can be implemented by following these steps.

Step 1. Select a text that is on the students' level but is dense enough that it is possible to ask a number of questions about it.

TABLE 5.1 *Comprehension Lesson Checklist*

Action	Fully	Partially	Limited	Suggestions
New strategy is pretested. Students who know 90 percent go to next element.				
Strategy is one that is needed for upcoming reading.				
Teacher explains strategy and its benefit.				
Teacher models strategy and engages in think-aloud.				
Teacher provides guided practice.				
Teacher provides independent practice and application.				
Teacher reviews strategy and arranges to have it applied to varied texts.				
Teacher assesses students' use of strategy and reviews as necessary.				
Teacher shows students how to integrate new strategy with previously taught strategy.				
Teacher discusses when and under what conditions strategy might be used.				
Teacher discusses with classes instances where students have applied the strategy.				

Step 2. Explain the ReQuest procedure to students. Tell them that they will be using a teaching technique that will help them better understand what they read. Explain that in ReQuest, they get a chance to be the teacher because they and you take turns asking questions.

Step 3. Survey the text with the students. Read the title, examine any illustrations that are part of the introduction, and discuss what the selection might be about.

Step 4. Direct students to read the first significant segment of text. This could be the first sentence or the first paragraph but should not be any longer than a paragraph. Explain that as they read, they are to think up questions to ask you. Students can make up as many questions as they wish. Tell them to ask the kinds of questions that a teacher might ask (Manzo, Manzo, & Albee, 2004). Read the segment with the students.

Step 5. Students ask their questions. The teacher's book is placed face down. However, students may refer to their texts. If necessary, questions are restated or clarified. Answers can be checked by referring back to the text.

Step 6. After student questions have been asked, ask your questions. Students' books are face down. You might model higher-level questioning by asking for responses that require integrating several details in the text. If difficult concepts or vocabulary words are encountered, they should be discussed.

Step 7. Go to the next sentence or paragraph. The questioning proceeds until enough information has been gathered to set a purpose for reading the remainder of the text. This could be in the form of a prediction: "What do you think the rest of the article will be about?" Manzo, Manzo, and Albee (2004) recommend that the questioning be concluded as soon as a logical purpose can be set but no longer than ten minutes after beginning.

Step 8. After the rest of the selection has been read silently, the purpose question and any related questions are discussed.

Students enjoy playing the role of the teacher and asking questions. Although they may ask lower-level questions in the early sessions, with coaching and modeling they can be led to ask higher-level ones. ReQuest provides a natural lead-in to one of the most carefully researched and highly effective techniques for building comprehension: reciprocal teaching.

Reciprocal Teaching

In reciprocal teaching, a group of students and a teacher read a selection and then discuss it. Students take turns leading the discussion. They use four highly effective comprehension strategies: predicting, question generating, clarifying, and summarizing (Palincsar & Brown, 1986).

1. Predicting. Students predict what information a section of text will present based on what they have read in a prior section. If they are just starting a selection, their prediction is based on illustrations, headings, or an introductory paragraph. They must activate their background knowledge to guess what the author is going to say next. Predicting makes them active readers and gives them a purpose for reading.

2. Question generating. Students locate the most significant information in a text so they can formulate worthwhile questions. Teacher modeling and prompting helps them to do this. The student discussion leader asks questions during the discussion of the selection.

3. Clarifying. Students note words, concepts, expressions, or other items that hinder comprehension, and they ask for explanations during discussion.

4. Summarizing. The student discussion leader retells the selection and highlights the main points of the selection. Summarizing also becomes a springboard for making predictions about the content of the next section.

Depending on students' ages, abilities, and previous experiences with the strategies, the teacher might introduce the strategies all at once, one a day, or even one a week (Gunning, 2005). It is not expected that students will become proficient in their use at this point. That will come when the strategies are applied in reciprocal teaching lessons. At first, the teacher plays a major role in the application of reciprocal teaching, modeling the four strategies, making corrections, and providing guidance when necessary. Gradually, the students take more responsibility for leading discussions and applying the strategies. In the initial stages, the group reads brief selections paragraph by paragraph or section by section. Later, they apply the technique to longer selections. The technique works especially well with informational text and content-area material but may be used with fiction.

Although designed for use with small groups, a whole class can use reciprocal teaching if it is adapted. In the adapted version, students use the headings to make two predictions about the content of the text they are about to read. After reading a segment, they write two questions and a summary, as well as list any items that require clarification. The predictions, summaries, and clarification requests are discussed after the selection has been read (Palinscar & Brown, 1986). If students are properly trained, they can use reciprocal teaching in paired readings, cooperative learning groups, and literature discussion groups (Oczkus, 2003).

A highly effective approach, reciprocal teaching leads students to a deeper processing of text. It focuses their efforts on constructing meaning, instead of just decoding words (Rosenshine & Meister, 1994). Because of this refocusing, reciprocal teaching has been especially effective when used with struggling readers. Oczkus (2003) reports gains of one to two years after just a few months of instruction. Cooper, Boschenken, McWilliams, and Pistochini (2000) also report encouraging gains and have produced a commercial program for struggling readers, Soar to Success (Houghton Mifflin), which uses reciprocal teaching and graphic organizers to foster improved comprehension.

Although highly successful, reciprocal teaching is not a complete comprehension program (Oczkus, 2003). Students also need to be guided in the use of inferring, imaging, evaluating, making connections with other texts they have read and personal experiences, using text structure, and appreciating the author's craft.

Since most students have been introduced to some or all of the strategies incorporated in reciprocal teaching, you can build on what they know. However, it takes time for teachers and students to become comfortable with reciprocal teaching. Chances are you won't see an improvement for several weeks. However, the improvement can be quite dramatic and so well worth the wait. To ease the implementation of reciprocal teaching, one reading specialist obtained copies of *Reciprocal Teaching at Work* (Oczkus, 2003) and encouraged middle school teachers to use them as a blueprint to implement reciprocal teaching.

Questioning the Author

A third highly effective collaborative technique is Questioning the Author (McKeown, Beck, & Sandora, 1996). In Questioning the Author, students read brief segments of text and then respond to teacher queries so that they are cooperatively constructing meaning as they process the text instead of reading the entire text and then answering questions. During the introduction of the techniques students are told that sometimes the author's meaning isn't clear, so they will have to ask themselves such questions as, "What is the author trying to say here?" Having students ask the author questions makes reading a more active process. Rather than simply extracting information from text, readers have to build a genuine understanding of the text (Beck, McKeown, Hamilton, & Kucan, 1997).

The teacher uses general queries to get the discussion started and to keep it moving. Initiating queries include, "What is the author trying to say here? What is the author's message? What is the author trying to tells us?" Follow-up queries are designed to help the students construct meaning. If a passage doesn't seem clear, the teacher might ask, "What did the author mean here? Did the author explain this clearly?" Questions could also be asked that help connect ideas that had been read previously: "How does this connect to what the author told us before? How do these two ideas fit together?" Other kinds of questions lead students to seek reasons. "Does the author tell us why? Why do you think the author included this information?" Questions might also help students see how what they are learning relates to what they know: "How does this fit in with what you know?" Questioning the Author queries incorporate accountable talk.

Accountable Talk

One of the most powerful techniques for fostering higher-level thinking skills and improved reading and writing for struggling as well as achieving readers is through talk. But not all talk is equal. For talk to be an effective means for learning, it should be accountable (Resnick & Hall, 2001). Through accountable talk, students learn to think carefully about their responses and to base assertions on passages from a text or other sources of information. Accountable talk respects and builds on what others say. Accountable talk takes place throughout the day in teacher-student conferences, in small-group discussions, in whole-class discussions, and in student presentations. Students are accountable to the learning community, to knowledge, and to rigorous thinking.

Accountability to the learning community
- Students stick to the topic and have as their goal the development of a topic or idea.
- Students listen to each other, acknowledge and build on others' contributions, and paraphrase or revoice the contributions of others.
- Students invite the contributions of all classmates.

Accountability to knowledge
- Students cite passages or examples to back up assertions.
- When using information from outside sources, students are careful to make sure that it is accurate.
- Students ask for clarification and explanation of terms and substantiation of claims.
- Students might challenge statements but not persons.
- Students note when more information is needed.

Accountability to rigorous thinking
- Students draw logical conclusions and provide proof for conclusions.
- Students make connections between ideas in a single text, between ideas in several texts, and between ideas in text and real world.
- Students use multiple sources of information.

- Students propose hypotheses and ways of investigating them.
- Students question, explain, compare and contrast, and question each other.

Teachers develop accountable talk by explaining, demonstrating, modeling, and coaching. They elicit accountable talk through a number of questions and probes.

- They seek clarification and explanation when called for.
- They ask for proof or justification for positions or statements.
- They recognize and help clarify erroneous concepts
- They interpret and summarize students' statements (Resnick & Hall, 2001).

Here are some prompts that help students carry on thoughtful, accountable discussions. The prompts might be used by teacher or students.

Drawing conclusions: What conclusion might we draw from these facts?
Making within-the-text connections: What is the connection between losing the game in the first part of the story and the way Shauna treats the new kid?
Making text-to-text connections: What other story that we have read reminds you of this one?
Making text-to-world connections: Do you know anyone like the main character?
Clarifying: Could you explain what you mean by that? I'm not sure I understand.
Explaining: Can you tell us step-by-step how that process works?
Predicting: What do you think will happen next? What makes you think so?
Hypothesizing: If we added salt, what do you think would happen to the freezing temperature?
Comparing: In what ways are the wars in Vietnam and Iraq similar?
Contrasting: How are the wars different?

Here are some prompts that might be used to facilitate a discussion. Most of these prompts are designed for teacher use. However, Affirming, Including, Agreeing, and Building would be used by students.

Elaboration: Would you please explain? Would you please tell me more? (Hyman, 1978)
Restating: Here is what you seem to be saying . . . A restating prompt is especially helpful for emphasizing a key point or clarifying an unclear statement. A restating prompt can also be used to keep a discussion on track (Hyman, 1978).
Summarizing: So far this is what the author has told us . . .
Affirming: I like the way you gave three examples to prove your point.
Including: We haven't heard from _____ yet.
Agreeing: I agree with Justin, because . . .
Building on what others have said: I'd like to add to what Justin said.

Disagreeing: I can see how Justin came to the conclusion that the main character was unselfish. But when I think of why he did favors for others, I believe that he was just trying to get on their good side. And here is why I think that.

Wait time: The best prompt of all is a moment or two of silence. After asking a question, pause a moment or two to allow the student to formulate a response. Typically, students, especially if they are struggling learners, are given a second or less to answer before the teacher moves onto a higher-achieving student. After the student has responded, pause again. Give the student the opportunity to elaborate. Research by science teachers (Lake, 1973; Rowe, 1969) has shown that pausing from three to five seconds results in fuller, more elaborated responses. Perhaps, more importantly, using wait time changes the teachers' perceptions of struggling students. When struggling students are provided with wait time, their responses are improved. They are more elaborated and more likely to be accurate. This, in turn, signals to the teacher that the students are more capable than he judged. Seeing that the students are more capable, the teacher expends more teaching resources on them and thus an upward spiral is created. And it all starts with three seconds of silence.

For talk to be an effective thinking skill builder, it must be substantive. The most effective talk involves discussing important and complex ideas of the type found in challenging content (Resnick, 1999). Therefore, struggling readers need the same high-level content that achieving readers receive. However, because struggling readers might have a more limited background and vocabulary, they will probably need more time and more carefully scaffolded instruction. The texts they read will also need to be made accessible.

Using Question-Answer Relationships (QAR)

An essential element in responding to questions is knowing where the necessary information is located. Some students might not realize or have the necessary skills to go back into the selection and find the answer to a question even when it is directly stated. Others may have difficulty putting together several pieces of information to answer a question. And some students might not realize that they must combine information from the selection with their own background knowledge to formulate a response. A common shortcoming in students' responses is the practice of relying strictly on one's background knowledge and not using information from the story at all. To help students use the correct source of information to answer questions, QAR (Question-Answer Relationships) was created. Questions are described as having the following four levels, based on where the answers are found (Raphael, Florio-Ruane, George, Hasty, & Highfield, 2004).

1. Right there. A very literal answer that is stated clearly in the book.
2. Think and search. Requires readers to make inferences, draw conclusions, or connect information from different places in a book.
3. On my own. Based entirely on readers' prior knowledge.

4. Author and me. Discovered by combining what the readers know with something the author says in the book. (p. 43)

Raphael (1986) recommends starting with two categories of answers: "in the book" and "in my head." This would be especially appropriate when working with students in kindergarten and first grade. "In the book" includes answers that are "right there" or require "think and search." "In my head" items are "on my own" and "author and me" answers. By second grade, students can use the two "in the book" strategies. By third grade, they can use all of the QAR strategies. Based on Raphael's (1986) suggestions, QAR might be presented in the manner described below.

Presenting QAR

Step 1. Introducing the Concept of QAR

Introduce the concept of QAR by writing on the board a paragraph similar to the following:

On September 6, 1620, 102 men, women, and children set sail from England for America. Many of the passengers were Pilgrims. Pilgrims are people who travel to distant places in search of a better life. The trip across the sea was long and hard. The Pilgrims were traveling on a small ship called the *Mayflower*. The *Mayflower* was built to carry only 60 people.

Ask a series of literal questions: "When did the Pilgrims leave? Where were they sailing from? Where were they going?" Lead students to see that the answers to these questions are "in the book."

Next, ask a series of questions that depend on the readers' background: "Why do you think they left in September? What makes you think that there were families aboard? Why do you think they were leaving England?" Show students that the answers to these questions depend on their knowledge of weather and traveling and families. Discuss the fact that these answers are "in my head."

Step 2. Extending the Concept of QAR

After students have mastered the concept of "in the book" and "in my head," extend the "in the book" category to include both "right there" and "think and search." Ask, "What was the name of the ship? How do you know that the ship was overcrowded?" Once students have a solid working knowledge of these, expand the "in my head" category to include both "on my own" and "author and me." The major difference between these two is whether the student has to read the text for the question to make sense. For instance, the question "What was it like below decks?" requires information from the selection and background knowledge of what happens when people live in crowded conditions and wear the same unwashed clothes. The question "How would you feel wearing the same clothes day after day?" involves only a personal opinion.

Step 3. Providing Practice

Provide ample opportunity for guided and independent practice. You might combine QAR and ReQuest. Model asking "in the book" and "in my head" questions and encourage students to compose similar questions.

Affective Component of Comprehension

Comprehension has an affective component. We find it easier to comprehend materials in which we have an interest. We read more carefully when seeking needed information. Intrinsic motivation results in deeper comprehension than extrinsic motivation. Intrinsic motivation has been defined as consisting of reading efficacy, importance, curiosity, involvement, and preference for challenging reading (Wigfield, 1997).

> Reading efficacy refers to the belief that one can be successful at reading. Importance of reading refers to how important reading is to the reader. Curiosity is the desire to learn about a particular topic of personal interest. Involvement refers to the pleasure gained from reading a well-written book or article on an interesting topic. Preference for challenging reading is the satisfaction of mastering or assimilating complex ideas in text. (pp. 22-23)

Extrinsic motivation refers to receiving external recognition for reading, reading for a grade or to complete an assignment, reading to outperform others, or reading so as to be able to share with others.

Intrinsic motivation leads to enhanced comprehension because students read more intensely (Wang & Guthrie, 2004). Spurred on by interest and curiosity, they concentrate more intensely and exert more cognitive effort into understanding. They are more likely to put forth the effort needed to overcome obstacles to comprehension. "In other words, effort and the exercise of higher cognitive skills assist them in understanding narrative texts in depth. Empirical studies have indicated that students with intrinsic motivation are more persistent and skillful in their academic activities" (Wang & Guthrie, 2004, p. 179). Students who are intrinsically motivated also read more.

Extrinsically motivated readers do not comprehend as well as intrinsically motivated students. Extrinsically motivated students

> tend to focus on receiving rewards and avoiding negative outcomes rather than learning from texts and employing deeper cognitive strategies to overcome challenges during reading. . . . Research has found that those students with extrinsic motivation were more likely to use strategies at a surface level. . . . (Wang & Guthrie, 2004, p. 180)

Of course, intrinsic motivation can be combined with extrinsic motivation. Students can read both for enjoyment and in anticipation of sharing with friends. However, achievement is enhanced when intrinsic motivation dominates. As part of your program, foster intrinsic motivation. When possible, give students choices in what they read. Find out what their interests are and provide materials that match those interests. Pique students' curiosity and ask challenging questions. Build their reading efficacy by teaching needed skills.

Boosting Low-Achieving Readers' Thinking and Comprehension

It is especially important that low-achieving readers be given instruction in higher-level thinking and comprehension skills. McDermott and Varenne (1995) found that teachers provided high-achieving readers with higher-level questions, but when working with lower-achieving students, these same teachers emphasized lower-level factual comprehension and also interrupted their students more frequently. Because they are behind, struggling readers need more, not less, instruction in higher-level reading and thinking skills. Study after study has demonstrated that when below-level readers are given systematic instruction in key strategies, they often perform as well as average readers. There should be a school wide, well-articulated comprehension program. Skills should be applied in the content areas as well as in language arts. This does not mean that content-area teachers become teachers of reading; it just means that they should teach those skills that foster learning in the content area. (However, content-area teachers may want to adapt the strategies presented here in ways that make them more appropriate for particular organizational patterns.) In fact, many skills are best applied to the content areas. With a common

BOX 5.2

Model Program: Instruction for Good Decoders Who Are Poor Comprehenders

During her six years as director of Title 1 programs in Douglas County, Colorado, Ellen Oliver Keene (Keene & Zimmermann, 1997) and other Title 1 staff members noticed that about 30 percent of students were adequate decoders and even fluent readers, but they had difficulty with comprehension. What's more, they didn't realize that they had a problem. "These children didn't know when they were comprehending. They didn't know when they were not comprehending. Many didn't know what they were supposed to comprehend when they read. Others didn't seem to know that text is supposed to mean something" (p. 18). This lack of comprehension was even seen when children were listening to read-alouds. They didn't seem to realize that they should be thinking about the illustrations or the text. They showed little interest in text-related meanings. To help build comprehension in these students, Zimmermann and others initiated a solution to the problem. The results of that quest, which includes a detailed program for fostering comprehension, is found in *Mosaic of Thought, Teaching Reading Comprehension in a Reader's Workshop* (Keene & Zimmermann, 1997). An overview of the comprehension program that was constructed is found in the booklet *Thinking Strategies for Learners* (PEBC Staff Developers, 2001). The program focuses on building students' awareness of effective comprehension strategies. It also stresses making connections between background knowledge, personal experiences, and texts; between different segments of text; and between different texts.

approach and using a common language, students will learn strategies more readily and apply them more consistently.

Building Background

In addition to teaching strategies and thinking skills, it is essential to build background. The more we know about a subject the better we're able to comprehend the selection written about that subject. Since informational texts are excellent background builders, your literacy program should include lots of reading and discussion of books that describe, explain, and explore.

Making Connections

Students learn more and retain their knowledge longer when connections are made between what they know and new knowledge. In high-performing schools, including a number that beat the odds, teachers helped students make three kinds of connections: connections within lessons; connections across lessons, classes, and even grades; and connections between in-school and out-of-school knowledge (Langer, 2004). One teacher made connections between a visit to a senior center and the composition of a character sketch derived from interviews with seniors. Later, students would create a character sketch for protagonists in a play. Another teacher helped students make connections between *The Glass Menagerie* and *A Raisin in the Sun.* Based on their discoveries, the students made connections between the family themes developed in these plays with family life in the real world.

Although these connections were made with secondary-level students, they can just as readily be made with elementary school students. In a somewhat simplified version, elementary school students are taught to make text-to-self, text-to-text, and text-to-world connections (Keene & Zimmermann, 1997). They make personal connections to the text that are drawn from their experiences; they make connections between text being read and texts previously read. They make connections to the world. To show students how to make connections, the teacher does a think-aloud in which she makes connections. Reading aloud from *The Two of Them* a story about a girl and her grandfather, the teacher explains that when she read about the grandfather dying, it reminded her of her grandfather's death. She urges students to make connections as they read:

> By remembering my own feelings, I could imagine what the little girl—the character—in this book might have felt. Because I understand the character's feelings, I understand the story better. It makes more sense to me and means more to me. When you go back to your own reading, remember to think about things the book reminds you of in your own life. When the pictures or the story remind you of your life, you're making a text-to-self connection. (Keene & Zimmermann, 1997, p. 57)

Later the teacher demonstrates how to make text-to-text connections when she discusses *Grandpa's Face* (1988) by Eloise Greenfield and compares this with *The Two of Them*. "This book reminds me of the book we read a few weeks ago called *The Two of Them*. Do you remember? The grandfather and his granddaughter are great friends in both books" (Keene & Zimmermann, 1997, p. 59). Later still, the class makes text-to-world connections when they make connections between a boy who was taught to read by a friend and the problem of illiteracy.

Putting It All Together: Using a GO! Chart

Although you might focus on a single strategy until students master it, comprehension is best fostered by the integrated use of strategies. An excellent device for integrating a number of strategies is the Graphic Organizer for Retelling (GO! Chart). The GO! Chart helps students to become aware of and apply the key strategies that proficient readers use. It helps students move up from a concrete comprehension to more analytical understanding (Benson & Cummins, 2002). The GO! Chart is 90 inches wide and is composed of six columns: predict/preview, vocabulary/inquiry, understanding, interpretation, connection, and retelling/organizing. A GO! Chart can be created in one session or over a period of days.

Preparing Students for High-Stakes Comprehension Tests

By definition, students in underperforming schools do poorly on high-stakes tests. In some instances, they do poorly because they are reading well below grade level or have very limited reading skills (see Chapter 6 for more information on test preparation). However, as explained in Box 5.3, sometimes students know the answers but are unable to formulate them in writing. An effective program of test preparation is embedded in the literacy program. As Farr (2004) explains, it doesn't teach to the test but teaches with the test in mind.

The first order of business in initiating a program of test preparation is to become acquainted with the test that students will be taking. Although tests vary from state to state, many are modeled on the National Assessment of Educational Progress (NAEP). In its latest framework, NAEP assesses four aspects of reading: forming a general understanding, developing an interpretation, making reader/text connections, and examining content and structure. These four aspects are assessed with three contexts or types of reading: literary text, informational text, and practical text. Table 5.2 shows the four aspects, sample questions, the kinds of strategies needed to answer these questions, and activities designed to prepare students for these kinds of questions. The table is based on work by Fountas and Pinnell (2001). Questions are drawn from the latest edition of the NAEP (National Assessment Governing Board, 2004).

BOX
5.3

Test Preparation: Personal Perspective

While working in a second-grade class, I noted that one of the children was crying. She was one of the last to finish her end-of-theme test. When I asked her what was wrong, she replied, "I don't know how to do this." The question that puzzled her was a constructed query that asked, "Could this story have happened in real life?" I asked her to read the question to see if maybe she didn't understand the question. She read it smoothly. Thinking that maybe she didn't understand the story, I asked her to read a few lines. She read those smoothly. We then talked about the story. The story was about a farmer whose hat blew off. I asked her if that could happen in real life. She replied that it could. We then discussed the part in which the farmer asks the squirrel if he saw his hat. She said that couldn't happen because animals can't talk. She said that the story was a fantasy. I suggested that she write down what she told me. However, her answer stated, "The story couldn't happen in real life. It is a fantasy." I was about to ask her to tell why it was a fantasy, when the teacher approached and reminded me that the student was taking a test.

Although I sensed the loss of a teaching opportunity, I halted the conversation. After all, it wasn't my classroom. But it made me wonder how many other students have the answer inside their heads but need some help in getting it out. I was quite certain that her answer would not receive full credit. She had failed to explain why the story couldn't happen in real life.

A few days later during a grade-level meeting with third-grade teachers, they complained that there was a problem with the unit theme tests. As they explained, the tests were poorly worded and so were confusing to the children. As a result, the children were performing poorly on them. I took them at their word. But they had created a problem for me. According to the grant application under which I had been hired, a promise had been made that the tests would be used to monitor ongoing progress. Thinking that perhaps I could edit the test to make the questions more understandable or even compose other questions, I took a look at the questions. The questions were fine. They asked students to explain their responses and give examples, but the wording was reasonably clear and the answers or the basis for them were in the selection. The teachers' gut feeling was that the students understood the selection, but were unable to compose an acceptable response. An examination of the test papers revealed that many of the students had not really responded to the questions. They supplied information but not the information that had been asked for or had not backed up their responses with details or examples from the selection. What the students needed was instruction in how to interpret and answer questions. I shuddered inwardly. I realized that it wasn't enough to bring these students up to grade level in reading. They also had to be able to answer high-level questions about what they had read. In some instances, comprehension was probably lacking. But in most instances, it seemed that students lacked the skills needed to explain their thinking. Although they understood the selection, they were unable to demonstrate their knowledge. They were failing the test despite knowing the answers. Unless something were done, they would fail the demanding state competency test, despite having grade-level skills. It was clear that we had to go beyond teaching comprehension skills and strategies and teach students to show what they knew. Tragically, students were failing tests that they should have passed.

It is clear from even this limited look at the type of questions being asked on today's high-stakes tests that today's students must be prepared to go well beyond literal comprehension. Key skills include the following.

- The ability to summarize
- The ability to generalize and draw conclusions based on facts, details, and examples
- The ability to make inferences based on facts, details, and examples
- The ability to support inferences, conclusions, and opinions based on information in the selection
- The ability to make connections between information in a selection and other reading or experiences that the reader has had
- The ability to analyze and describe the structure of a piece, including literacy elements that were used to compose it
- The ability to make and substantiate judgments about a piece
- The ability to skim over or search through a selection to locate needed information, such as examples, to show what kind of a person the main character is

Students should be taught these skills and provided with many opportunities to apply them. In whole-class and small-group discussions, students should be asked questions such as the following.

For fiction pieces:
What was this story all about?
What was the author trying to tell you in this article?
What kind of a person was the main character?
How do you know that the main character was kind but lazy?
Give examples that show the author was kind.
Do you know anyone like the main character?
How is that person like the main character?
Have you read about any character who is similar to the main character in this story?

What did the author do to make the story exciting?
What special techniques did the author use?
How did the author prove her or his point?
Was the author fair? Why or why not?

For informational pieces:
- What was this article about?
- What was the author's main point?
- How did the author prove his or her point?
- What did you learn from this article?
- What are the main steps in . . . ?
- What might happen if you left out step 2?
- What causes _____?

TABLE 5.2 Sample Constructed Response Questions

continued

Questions	What the Test Taker Needs to Do	Preparation
Forming a General Understanding		
After reading this article, what do you think is the most important information about the Anasazi?	Skim over the article to locate all the important information. Reflect on all the information in the article and select a piece of information that is most important. Decide why the information selected is more important than other information. Supply a reason for your choice.	Read informational articles and discuss the main idea and the most important supporting details. Discuss why some details might be more important than others.
Write a paragraph telling what this story is about.	Go back over the selection and note the story problem, key plot elements, and solution to the story problem.	Read stories and retell them in sequential order. Use knowledge of story structure to summarize a story.
Write a paragraph telling what this article generally tells you.	Read informational pieces. Go back over a selection and locate or infer and state the main idea and key supporting details.	Read informational pieces, identify or construct main ideas, and note supporting details. Summarize informational text.
Developing an Interpretation		
What do Turtle's actions at Spider's house tell you about Turtle?	Consider Turtle's actions and draw conclusions about his main character traits. State the traits and cite support from the story for each one.	Read fictional pieces and biographies and make judgments about characters and people based on their actions. State the character traits and the actions that suggest the traits.
The three moves made by the Anasazi are listed below. Explain the possible reasons that were suggested in the article for each move.	Go back over the article to get more information about the moves and make inferences about why the moves were made. Is based on information in the article but goes beyond it.	Read articles and stories and draw conclusions about events and decisions.

FIGURE 5.2 *Sample Constructed Response Questions (continued)*

Questions	What the Test Taker Needs to Do	Preparation
What does this idea imply?	Reflect on an idea and its implications based on information in a selection. State the implication and supporting reasons from the selection for composing that implication.	Read informational text and draw inferences about the text. In discussions, state the implications and the reasons for making the implications.
Making Reader/Text Connections		
Think about Spider and Turtle in the story. Pick someone you know, have read about, or have seen in the movies or on television and explain how that person is like either Spider or Turtle.	Analyze the character of Spider or Turtle and extract at least one essential trait or behavior, think of a real or fictional character who has that trait, and explain how that real or fictional character demonstrates that trait.	Read biographies and fictional pieces and compare the character or person to other fictional characters or real people. Explain the similarities.
Who do you think would make a better friend, Spider or Turtle? Explain why.	Pick the character who has a trait that would suggest that he would be the better friend and use evidence from the story to support the choice.	Read stories and discuss character traits and have students provide evidence from the selection that the person possesses the traits.
Do you think Turtle should have done what he did to Spider? Explain why or why not.	Make and express a judgment about the appropriateness of Turtle's actions and express and explain this judgment with details from the selection.	Read stories and make value judgments about the appropriateness of actions. The discussions require students to explain or justify their judgments. The judgments and explanations should be based on information contained in the selection.

continued

IGURE 5.2 *Sample Constructed Response Questions (continued)*

Questions	What the Test Taker Needs to Do	Preparation
After reading this article, would you like to have lived during colonial times? What information in the article makes you think this?	Reflect on the information in the article, form an opinion based on that information, and support opinion with facts contained in the article.	Read fictional and informational pieces and form opinions based on that reading. In discussions, state opinions and provide support for them. The support is based on information in the selection.
Examining Content and Structure		
There is a saying, "Don't get mad, get even." How does this apply to the story?	Reflect on the story to determine why Turtle had reason to be mad and then determine what Turtle did to get back at Spider for tricking him. Explain both how and why Turtle got revenge.	Read and discuss the structure and content of trickster tales and fables. In discussions, talk over how the characters tricked each other. This might require making inferences since the tales typically imply that characters have been tricked but don't specifically state it.
Does the author use (irony, personification, humor) effectively? Explain.	Reflect on the literary element in question and its use in the selection. Make a judgment about its effectiveness, state the judgment, and explain the judgment based on details in the selection.	Literary techniques are introduced and discussed and examined in literary works. Students note and discuss the presence of these techniques and their effectiveness.
Imagine that you are living with the people of Mesa Verde during the 1200s when they left the mesa. Some of your friends and neighbors do not want to leave the area. Based on information in the article, what would you tell these people to convince them to leave?	Skim back over the article and determine why it is important to leave Mesa Verde. Use this information to provide reasons why the people left.	Read stories and articles and determine reasons why people in the stories or articles should take certain actions. Probe for specific reasons (the outlaws are on their way) when students give general ones (your lives are in danger).

- What happened as a result of _____?
- How might you use the information in this article?
- Did you think the information was presented fairly? Why or why not?
- How was the information organized?
- What comparisons did the article make?
- What were the effects of _____?
- In what order did the main events take place?
- In what order should the steps be carried out?
- Based on information in the article, what would you do if _____?
- What is the meaning of the word _____?

Above all, ask students to explain, justify, and give examples and proof. Stress the need to use information from the selection and not simply from their own experience. However, do encourage students to make connections between events and characters in a story, between different selections and different authors, and between information from reading and real-world experiences. Most of the skills listed are worthwhile ones and should be part of any literacy program. These might be integrated into normal instructional activities so that they become a part of students' repertoire of reading, writing, and discussion strategies. Many of the items might be used for comprehension and discussion questions. Most would make thoughtful prompts for reading journal entries. Questions of this type might also be used in end-of-unit assessments. Your quizzes and tests might be constructed so they incorporate the kinds of strategies assessed on the high-stakes assessments. Activities that naturally foster the skills and strategies needed to cope with constructed responses include the following.

- Increase opportunities for discussions.
- Guide students so that they increase the depth and breadth of whole-class, small-group, and paired discussions.
- Foster the use of accountable talk so as to develop thinking and language skills.
- Read a variety of fiction and nonfiction.
- Develop vocabulary and word analysis skills so that students have a better chance of being able to understand challenging test selections.
- Reread selections for specific purposes, such as to provide support for an opinion.
- Compare and contrast characters, plots, events, authors.
- Make connections.
- Encourage students to read, read, read. Make reading so exciting that they read willingly on their own and can't wait to talk over their reading.

Planned Test Preparation

Although the best preparation for a high-stakes test is a balanced, well-planned program of reading and writing, students should also receive some direct preparation for high-stakes tests, especially if they contain unfamiliar formats or seek responses that are on a higher level than students are used to constructing. A planned program of test preparation includes the following steps.

Step 1: Analyze the demands of tests that your students are required to take and compare the demands of the tests with the skills and strategies that are taught. Add skills if necessary. Integrate the teaching of needed skills into your curriculum.

Step 2: Analyze students' test-taking abilities.

Step 3: Because responding to tests is a unique genre, it should be treated as such and so taught in a systematic fashion. Discuss with students the importance of being able to respond to test questions. Share experiences that you have had and explain how you learned to take tests. Discuss any concerns that they might have.

Step 4: Model how you would go about responding to a test question. Select a relatively easy test question. Show how you would read the directions, read the selection, and read the test question. Using a think-aloud procedure, explain what is going on in your mind as you respond.

Step 5: Create a rubric for assessing your response to a practice test question. Using the rubric, involve the class in assessing the response.

Step 6: As a group, have the class cooperatively respond to a similar test question. Use the rubric as a guide.

Step 7: Provide guided practice as students respond to similar test questions. Initially, give extra assistance or scaffolding. Have students complete partially finished responses. Have students complete items in which the lead sentence and a detail have been supplied and they must add two more supporting details. Two aids that you can use are the answer organizer and the answer frame (Boyles, 2002). In the answer organizer, you lay out step-by-step what students are to do: Write the topic sentences first, add three supporting details, write a concluding sentence (see sample in Figure 5.7). Answer frames provide even more assistance than answer organizers do. In the answer frame, you fill in a portion of the answer and have students finish it. In addition to providing step-by-step directions, the answer frame shows the students what words to use (see sample in Figure 5.8). Answer frames help students who would not be able to complete the task without that level of support (Boyles, 2002). As students learn how to formulate responses, answer frames should be reduced and gradually eliminated. Boyles (2002) estimates that students should complete five assisted exercises before attempting to create a response on their own.

Step 8: Have students take a practice test. Using the rubric, analyze responses and provide additional instruction as needed. Provide individual guidance to students who do not "pass" the test. If possible, provide sufficient guidance and practice so that they do pass a retest.

Step 9: Have students apply their skills by taking a real test. Although the test might be used to obtain a grade, also use it as a learning experience. Provide corrective instruction to students so that they improve sufficiently to

To answer the question above, follow these steps:

1. Write a topic sentence that tells the people it is important that they leave.
2. Go back over the article and select reasons why the people should leave. List at least three reasons.
3. Put each reason in a sentence. Use the words *first, second,* and *third* to number the reasons.
4. Write a closing sentence that strongly states how important it is to leave.
5. Read over your answer. Make sure it is clear and has three or more reasons.

FIGURE 5.7 *Answer Organizer*

achieve a passing grade or better. Adopt a mastery approach. Look at tests as a means of providing information on which to base instruction rather than as a device for grading. Reteach those skills that students had difficulty with until they have mastered them to the point where they can pass the test.

On a regular basis, perhaps once a week, provide instruction in responding to on-demand prompts. Tie this instruction in with your overall literacy program. If you are emphasizing summarizing, introduce a question that involves summarizing. If you are focusing on developing characters, pose a question that asks students to cite examples to show what kind of a person the main character was. Don't attempt to cover all response types in a single year. The most ambitious program could probably cover one a month, but five to eight would probably be a more realistic goal.

Planning a Program

Which response types should you teach? That depends on students' level of literacy development, your literacy program, and the demands of the high-stakes tests that students will be taking. Your response instruction will be much more effective if the school has created a curriculum that has a scope and a sequence. Sample response types can be found in Table 5.2.

I know you love your beautiful homes, but you must leave. First of all, because of the cold and the drought and the soil washing away, _____. Second of all, because many of the animals in the forest have gone away, _____. Last of all, because our people have not been getting enough food, they _____ and they _____. For all these reasons, it is time to move to a better place.

FIGURE 5.8 *Answer Frame*

Assessing the Thinking Skills Component of Your Program

Although frequently neglected, thinking skills form the basis for comprehension and become more important as students move up through the grades and are called on to read increasingly complex materials. Use the checklist in Table 5.3 to determine strengths and weaknesses of the thinking skills component of your program.

TABLE 5.3 *Thinking Skills Development Checklist*

	Fully	Partially	Limited	Suggestions
Students' thinking skills are assessed indirectly through observation and analysis of students' writing and discussion.				
Thinking skills are integrated into every area of the curriculum.				
Teachers develop thinking skills through think-alouds, demonstrations, and questioning.				
Students are asked questions on a variety of thinking levels.				
Students are given tasks that require higher-level thinking.				
Students are asked to make inferences, draw conclusions, substantiate conclusions, make comparisons, make predictions, detect bias, and engage in similar activities that develop thinking skills.				
Teachers use techniques such as Questioning the Author that develop thinking skills.				
Students are given challenging content to read and write about.				
Students are given discussion assignments that foster higher-level thinking.				
During discussions, students are asked to explain their thinking and support their responses.				
Students are given writing assignments to foster higher-level thinking.				

6

Building Background through Informational Reading and Writing

According to her analysis of contemporary basal reading systems, Walsh (2003) concludes that they don't do a very good job building background knowledge and vocabulary, two prime components in comprehension. Basals focus on familiar topics and so don't introduce many new ideas to students. Although some literacy authorities might disagree, Walsh also judges that too much time is spent teaching strategies. As she explains, "They miss opportunities to develop word and world knowledge by offering and exploiting content rich themes" (Walsh, 2003, p. 24). In her judgment, more time should be spent building background. She recommends that teachers read challenging selections to students. She recommends reading selections to students that are two years above their students' grade or reading levels. She also recommends that more time be spent developing background and word knowledge introduced in the read-alouds.

> Developing knowledge in a particular domain and becoming comfortable using its specialized vocabulary depends on devoting time to selected topics—time in which new ideas and concepts can be built and contemplated; time to progress from introductory to more detailed texts; time to discuss new information and concepts; and time to repeatedly hear and practice using the vocabulary of the domain in a variety of contexts. (Walsh, 2003, p. 27)

Importance of Informational Text

Reading informational texts provides a range of benefits. Informational texts can be motivating. Research suggests that children enjoy reading informational text as much as narrative text (Kletzien & Szabo, 1998). Some children actually prefer informational text to fiction (Duke, Bennett-Armistead, & Roberts, 2003). As Duke (2003) notes, "Informational text can capitalize on children's interests and curiosities, provide opportunities for children to apply and further develop areas of expertise, and provide valuable links to children's home literacy experiences" (p. 162). Informational text also builds background and vocabulary and the language of explanation and description. To learn how to use the discourse of a particular genre, it is necessary to have been exposed to that genre. Reading science books helps children learn about scientific discourse just as reading narrative helps children understand how stories are structured. When fairy tales are read to them, young children learn structures such as "once upon a time" that are found in fairy tales (Purcell-Gates, 1988). Children who start school with little experience with fairy tales or other narrative pieces have to learn narrative discourse (Purcell-Gates, McIntyre, & Freppon, 1995). Children who have informational text read to them pick up the discourse of informational writing. For instance, when retelling an informational text about firefighters, they use structures typically used in informational texts: "Firefighters fight fires," which is a general statement of information as contrasted with "The firefighter is fighting a fire," which is the kind of statement more likely to be found in narrative text. As Duke (2003) admonishes, "Schools must provide students with experience with the specific genres of written language we wish them to acquire" (p. 166). In other words, if we don't give them informational as well as narrative text, they may have difficulty reading and writing informational pieces.

Need for More Informational Texts for Underachieving Students

The importance of informational text for all students, but especially underachieving youngsters, is obvious. Unfortunately, Duke (2003), in her study of the presence of informational text in first-grade classrooms, found a scarcity of informational texts. Based on four visits to each of twenty classrooms, she found that only 2.6 percent of the material displayed on walls was informational; slightly less than 10 percent of the books in classroom libraries were informational. On average, only 3.6 minutes a day were spent talking about informational books during whole-class activities. In seven of the twenty classes, no time was spent with informational text. In schools in impoverished neighborhoods, the scarcity of informational text was even greater. These schools had only about half the number of informational books in their classroom libraries that the more privileged schools had. And the students spent even less time than their middle-class counterparts reading and discussing informational text. This finding may help explain the higher incidence of the fourth-grade slump among low socioeconomic status (SES) children.

Duke and Kays (1998) recommend including informational books in read-alouds. Through listening to informational books, children pick up the language of expository writing. They also learn the content conveyed by the text. In their study, Duke and Kays (1998) found that after hearing a book about potatoes, earth-

BOX
6.1

Model Program: The Emotional Power of Informational Text

Reading informational text can have a strong affective impact. Laurence Pringle, the author of more than one hundred children's books, reports that he is no longer surprised when students tell him that they feel very sad or even cry after reading his seventy-seventh book, *An Extraordinary Life: The Story of a Monarch Butterfly* (1997) (Livingston et al., 2004). When well written about a carefully chosen topic, informational text can be as powerful as fiction and can evoke an emotional response.

Informational text is an important element in closing the gap. Informational text builds background and vocabulary in a way that fiction can't. As Livingston and colleagues (2004) note, "The proliferation of new nonfiction books holds children's attention, develops their curiosity, and contributes to their knowledge base, spurring future investigations into informational reading" (p. 584). Their article, "Nonfiction as Literature: An Untapped Goldmine," has a description of a number of outstanding informational books (Livingston et al., 2004).

worms, spiders, or all-terrain vehicles, children were able to draw fairly detailed illustrations of what they had heard. First-graders were able to create rich retellings about informational texts that had been read to them (Moss, 1997).

Fostering the Reading of Informational Text

Reader's theater. One imaginative device for summarizing an informational book's content and also its vocabulary is through reader's theater. Livingston, Kurkijan, Young, and Pringle (2004) adapted *It's a Hummingbird's Life* (Kelly, 2003) so as to present the main facts about hummingbirds and key vocabulary. In reader's theater, students dramatize poems, short stories, biographies, or even excerpts from social studies and science texts. Using teacher-created reader's theater presentations as a model, groups of students can create their own presentations, thus combining practice in summarizing and writing with building background, vocabulary, and speaking and listening skills. Reader's theater works especially well with low-achieving readers because it provides them with the opportunity to reread a text several times so that they become thoroughly familiar with it.

Reader's theater begins with a careful reading and discussion of the selection and is followed by the preparation of a script and its performance. Students discuss how they want to rewrite the script. In most instances, dialogue from the selection should remain intact. Narrative portions from the selection might be summarized, especially if they are lengthy, or they may be translated into dialogue. For the sake of clarity, additional narration may need to be written. Narrator's lines can be added as needed to introduce scenes, provide transitions, or summarize events. Students can highlight their dialogue with markers (Hoffman,

1993). Reader's theater is relatively easy to implement because it can be brief, does not require students to memorize lines, and does not require sets or costumes.

Favorite authors. Students might be encouraged to select favorite nonfiction authors such as Laurence Pringle or Seymour Simon. Laurence Pringle has a Web site that provides biographical information and reviews of a number of his one hundred books (http://www.author-illustr-source.com/laurencepringle.htm). Most of the better-known children's writers also have Web sites.

Each year thousands of informational books for children are published. Many publishers have produced extensive series of informational books. One of the best known is the Read About Science series (HarperCollins), which explores dozens of science topics. Using a question and answer format, Don't Know Much About series by Kenneth C. Davis fosters an active, reading style. The series comes in two formats: picture book for younger readers and lengthier text for middle schoolers. Table 6.1 lists other informational series.

Need for Both Narrative and Informational Text

In discussing her research, Duke (2003) urges teachers to increase the amount of informational text students read. However, she warns against spending less time

TABLE 6.1 *Informational Series*

Series	Grade Level	Publisher
Animals in Danger	2-3	Heinemann
Community Workers	2-3	Compass Point
Cornerstones of Freedom	5-6	Children's Press
Dear America	4-6	Scholastic
Enchantment of the World	7-9	Children's Press
Eyewitness Books	4-8	Dorling Kindersley
My Health	5-6	Watts
Our Solar System	4-5	Smart Apple Media
Planet Library	5-6	Lerner
Read and Learn	1-2	Heinemann
Revolutionary War Leaders	4-7	Chelsea
Rookie Read-about Science	1-2	Children's Press
Science of Weather	3-4	Carolrhoda/Lerner
True Book	4-5	Children's Press
Visit To (countries)	2-3	Heinemann
Visit To (farm, doctor, etc.)	1	Capstone
Welcome Books	1-2	Children's Press

with narrative text so that more time can be spent with informational text. This is self-defeating. Students should simply read informational text in addition to narrative text. In her study, Duke (2003) found that worksheets took up nearly 22 percent of written language activity. Low SES students also spent 17 percent of their time working with individual letters, words, and sentences that were not part of a story or similar context. The figure for higher SES students was 9 percent. Some of the time spent in lower-level skills might well be replaced with time spent reading informational text.

Themes: Reading in Depth

Unfortunately, much of the reading that students do is fragmented. The selections they read jump from topic to topic. They read just enough about the sun, storms, or mosquitoes to get a brief overview of the topic. Because their knowledge is shallow, it fades from memory. Students don't get deeply enough into the topic to really understand it, to become interested in it, or to want to explore it in more depth. They don't learn the vocabulary associated with the topic because there is insufficient exposure to the words. Had they explored the topic in depth, they might have encountered key words a dozen times or more. This would have fostered a deeper understanding of the words and also a more rapid recognition of them. However, topics or texts should be interesting to students so that they want to spend time with them. As Hirsch (2003) comments, "These texts and topics must be compelling enough that both the teacher and the children want to talk about what they read, and deep enough that there is enough reason to revisit the topic" (p. 14).

Time spent on topics will vary depending on the nature of the topic and age of the students. Primary-grade students may spend a week on a topic, whereas middle school students may spend two or three weeks on a topic.

Extended time on a topic should build fluency as well as vocabulary and comprehension. Because many of the same words will be repeated, the text will gradually become easier as the readers become more familiar with the words and so the reading becomes more automatic (Hirsch, 2003).

Hirsch (2003) found that extensive reading in an area also improved writing. He speculated that because students acquired a depth of knowledge, they could more readily draw on that knowledge as they wrote. Because they had to devote less energy to thinking about the content, they had more cognitive energy to use composing their message. In addition, they would be more familiar with the vocabulary of the topic and the language used to explain it.

Using the Content Areas to Close the Gap

To raise scores on mandated tests, some schools have limited or even curtailed instruction in the content areas and use the time instead to work on test preparation exercises. This is a misguided practice. Actually, content-area reading is an outstanding means for closing the gap. Content-area materials offer an unparalleled opportunity to increase vocabulary, build background knowledge, and foster comprehension. In fact, if you don't look at the title of today's content-area books, you might mistake them for reading improvement texts. In *Scott Foresman's Social Studies*, for instance, students are taught a target reading strategy that will assist them as they read the chapter (Boyd et al., 2003). In a chapter on the American Revolutionary War, students are taught to recognize cause-and-effect structure and to make use of this structure to comprehend the text. After being taught the skill in the context of an article on events leading up to the Revolutionary War, they apply the skill throughout the chapter. Questions build on the skill and lead students to apply it. For instance, students are asked such questions as "What effect did the Sons of Liberty have on the Stamp Act? What caused British leaders to pass the Townshend Acts?" Graphic organizers also reinforce skill as students fill in missing causes on a cause-effect organizer. Writing is used to foster learning. Students are asked to pretend that they are a member of the Virginia House of Burgesses and write a speech opposing the Stamp Act.

Using Science to Build Reading Skills

One problem with reading in the content areas is that the texts are often too difficult for struggling readers. However, the texts can be made more accessible if needed background is built before students read them. Here is how this might be done in science. Typically, students view science demonstrations or engage in experiments or other activities after reading the text. However, if the demonstrations or experiments were conducted before the reading of the text, they would provide preparation for the reading of the text. One program that implements this principle is FOSS (Full Option Science System). As the creators of the program explain:

> We believed that reading was important but that what one learned from reading would be enhanced if it came after hands-on experience. Reading is richer and has more meaning when students bring to the written word knowledge and enthusiasm developed through first-hand experiences. We wanted students to learn science by doing science and then enter into library resources to extend what they learned through printed materials.
>
> Reading enriches and extends the FOSS activities with objects, organisms, and materials that can't be brought into the classroom. Reading brings students in touch with the historical discoveries that laid the foundation for their own investigations. Reading allows students to share the adventures of others grappling with or using the science principles they have been working with in the classroom. Reading provides technical information for trying to build equipment or conducting investigations to continue their inquiry into the subject at hand. (FOSS, 2004a)

Although FOSS is a hands-on curriculum, activities are accompanied by reading materials. Each FOSS module has a FOSS Science Stories book written specifically for that module. The materials have eight to twelve individual stories or articles that correlate to each module. The selections include the following elements.

- Related historical and biographical readings
- Fictional tales, myths, and stories about students doing interesting things with science
- Expository text that extends key concepts
- Technical readings in which students follow instructions or read technical explanations of scientific principles (FOSS, 2004b)

Just as reading can add power to science learning, science can add power to reading and writing. In FOSS and other well-designed programs, students are taught the vocabulary of science and key critical thinking skills. They draw conclusions, note likeness and differences, and categorize phenomena. The skills, knowledge, and vocabulary that they acquire foster comprehension. In fact, noting likenesses and differences has been cited as a powerful, high-payoff comprehension skill (Marzano, Gaddy, & Dean, 2000). Science programs also build language as students discuss observations and conclusions and explain phenomena. FOSS has student sheets that help students organize and discuss data. Not surprisingly, students who have taken part in FOSS have higher reading scores than those who haven't. Fifth- and sixth-graders who had been in the program for four years outscored their non-FOSS counterparts by 13 percentile points (Valadez & Freve, 2002). There are very few reading interventions that yield gains of that magnitude.

Perhaps, most important of all, science fosters language development and higher-level thinking and writing skills. Science investigations offer opportunities for students to think critically, to apply what they read, and to develop written and verbal communication skills. It is unfortunate that teachers are currently being asked by administrators to increase the instructional time devoted to language arts at the expense of time for science and social studies. Teachers should be encouraged to use science and social studies to apply reading and writing skills in challenging contexts.

Although FOSS has been highlighted because it is a university-sponsored, high-quality program, any high-quality science program can be used to achieve the same results. The important point is that while the study of science is valuable in its own right, it is also an invaluable means for closing the literacy gap. As noted earlier, social studies can also be a vehicle for improving reading skills. In her review of the research, Wade (1983) found that when teachers taught reading skills as a means for increasing students' knowledge of social studies, students' performance in both areas improved.

Providing Preparation for Reading Content-Area Texts

From third grade through twelfth, the typical student reads thirty thousand pages from science, math, and social studies textbooks (May, 1986). Unfortunately, many underachieving as well as many achieving students are not prepared to read content-area materials. With its more complex structures, technical vocabulary, and conceptual demands, content reading is more intense. In some ways, learning to read in content areas is akin to learning a foreign language. As Postman (1979) reminds us, "Biology is not plants and animals. It is language about plants and animals. History is not events. It is language describing and interpreting events. Astronomy is not planets and stars. It is a way of talking about planets and stars" (p. 165). Because of the complexity of content-area reading and the key role that it plays in education, especially in grades 4 and beyond, students should begin learning to read content-area material in the primary grades.

Improving Access to Texts

Unfortunately, some students are reading so far below grade level that building background and using supporting aids will not be sufficient to make the texts readable. Most textbook series have the text recorded on a CD-ROM so that students with weak reading skills can read along with the CD. (Recorded textbooks are also available for students with reading disabilities, regardless of cause, from Recording for the Blind and Dyslexic (RFB&D) at http://www.rfbd.org. RFB&D is a private organization, so there are fees involved and playback equipment must be purchased.) Although the recorded versions of texts can help students who lack decoding skills, they can't compensate for students who don't recognize the words when they hear them. If students don't understand the language when they hear it, then recorded text will not make up for their deficiency.

For students for whom the language is too difficult, you might want to obtain easy-to-read texts. The following publishers have a wide variety of texts for below-level readers: American Guidance Services, Globe Fearon, Phoenix Learning, and Steck-Vaughn. Another option is to use easy-to-read trade books written on key topics. A third option is to rewrite portions of the text to make it more accessible.

Using Writing to Close the Gap

Writing skills should be developed for their own sake. Writing is an essential literacy tool. However, writing is a way of learning and also developing language skills. As such, it is a powerful tool for closing the gap. In 90/90/90 schools, 90 percent or more of the students are eligible for free or reduced-price lunches and are members of ethnic minority groups, but also meet academic standards in reading or another area (Reeves, 2000). A key element in 90/90/90 schools is an emphasis on nonfiction writing. Students are required to produce an acceptable piece of writing on a periodic basis. For elementary schools, this is once a month. For secondary schools, it is once a quarter. After being provided with thorough guidance and instruction, students write a nonfiction piece. Nonfiction pieces must include information that students do not already know so that the project becomes a genuine quest for new knowledge. The format can vary and might include reports, a persuasive editorial, a biography, or an explanation of a scientific process. In writing their pieces, students not only increase content knowledge but they also develop thinking and writing skills.

Use of a Common Rubric

Writing is a whole-school activity and is assessed using a common rubric. The rubric highlights key characteristics of effective writing. It provides clear standards for writing and clear standards for assessing (Reeves, 2003). Teachers would meet to assess papers or exchange papers so assessment was the result of applying the rubric rather than simply using highly subjective judgment. Disagreements about scoring generally arise when teachers use implicit criteria rather than stated criteria or the criteria are not specific enough. For instance, a teacher might judge a paper partly on neatness, which isn't one of the stated criteria. Or a criterion such as "fully develops ideas," which lacks specificity, is interpreted in different ways by different reviewers. By talking over standards and disagreements, teachers can clarify the criteria and refrain from adding criteria that are not stated.

The rubric is geared to students' grade levels and English proficiencies. A five-sentence piece might earn a young English learner a proficiency designation, whereas an older native speaker might be required to a write a three-page piece. The principal and teachers regularly discuss and share students' writing to maintain their focus on key characteristics of students' writing. Students are expected to live up to the rubric's provisions. They are required to revise and edit as much as necessary to produce an acceptable piece. Writing assignments are not treated as work samples to be graded but as opportunities to build essential skills.

Another characteristic of 90/90/90 schools is an emphasis on written responses in performance assessments. The emphasis on written response has a double payoff. "First, students process information in a much clearer way when they are required to write an answer. They 'write to think' and, thus, gain the opportunity to clarify their own thought processes. Second, teachers have the opportunity to gain rich and complex diagnostic information about why students respond to an academic challenge the way that they do" (Reeves, 2000 p. 190). By assessing students' written responses, teachers are better able to determine what concepts and skills students grasp and which they are having difficulty with. In keeping with the 90/90/90 schools' emphasis on writing, the National Commission on Writing (2003) recommends that the amount of time devoted to writing be doubled and that students write in each subject area.

Increasing Writing Time

Elementary schools devote three hours or less each week to writing (National Commission on Writing, 2003). Writing time can be doubled by having students write in all subject-area classes and by writing at home. Students might be asked to write 15 minutes a night, four nights a week. Schools should also develop common expectations about writing. In commenting on the importance of writing for learning, the National Commission on Writing (2003) states:

> If students are to make knowledge their own, they must struggle with the details, wrestle with the facts, and rework raw information and dimly understood concepts into language they can communicate to someone else. In short, if students are to learn, they must write. (p. 9)

Not All Writing Is Equal

When it comes to literacy and cognitive development, not all writing is equal. Students and writing programs sometimes get bogged down in recounts. In recounts, students tell about a personal experience they had, or about a book they read, or about a TV show or movie they saw. Prevalent in the early grades, recounts persist into the middle grades unless students are guided into more demanding and more rewarding kinds of writing. In their study of writing, Langer and Applebee (1987) found that through writing, students gain new knowledge and review, reflect on, and extend ideas. However, the level and extent of the benefit depend on the level and extent of the writing. Simply locating and recording information is of limited benefit. Writing that requires reflection is of much more benefit. The most beneficial writing tasks are those that require comparing, contrasting, concluding, and evaluating. In other words, those that require students to do something with the information result in deeper understanding and learning than those that merely involve a retelling, as recounts do. Students should write in the content areas as well as in language arts class. History lends itself to comparing, contrasting, and evaluating. Science lends itself to describing and explaining.

Writing Requires Instruction

In writing, practice doesn't necessarily make perfect. Students don't make progress until they are challenged to compose more complex forms. Writing is a complex skill. Students need careful guidance, direct instruction, and experience writing in a variety of modes. They need to be coaxed out of their comfort zones so that they attempt new genres and new techniques. As in other areas of literacy, a carefully planned systematic program that builds on students' interests works best. A checklist for assessing the quality of the writing program is presented in Table 6.2.

Model Programs

A well-crafted program for the primary grades is *Units of Study for Primary Writing: A Yearlong Program*, which was created by Lucy Calkins (2003) and members of the Teachers College Reading and Writing Project, Columbia University. This is an intensive step-by-step program. But its most compelling feature is that it is based on extensive work with students in some of New York's poorest schools. It demonstrates convincingly that given effective instruction, the poorest of children can achieve at high levels.

A high-quality program for grades 3-6 from the same source is *Teaching the Qualities of Writing* (Portalupi & Fletcher, 2004). *Teaching the Qualities of Writing* is

TABLE 6.2 *Writing Lesson Checklist*

Action	Fully	Partially	Limited	Suggestions
Teacher uses process approach.				
Students are divided into guided writing groups according to needs.				
Writing strategy is introduced with examples. Teacher explains value of strategy.				
Teacher models strategy and engages in think-aloud.				
Teacher provides guided practice.				
Students apply strategy in their writing.				
In conferences, teacher focuses on use of newly taught strategy.				
Teacher assesses students' use of strategy and reviews as necessary.				
Writing-on-demand is presented as a separate genre.				

also based on extensive work with teachers and students in the New York area. It includes a well-thought-out overview and rationale for the program, 10 cycles or units of instruction that stress genres, including writing to a prompt; 112 lessons; resources for lessons; and practical suggestions and forms for assessment. But the most valuable part of the program is a series of 24 writing samples that the authors JoAnn Portalupi and Ralph Fletcher discuss. This provides an excellent tutorial in what to look for in students' writing and suggestions that can be used in instruction. Also of particular value is an Instructional Challenge Chart that lists areas that need improving, samples of students' writing that illustrate the challenges, and lessons that can be used to provide instruction in the needed areas.

Assessment is thorough but carefully embedded in the program. Instruction is based on students' strengths and weaknesses as revealed in conferences and in their writing. However, the authors caution against going overboard.

> Assessment, while key to effective instruction, can be a risk when valuable time for learning gets usurped by an overzealous attention to assessing growth. Because we believe students learn in the acts of reading, writing, and talking, the best assessment of their growth happens closest to these actions. Teachers who listen closely as students talk about their writing gain an understanding of their students' skills: assessment happens moment to moment. In addition to daily ongoing observations, it helps to step back and take a slower look at a collection of children's work over time. (Portalupi & Fletcher, 2004, p. 44)

Based on carefully planned staff development, *Teaching the Qualities of Writing* should improve teachers' teaching skills as well as students' writing skills.

Assessing the Reading and Writing Informational Text Component of Your Program

Because it builds background, vocabulary, and skills, reading and writing informational text is an essential part of any program that is designed to beat the odds. Use the checklist in Table 6.3 to determine the strengths and weaknesses of the informational text component of your program.

TABLE 6.3 *Assessment Checklist for Reading and Writing Informational Text*

Action	Fully	Partially	Limited	Suggestions
Students are encouraged to read informational text.				
Informational text is included in read-alouds.				
The classroom library contains a large number of informational texts on a variety of topics and on a variety of levels.				
The classroom library contains trade books on key topics covered in the content areas.				
Guided reading sessions are frequently devoted to informational texts.				
Students are taught key skills for reading informational text.				
Students write expository and persuasive as well as narrative text.				
Students are taught skills needed to write a variety of types of narrative and informational text.				
Students use writing as a learning tool.				
A common rubric is used by all teachers to assess writing.				
Students read content-area materials that are on the appropriate level.				
Students are taught content-areas skills and apply skills taught in language arts class to the content areas.				
Students develop content-area vocabulary.				
Students read content-area trade books.				

7

Using Extensive Reading to Close the Gap

The most effective initiative to optimize a program and provide necessary practice is the simplest. It requires no expenditure of funds, no additional staff, no complex techniques, no reorganization, no lengthy in-services. The quickest and best thing you do to boost the reading abilities of all students is to increase the amount of time they spend reading. Earlier in my career, I taught a summer school reading improvement program to middle school students. Time was limited. I had just six weeks of daily sessions that lasted for 90 minutes. However, my students made good progress. An essential element in the program was a requirement that students spend a significant amount of time reading. In those days before Sustained Silent Reading, classroom sessions were set up primarily to teach and practice skills. Realizing that 90 minutes of instruction and practice was not going to accomplish much, I set up a classroom library and made voluntary reading at home a key element in the program. The impact of the 90-minute sessions was multiplied by the reading that the students did on their own. My post-test results were so encouraging I felt as though I had cheated. I sensed that my students' good showing was more the result of their outside reading than my classroom instruction. In retrospect, it was most likely a happy combination of both.

Reading just 10 extra minutes a day improves reading performance (Anderson, Wilson, & Fielding, 1988). However, previewing the vocabulary and discussing the selection after it has been read will optimize the benefit. Extra reading builds background, vocabulary, and skills. Researchers also have found that higher volumes of reading foster cognitive development (Cunningham & Stanovich, 1998). Reading widely not only makes you more knowledgeable; it also makes you smarter. As Cunningham and Stanovich (1998) conclude: "All of our studies have demonstrated that reading yields significant dividends for everyone—not just for the 'smart kids' or the more able readers. Even the child with limited reading and comprehension skills will build vocabulary and cognitive structures through reading" (p. 7). They recommend that we "provide all children, regardless of their achievement levels, with as many reading experiences as possible. Indeed, this becomes doubly imperative for precisely those children whose verbal abilities are most in need of bolstering, for it is the very act of reading that can build those capacities" (Cunningham & Stanovich, 1998, pp. 6-7).

Lack of experience reading might produce another phenomenon, the slow reader. Tim Rasinski, an expert on fluency, found that middle grade readers in a high-poverty school were reading with good accuracy but at a slow rate (personal communication, December 3, 2003). Slow reading rate typically results in diminished comprehension. It also means that because they're reading slowly, students won't encounter as many words and so won't benefit as much from their reading.

Unfortunately, the amount of reading that students engage in varies widely, with the poorest readers reading the least. One study found that the average fifth-grader spends about 30 minutes a week engaged in independent reading, which is less than 5 minutes a day (Anderson, Wilson, & Fielding 1988.) The heaviest readers spend more than an hour a day reading. Students in the lowest 20th percentile average less than a minute a day engaged in independent reading. Students at the 20th percentile in terms of volume of reading read about 21,000 words a year. Stu-

BOX

7.1

Exemplary Program: Just Read

An effective voluntary reading program starts with access to books. An excellent example of a program that used voluntary reading to boost achievement is Just Read (Joyce & Showers, 2002). Just Read began with conversations among teachers and other staff members who were dissatisfied with the amount of reading that students were doing. They discussed the importance of outside reading and how much outside reading they thought their students were doing. Curious about their speculations, they began gathering data on students' outside reading. They discovered that many of the students were doing very little reading. About one in ten were doing no outside reading.

A program of voluntary reading entitled Just Read was initiated. The program was based on data. A survey of students' interests was used to obtain additional books for classroom libraries. Motivational talks and discussions were held. Students were provided with individual guidance and encouragement. Reading logs were collected weekly. Data from the logs was used to adjust the program and also to "celebrate successes." Parent support was enlisted. Parents not only encouraged their children to read; they also sent in ideas for motivating voluntary reading, and they sponsored events, such as book fairs and book trading days, that fostered added reading. Ads for books were posted in school hallways. T-shirts with the Just Read logo were obtained. Charts were used to show increases in the number of books read. The amount of reading increased dramatically, but not in all classrooms. Some teachers were more effective than others in motivating voluntary reading. Additional assistance was provided for teachers whose students lagged behind in their outside reading. The number of nonreading students dropped from more than 11 percent to just 3 percent.

Both reading and writing scores rose dramatically. Average score before the initiative was at the 48th percentile. After the initiative, it was at the 66th percentile. Surprisingly, writing scores also took a leap upward. The initiative itself became embedded in the school's curriculum so that fostering wide reading became a permanent goal.

dents at the 90th percentile read nearly 2 million words. The heaviest readers read more than 4 million words a year.

Extra Reading Is Needed to Close the Gap

The more text that students read the better their reading should become. Unless struggling students are reading on a continuous basis, they probably won't make adequate progress. How much should they read? For students in grade 4 and beyond, New Standards (National Center on Education and the Economy and the University of Pittsburgh, 1997) sets a goal of 25 books per year, which seems reasonable. Guthrie (2004) estimates growth based on the amount of time students spend reading, both in school and out. Based on observations, questionnaires, and studies, Guthrie speculates that the average student in grade 4 reads about 2 hours a day. This includes 30 minutes in language arts, 30 minutes in the content areas, 30 minutes during self-selected reading, and 30 minutes at night doing homework or voluntary reading. With reading a total of 2 hours, the student achieves an average score on the typical standardized test. Students who read more achieve higher scores; students who read less have below-average scores. A fourth-grade student who has been reading just 60 minutes a day will be at the second-grade level. A student who reads 3 hours a day will be at the sixth-grade level. Each 30 minutes of additional reading is associated with about a year's growth in reading. However, assuming that students have been reading at an extended rate since second grade, a fourth-grader would have to read an additional 270 hours (30 minutes times 3 years) to gain a year's growth. Of course, this is very approximate, but it can function as a rule of thumb.

Setting Aside Time for Self-Selected Reading

Although there is widespread agreement that setting aside time for self-selected reading (SSR) is a valuable activity, its value can also be enhanced. If students are simply daydreaming, thumbing through picture books, or getting bogged down in a text that is too hard, they are not deriving any benefit. As originally proposed, SSR programs were relatively passive. Everyone simply read. However, SSR programs work better when the teacher takes time to introduce and recommend new books, helps struggling readers select appropriate materials, discusses the students' reading at the end of the session, and holds them accountable for what they have read (Marshall, 2002). Holding students accountable does not mean giving them quizzes, asking for summaries, or requiring book reports. It can be as simple as filling out log sheets, such as the one shown in Figure 7.1.

SSR can be a value-added activity if students become so intrigued by a book that they take it home and read it. Then they are extending your efforts by reading on their own time, which is one way to catch up. SSR also works better if you have plenty of interesting books, periodicals, and other materials to choose from.

The purpose of SSR is to help students discover the joy and satisfaction of reading. SSR also provides time for students to learn how to select books, to apply reading skills, to build background knowledge, and to foster fluency. Initially time set aside for SSR might be only 10 minutes but can be lengthened to 20 to 30 minutes. As originally conceived, during SSR everyone stopped whatever they were doing and read. The object was to highlight reading and have the teacher model reading. However, many teachers have found that SSR is more effective if they take a more active role. As one middle school teacher explains:

> There is no way to help students choose the right book, watch them choose books, talk with them about their reading, read to them, or listen to them read if you are at your desk behind a book. (Marshall, 2002, p. 8)

This doesn't mean that the teacher won't spend some time reading. However, in revised SSR, the teacher does the following.

- Motivates reading by taking a few minutes to read a portion of a chapter aloud, highlight a few books, or point out newly arrived books.
- Observes students to make sure that they choose books that are interesting and on their own levels.
- Holds individual or group conferences with students. The conferences are of the type that adults might have when discussing a book that they are reading. There is no checking for understanding or time spent building skills. Focus is on reading for enjoyment. This is a good time to find out what kinds of reading students like to do so that the teacher can obtain materials that match their interests.
- Holds students accountable for their reading. Students keep a record of their reading. In their reading logs, which are kept in folders in the classroom, students note the title and author of the book they are reading and the number of pages read each day. Students can write a brief comment about what they have read, but you might want to make this optional. After finishing a book,

Name _____ Class _____

Reading Log

Date	Title	Pages Read	Comments

FIGURE 7.1 *Reading Log*

they should fill out a review sheet in which they briefly give their opinion of the book. Reviews can be kept on file or posted so that students can consult them when selecting a book. A list of recommended books should be posted. Favorite books might be given a gold seal.

- At the end of SSR, briefly discusses the reading that students did and perhaps encourages them to continue their reading at home.

Independent Reading: A Structured Version of Voluntary Reading

In this version of SSR, Fountas and Pinnell (2001) include student discussion and written response. Independent reading is a modified version of individualized or personalized reading, which dates back to the 1940s and 1950s. Key elements include a minilesson in which a skill such as selecting appropriate books, previewing a selection, or using a glossary is briefly presented. An overview of the session's activities, independent reading, and conferring are also essential elements. While the students are reading silently, the teacher confers for a few minutes with individual students. The session ends with a group sharing of what they have read. Students also evaluate their personal work and how well they worked together (Fountas & Pinnell, 2001).

If you are an experienced teacher, you have probably already concluded that while highly effective, a program of independent reading requires a host of skills a careful introduction and management if it is to be successful. Done right, independent reading is a dream; done poorly, it can be a nightmare. To implement independent reading, follow or adapt the following steps, which are based on work by Fountas & Pinnell (2001).

Implementing Independent Reading

Step 1: Obtain and classify books

The first order of business is to obtain interesting reading materials on the students' levels. To do this, find out what levels your students are reading on. Expect a range. For a fourth-grade class, materials might range from a second- to a sixth-grade level. Then determine students' reading interests and their attitudes toward reading. Through observation, classroom discussions, and conversations with individual children, explore students' interests. Find out who likes adventure, who likes sports, and who prefers stories about animals. Obtain materials that reflect your students' interests and that are on the levels your class will most likely need. Books should be leveled and marked. Insofar as possible, deemphasize book levels. Instead, stress selecting books that students can read smoothly or that will help them grow as readers (Calkins, 2001). Instead of saying, "You need to read books that have a blue dot," say, "You might be able to read a blue dot book faster and more smoothly" or "Why don't you try a blue dot book for now and try the green dot books after you read some blue dot ones?" Or you might ask, "Is this a stop and go book? Are you stopping a lot to try to figure out hard words? Try a blue dot book. You won't have so many stops" (Calkins, 2001). You don't want to stigmatize below-level readers, but at the same time, you want them reading books that they are comfortable with and that foster maximum growth. As explained in Chapter 3, there are numerous sources for leveled books. There are also a number of leveling systems. At Urban Elementary, teachers found Renaissance Learning's ATOS (Advantage-TASA Open Standard) (http://www.renlearn.com) easy to use and sufficiently accurate for books beyond the first-grade level.

You might not level all books. If a small number of books are not leveled, this provides students with the opportunity to pick books from a variety of levels and also to use their book selection skills (Calkins, 2001). However, not leveling any books can be disastrous. Calkins (2001) recalls visiting classrooms in which students stumbled through books that were not leveled; as a result, students had picked books that were frustratingly difficult.

Step 2: Set up a classroom library

Once books have been obtained and marked, set up a classroom library and reading area. Whenever possible, books should be displayed with their covers facing outward to attract prospective readers. Books should be organized by level and topic. Books might also be arranged by author. Gary Paulsen books might be placed in a separate bin, as might detective stories or books about pets. When setting up a library, take a hint from retailers. Don't restrict books to the book or library corner. Set up book displays next to areas of interest. In general merchandise stores, band-aids are stocked near the fish hooks as well as the first-aid aisle. Buyers of fish hooks see the connection, and the purchase of band-aids increases. In similar fashion, put books on tropical fish next to the fish tanks and books on magnets next to the magnet display. In your displays, include nonfiction as well as fiction, electronic texts along with hardcopy text. Also stock the library with popular periodicals, such as *Sports Illustrated for Kids, National Geographic World,* and *Ranger Rick.*

Step 3: Set up a management system

Explain to the class the purpose of independent reading and how the materials are organized. Set up a system for obtaining books and returning them. It is generally a good idea to have students select and check out their books before the independent reading period begins so that they are ready to go as soon as the session starts. Some teachers have students obtain five or so books at the beginning of the week. These become the basis for the week's independent reading. Encourage students to check out more than one book. If it turns out that they don't like their first selection, they have a backup. Calkins (2001) advocates creating "bookshelves," which are magazine boxes or other suitable containers. The bookshelves hold the students' books, bookmarks, conference record sheets, and book logs. One school has students keep their books in cloth bags, which are hung on the backs of their chairs.

Involve students in setting up checkout procedures and rules so that they acquire a sense of ownership of the classroom collection. Keep the rules simple; if they are complicated and punitive, they will discourage borrowing (Wilson, 1986). Unfortunately, some books will be lost or damaged. Consider this part of the cost of "doing business." Do not charge late fines or fees for lost or damaged books; these could be a genuine hardship for some children. Instead, have a talk with students about being more responsible. If it is not a hardship, students could contribute replacement books, which do not necessarily have to have the same titles as the lost books. Put students in charge of keeping track of books; they can handle checking in, checking out, and putting books away.

Stress that reading time is quiet time. Explain that it is hard to concentrate when someone is talking. Also explain that they will be given time to talk about their books at the end of independent reading time.

Set aside a time each day for independent reading. It might be 20 to 30 minutes. However, it might be necessary to build reading "stamina," especially for younger children. Calkins (2001) recommends partner reading to build stamina. Partners should be on the same approximate reading level or the stronger reader will dominate the session. In partner reading, one student selects a book, but the other student decides how the book is to be read: taking turns (you read a page; I'll read a page); taking parts (I'll be the mouse; you be the lion—only works with certain books); choral reading (both read together).

Step 4: Teach students how to select books

Model the process of selecting a book. Discuss how you get a sense of its contents by examining the cover, finding out who the author is, reading the blurb on the jacket, glancing through the book, and reading selected parts. Brainstorm ways in which students have chosen books. Also have some of your proficient book selectors demonstrate how they choose books. Discuss both the need to pick a book that is interesting and a book that is just right. To pick a book that is just right, encourage students to read a page or two to see if they know most of the words and understand what the book is saying. Post book selection suggestions and, from time to time, have students explain how they happened to select an especially interesting book. Guide students, especially those who are reading below grade level, as they select books. Have them read a passage or two. If the passage seems too hard, suggest an easier book.

Book selection is the key to successful independent reading. If students succeed in finding books that capture their attention, then discipline problems fade away. They are too interested in their reading to have time for talking or making mischief.

Step 5: Teach students how to talk about books

After they read, students gather in pairs or groups of three or four and talk about their books. They buzz each other. So that the buzz may be profitable, give students a prompt beforehand. You might ask them, for instance, to attach stick-on notes to two passages that they would like to share. During the buzz, they read the passages that have been marked and explain why they chose them. They also ask each other questions. Before engaging in book buzz, students are taught to listen attentively, ask questions after each presentation, and take turns. Although they are taught to be respectful of each other, they also learn how to provide support for their statements and how to politely voice opposing opinions.

Why is it important for students to talk about books? Calkins (2001) explains:

It is by talking about books that children learn to conduct a dialogue in their minds, to think about books even when they read alone. In our reading workshops, partnerships support talking, and therefore thinking about texts. (p. 75)

Step 6: Teach students how to respond to books
Using open-ended prompts, such as locating and explaining favorite parts, or more specific prompts, students are provided with a purpose for reading and discussing. For independent reading, the prompt is typically open-ended and general. Responses need not be written but might be simply marked with a stick-on note. Possible prompts include the following.

- Mark two passages that you would like to share.
- Mark two passages that are interesting.
- Mark two passages that are funny, exciting, or sad.
- Mark two passages that tell you things you didn't know.
- Mark two passages that you think the others in the group would like to hear.
- Mark two passages that contain interesting language.
- Mark two passages that give you information you can use.
- Mark one or two passages that tell about a place that you would like to visit.

The purpose of the sharing is to motivate reading. After reading a good book, we enjoy sharing with others. Hearing others talk about books entices us to read the books. The discussion is not about building skills or vocabulary; it is about experiencing and sharing the joy of reading

Step 7: Teach students how to work together
With the class, create a series of guidelines for working together. Guidelines include having books available for reading, reading silently, and holding questions or concerns until the teacher is available (unless it's an emergency).

Step 8: Teach students how to write recommendations
Recommended books are placed on a special shelf or rack. Model how you would go about deciding whether to recommend a book and how you would compose a recommendation.

Independent Reading in Action

Does independent reading work? It works extremely well. Here is what it looks like in an inner-city third-grade classroom. At the beginning of the session, the teacher asked students to make a connection between something they read in the books and something in their lives. The teacher began the lesson by modeling connections she had made. She discussed how the dog in this story she had read was similar to a dog she owned. Students were asked to use stick-on notes to mark two passages in which they made connections and which they would like to share with their group.

Although the students had taken their books home with them the night before to continue their reading, all of the students but one had remembered to bring their books to class. The student who had forgotten was allowed to select another book but was reminded to bring in the book he had forgotten. The classroom library was extensive. Books were available on a variety of topics but were also leveled. Although several students were reading on a first-grade level, there were appropriate books for them. Students were also allowed to "abandon" books in which they had lost interest. Only one student requested permission to abandon his book. Having lots of books on appropriate levels and teaching students how to select books lessens the problem of having students pick books that are too hard or lacking in appeal.

While the students read silently, the teacher held conferences with individuals. Students were asked to tell how they liked their books and what had happened in their books, if they were reading fiction, and what they were learning, if they were reading nonfiction. At the conclusion of the discussion, they were encouraged to predict what would happen next or to tell what they would like to learn.

At the teacher's signal, the students engaged in Buddy Buzz. They discussed their book with a small group. They were reminded to give the title, talk about the two passages they had marked, and to explain why they had chosen those passages. At the conclusion of each student's sharing, the other members of the group asked questions. During Buddy Buzz, the teacher visited groups, listened to their discussions, and made helpful suggestions.

At the end of the session, students discussed why other people might enjoy the book they were reading. Several students cited reasons why they thought others might like their books. The teacher then asked students if they would like to read anyone else's book. One student wanted to find out more about Hawaii. Several students were interested in finding out what happened to the princess who was in a deep sleep. There was a spontaneous clamor for the book in which a boy had put bugs in a bully's pants. They begged the teacher to show the page and read it aloud. Needless to say, as the result of the discussion, the students sought out several of the books that had been mentioned. For them, reading had become a source of enjoyment. When that happens, students' reading is sure to take off.

At the end of the session, the teacher modeled writing of a letter explaining why she thought others might enjoy the book that she had just read. Students then wrote a similar letter in their response journals.

Materials

Much of the success of your voluntary reading program will depend on the kinds of materials you have available. Marshall (2002) found that students' enthusiasm was rekindled when she involved them in selecting books for the classroom library and when she obtained books that were both interesting and on the appropriate levels. She discovered that struggling readers were turned off when they encountered books that were too difficult for them. Materials should reflect your students' interests and reading levels. Make sure you have plenty of materials for struggling readers. Have recorded books available for students who might not be able to read the book on their own or for those who would like to read in that way. By opening up recorded books to everyone, you don't stigmatize students who might read recorded books because they lack the skills to read them on their own. For lists of recommended books, go to Renaissance Learning at http://www.renlearn.com/, click on Order Quizzes, and then click on Recommended Reading Lists. Another good source for recommended classroom libraries is the Field Guide to the Classroom Library at http://fieldguides.heinemann.com/how/libraries/b.asp. The lists have been compiled by teachers working in the Teachers College Reading and Writing Project.

Reading should not be restricted to books. Reading is reading. Reading magazines and Internet sites is just as beneficial as reading a chapter book or a novel. Students who like sports and read *Sports Illustrated for Kids*, which is written on about a fifth-grade level, will encounter just as much print as they would reading a brief novel. A good use of funds would be for classes to select and subscribe to two or three periodicals, which could then become part of the class library.

Organization

In general, there should be no exchanges during the SSR sessions, and all students should be involved in reading. Material to be read should be selected before the session starts, and students should choose more than one book or magazine in case their first choice proves to be dull. Students should handle checkout procedures for materials. There should be no book reports of any kind. There should be inviting places set aside for reading print books as well as recorded books or e-books. Use a timer to regulate the length of sessions.

Gear activities to the level of the students' reading development. Students whose reading is very limited may not benefit from SSR or even reading with a partner. Have them read along with a recorded selection or a CD. Novice and struggling readers need lots of experience with contextual reading (Carbo, 1997).

Reading Appropriate Level Books for Maximum Gain

Gains for students who read voluntarily can be quite substantial. Based on their analysis of studies, Lewis and Samuels (2003) found that independent reading was "especially beneficial for students at earlier stages of reading development: students in lower grades, those experiencing difficulties learning to read, and students learning English as a second language. The value of reading was also greater for students in rural and urban schools" (p. 2). Students who read voluntarily gained between two-fifths and three-fifths of a standard deviation over students who did not engage in voluntary reading. This translates into a gain of between 14 and 20 percentile points.

Gains are highest when students understand almost all of what they read. As Paul (2003) comments, "It's not practice which makes perfect, but successful practice which develops successful readers" (p. 38). Even reading easy books can result in gains. As Paul (2003) points out, "Trade books often contain vocabulary that is more advanced than the book level (i.e., third-grade book with some sixth- to seventh-grade vocabulary words)" (p. 43). Although tackling a difficult book on occasion can bring about gains, by and large, students gain the most when the books they read are on their level, when the reading is relatively easy.

Finding books on the appropriate level for struggling readers can be a challenge. Each year, approximately ten thousand children's books are published. There is a wealth of reading materials available. Unfortunately these reading riches are not evenly distributed. Most trade books are written on or above the expected grade level of the intended audience (Gunning, 2000). For instance, books that appeal to fourth-graders or that have fourth-graders as their main characters are generally written on a fourth-grade level. There are relatively few trade books for below-level readers. Finding a book on a fourth-grade level that would appeal to a fourth-grader is relatively easy. Finding a book written on a second-grade level that would appeal to a fourth-grader is a challenge. However, unless given books on their level, struggling readers fail to thrive. The following school publishers have created series of high-interest, low-readability books:

American Guidance Services	Lake Education
Children's Press	Perfection Learning
Don Johnston	Steck-Vaughn
Globe-Fearon	Sundance
High Noon	

Motivating Voluntary Reading

Having available lots of interesting materials on appropriate levels is the first step in motivating voluntary reading. However, there are a number of other steps that can be taken to foster wide reading.

The Role of Discussion in Fostering Voluntary Reading

The opportunity to talk about reading is highly motivating. In a study comparing sustained silent reading with individualized reading in which students have conferences with the teacher and also with individualized reading in which students have conferences with each other, the students who discussed books with peers did significantly better on reading achievement tests. For the peer conference group, reading became an important activity, at least in part, because it was something that these students shared with other students (Manning & Manning, 1984). As Wilson (1992) comments:

> Reading becomes something that students do because of friendship, because their friends read. More important, sharing their thoughts and feelings about books becomes part of the intellectual currency of their social relations within the classroom. Reading becomes part of the culture of the classroom. (p. 163)

The Role of High-Quality Instruction

High-quality instruction also fosters voluntary reading. Students who are taught a variety of comprehension strategies read more. Having a command of strategies enables students to comprehend materials that they encounter at school and at home. Because reading is a successful experience, they are motivated to read on their own. As Lewis and Samuels (2003) comment, "When students are successful, it leads to additional growth and improvement. Children are motivated to do that which they can do well" (p. 16).

In addition, teachers "who emphasized the importance of comprehending and learning from books probably created greater interest in books and fostered students' motivation to read" (Guthrie et al., 1995, p. 23). In his study of outside reading, Paul (2003) found that both the amount and quality of students' reading is dependent on the quality of instruction rather than on students' abilities.

> The fact that the teacher/classroom determines far more gain than beginning reading ability . . . is very good news. If the students' beginning ability was the key factor, then the teacher could do very little to impact student performance. However, this analysis shows that the teacher is key and can do a great deal to improve student performance. (Paul, 2003, p. 34)

The Role of Follow-Up Quizzes

Some programs for promoting reading use quizzes to motivate and assess students' independent reading. Using quizzes has several advantages. Quizzes can be motivational. They also provide an objective check as to whether students actually read the book. In addition, knowing that they will be quizzed, students will probably read a bit more carefully. In addition, quizzes serve as a monitoring device. Low marks on quizzes indicate that the books are too hard for the students.

However, there is a downside to using quizzes. Commercial quizzes are multiple-choice and so tend to stress lower-level details. In addition, quizzes make independent reading seem like a school assignment and so might interfere with the goal of instilling a love of reading in students.

The best known of the commercial quiz programs is one created by Accelerated Reading. Accelerated Reading has more than 65,000 AR Reading Practice Quizzes. Book Adventure is similar to Accelerated Reading except that it is free. Book Adventure has quizzes for more than 8,000 books. After reading a book, students can choose to take a brief multiple-choice quiz. If students want help selecting a book, they can click on any five of thirty-eight categories that include action, adventure, biographical, families, fantasy, funny, science, and sport and recreation. They also enter a grade level and check whether they want easier books, books at grade level, challenging books, or books at any grade level.

The Role of the Media Specialist

The role of the media specialist is key. Based on a study of 221 library media centers in Colorado, Lance (1994), an expert in school library services, found that the quality of the library as measured by the amount of staff hours available and the size of the collection has a powerful impact on the school's achievement in reading. Based on more recent research results in more than a dozen states, Lance concludes that schools with stronger library programs average between 10 and 20 percent higher scores on standardized tests (*Reading Today*, 2004). This was true regardless of whether the library was located in a poor school or an affluent one. Schools in which the media specialist played an active teaching role did better than those whose media specialist did not. In Texas, schools with librarians had 10 percent more students passing the state tests than did schools without librarians (Smith, 2001). As students move up through the grades, the presence of an effective media center becomes more of a factor in achievement.

Although classroom teachers should have libraries of their own, it is the media specialist who can help them refresh their collections, alert them to newly published books, help them assemble books for a unit theme, advise them as to readability and suitability of books, suggest ways to motivate wide reading, and help them take responsibility for a voluntary reading campaign.

A key goal for the media specialist should be to increase circulation. He should keep a record of number of books circulated. A related goal would be to broaden the base of those checking out books. Typically, the best readers are those who check out the most books, which is, in part, the reason they are the best readers. The media specialist should keep statistics not only on how many books are circulated but how many students are checking out books.

To close the literacy gap, it is essential that struggling readers do a lot of reading on their own. One way of fostering free reading among struggling readers is to guide them to books that they would want to read and can read. The media specialist should be knowledgeable enough about the school's reading program so that he can ask a prospective borrower what book she is currently reading and then help the student choose a book that is on the same approximate level. Of course, this procedure needs to be flexible. Students might choose to read a book on a level that is lower or higher than their instructional or independent reading level. It will be essential that the library have books that appeal to a wide variety of interests and reading levels. It is especially important to have a varied, intriguing collection for struggling readers.

The school media center should be a warm, welcoming place with hours set that are most convenient for potential borrowers. The library should be open before school, during lunch hours, and after school. To foster reading during the summer, keep the library open, if just for a few hours each day or even just one day a week. The library should be open to service after-school, Saturday, and summer programs. If the library can't be kept open during the summer, another possibility is to allow students to take a number of books home during the summer months (Allington, 2001).

Using an economics analogy, book circulation will give you the biggest bang for the buck. But there is a price to be paid. You must expand and maintain your collection. And you must tolerate a certain percentage of lost, damaged, or unreturned books. In a misguided attempt to protect the collection, some schools do not allow books to circulate. Unfortunately, this tends to happen in the poorest of schools where students are most dependent on the library for a source of reading materials. These schools have lost sight of the mission of the media center. It is to foster literacy and develop a love of reading. It goes without saying that students should be taught to be responsible for the books they check out. But library policies should foster responsibility without being so punitive that students are afraid to check out books lest they lose one or, if they lose a book, their borrowing privileges are revoked or suspended.

Coping with the Lost Book Problem

One way of coping with the lost book problem is to follow the example of Internet services that loan out DVDs. Members are allowed to borrow three to five videos at a time. Each time a video is returned, another video may be borrowed. Students might be given the same borrowing privileges. Often borrowing privileges are suspended as soon as the student fails to return a book. This cuts the students off from a main source of reading material. For impoverished students, this might be the only source of outside reading material. For some families, paying the replacement cost of a lost book might be too great a financial burden. They might forbid their child from borrowing books lest they be lost. With the three-book allowance, children will be able to retain their borrowing privileges even if they have lost one or two books. To cope with the problem of fines or replacement costs that might be prohibitive, you might charge a nominal replacement cost of $1 or you might allow students to replace a lost or damaged book with any book. These policies could be readily implemented in classroom libraries and might also be implemented in school and public libraries. Whatever policy is adopted, it should not inhibit the flow of books.

As part of the collection, you might have books that are old or somewhat damaged or that have been donated and that students might have for free. If the supply is limited, you might place a limit on the number of books that can be taken but allow students to trade in books that they have read for books that they haven't read. Focus on Literacy, a highly successful intervention program in Philadelphia, allows for lost books (Gill, 2004). The program budgets one-quarter of its book budget for lost books.

Impact of Book Discussion Groups

Book discussion groups allow for the differentiation of instruction and foster added reading. In literature discussion groups, students meet and discuss pieces of literature that they have read. Students may have some choice in the books they read, or the teacher may make the selections. Each group may be reading a different book, or all the groups may be reading the same text. Discussion groups, which are also known as literature circles, literature study groups, conversational discussion groups, and book clubs, provide opportunities for students to discuss their reading in much the same way that a group of adults might converse about a book that they have read. Groups might be teacher directed or student directed or some combination of the two. By having students conduct the circles themselves, with some guidance from you, this frees you up to work with other groups of students. By having students read their literature circle selections at home instead of at school, you can increase the amount of time they read. Because they know the members of the group will be relying on them to have completed the required reading so they can take part in the discussion, students are more likely to complete literature circle reading than reading assigned to the whole class (Bjorklund, Handler, Mitten, & Stockwell, 1998).

In most literature discussion groups, students choose the books that they want to read, so this fosters motivation. Typically, the teacher allows students to select from five or more books. The teacher provides an overview of each one and time for students to browse the books. Students then list their top three choices. Based on students' selections, four or five groups of five to six students are formed. The teacher forms groups that are heterogeneous but matches below-average readers with books that they can handle. Students are taught how to hold discussions. It takes about five meetings before students are able to function adequately as a group (Almasi, O'Flahavan, & Arya, 2001).

Students might respond to prompts as they read: "Does the main character remind you of anyone that you know? Was there anything in this part of the novel that surprised you or confused you?" Or they might fulfill roles in much the same way that a cooperative learning group operates. Key roles are the discussion leader, summarizer, literacy reporter, illustrator, word chief, and connector (Daniels, 2002). The discussion leader develops questions for the group and leads the discussion. The summarizer summarizes the selection. The literacy reporter locates colorful language. The reporter can read the passages out loud, ask the group to read them silently and discuss them, or, with other members of the group, dramatize them. An illustrator depicts a key part of the selection with a drawing or graphic organizer. The word chief locates difficult words or expressions from the selection, looks them up in the dictionary, and writes down their definitions. At the circle meeting, the word chief points out and discusses the words with the group. The connector finds links between the book and other books the group has read or with real events, problems, or situations. The connector describes the connection and discusses it with the group. Students periodically switch roles so that each member of the group experiences all the roles. As students grow more experienced, role sheets can be phased out.

Responding to Literature

In addition to responding to literature through discussions, students compose written responses. Responses can be as simple as marking an exciting or confusing passage with stick-on notes or as elaborate as writing a letter to the teacher. Responding in writing deepens students' understanding because it provides an opportunity for them to reflect on their reading. It also helps them to organize their thoughts and feelings. If the teacher responds, students can be led to deepen and broaden their responses. In an analysis of the dialogue of one fourth-grade student and her teacher, Fountas and Pinnell (2001) concluded that the student was learning to see the value of biography, learning how to seek out big ideas, discovering how biographers chose their subjects, and learning the characteristics of biographies. She was also learning how to make personal and textual connections and developing as a reader. In an examination of a number of journals completed by students in grades 3 through 6, Fountas and Pinnell (2001) found that through completing entries in response journals, students went well beyond merely recounting the main events in a story. They made connections with characters, came to appreciate the author's craft, related stories to their own lives, compared the world of the story to their world, and explored issues raised by their reading. Responding leads students to a deeper level of inquiry and reflection:

> Indeed, we've found that journal responses reflect thinking beyond a literal recall of the text. Indeed, we've found that student response journals almost without fail reveal deeper analytical thinking and a more sophisticated synthesis of ideas than students produce when they are asked to answer a list of comprehension questions. (Fountas & Pinnell, 2001, p. 179)

Students' responses can be open-ended or the result of a prompt. Parsons (1990) suggests the following types of questions, some of which have been altered slightly.

- What surprised you about the section that you read today? How does it affect what might happen next in the story?
- As you read today, what feelings did you experience in response to events or characters? For example, did you feel anger, surprise, irritation, or disappointment? Why do you think you responded that way?
- What startling, unusual, or effective words, phrases, expressions, or images did you come across in your reading that you would like to have explained or clarified?
- What characters and situations in the story reminded you of people and situations in your own life? How are they similar, and how do they differ?

Other prompts that might be used include the following.

- How does this book compare with other books that you have read?
- What did you learn from this book?
- Would you recommend this book to others? Why or why not?
- How does this book compare to the movie version?
- If this book were made into a movie, would you go see it? Why or why not?
- If you were part of the book, which character would you like to be?
- If you were the author's editor, what would you say to her or him?

Prompts might tie in to what you are teaching. If you are teaching character development, provide a prompt that asks how the author developed his characters. If the class has been studying images or themes, pose prompts about these elements. Two other response prompts that might be used are "What if . . . " and "If I were in the story. . . ." In the "What if . . . " response, readers speculate what might have happened if a character had taken a different course of action or if a key event in the story had been different. In the "If I were in the story . . . " response, readers tell what they would have done if they had been a part of the story's action (Raphael & Boyd, 1997). The student might assume the role of one of the characters in a selection and write as though she were that character. A student assuming the role of Carlie in *The Pinballs* (Byars, 1977) might tell how she felt when she saw how sick Harvey had become.

In dialogue journals, students write to the teacher and the teacher responds, or pairs of students might write to each other. The journal writing should be a genuine exchange between teacher and student and not simply an assignment to be completed. As Fountas and Pinnell (2001) explain, completing a response journal is not a homework assignment or a test to discover whether the student completed the reading; it is a written conversation between teacher and students. To help students get the most out of their dialogue journals, model the writing of responses and have the class practice composing responses to stories that all have read or that you have read to them. As you read journal entries and see a need for more reflection or supporting opinions, model how that might be done.

In your response, affirm the students' opinions and observations. Include personal observations. Play the role of a fellow reader engaged in a conversation about a piece of writing. But be a mentor, too. Ask questions that guide the students into deeper reflection. Ask questions about comments that are not clear: "I wasn't quite sure what you meant when you said . . ." Above all, be encouraging. For a detailed description of response journals and practical suggestions for implementing them, see Chapter 10 of *Guiding Readers and Writers Grades 3–6* (Fountas & Pinnell, 2001).

How often should students respond? Some teachers ask students to respond five times a week. Fountas and Pinnell (2001) recommend that students respond once a week. There are merits to both. However, if you are closing a gap, you need to require more of your students. You might ask them to respond two or three times a week (but more often if they wish). But they turn in their response journals just once a week. You might color code the journals and have just five or six turned in each day so that you aren't overwhelmed with journal reading.

Schools in Chicago that used literature circles as part of a reading-writing workshop showed significant gains on citywide reading tests (Daniels, 2002). In one school, the number of students reading at the national average tripled. For more information on book discussion groups, refer to one of the following sources.

Literature Circles.com
http://www.literaturecircles.com/
Features book recommendations, classroom management ideas, links to related sites and organizations, and tips from veteran literature circle teachers from Chicago's Center for City Schools.

Literature Circles Resource Center
http://fac-staff.seattleu.edu/kschlnoe/LitCircles/
Provides an overview of literature circles and suggestions for organizing circles, choosing books, holding discussions, and fostering responses.

Assessing the Extensive Reading Component of Your Program

Extensive reading builds background, vocabulary, reading skills, and fluency. In fact, extensive reading is the single most effective means for closing the literacy gap. Use the checklist in Table 7.1 to determine strengths and weaknesses of the extensive reading component of your program.

TABLE 7.1 *Assessment Checklist for Extensive Reading*

Action	Fully	Partially	Limited	Suggestions
Students read for at least 60 to 90 minutes in school each day.				
Students read at least 30 to 60 minutes at home each night.				
The classroom has a well-stocked, inviting library with books on a variety of levels.				
Students are encouraged to read in all subject areas.				
Students are shown how to select reading materials.				
Students are encouraged to talk about their reading.				
Extensive reading is used in lieu of workbooks or worksheets.				
Students use logs or other devices to keep track of their reading.				
Extensive reading is a priority in the school.				
Teachers keep track of students' reading.				
Parents are encouraged to help their children obtain books.				

8

Phonological Awareness and Word Analysis

Although the construction of meaning is the ultimate aim of reading, reading is built on the ability to swiftly and accurately translate printed symbols into their spoken equivalents. Decoding, in turn, is based on the ability to detect individual sounds in words. Solid bases of phonological awareness and word analysis skills are prerequisites for comprehension.

Phonological Awareness

Both phonological awareness and letter knowledge are essential building blocks for beginning reading. However, letter knowledge tops out. Once students master the twenty-six letters, upper- and lowercase, there's nothing more to be learned. Phonological awareness exists along a continuum, which begins with rhyming for most students or beginning sounds for some students, followed or accompanied by segmentation of sentences into words, words into syllables, words into onset-rime (the rime is the part of the word that rhymes: the *at* in *cat* and *bat*; the onset is the part that comes before the rime: the *c* in *cat* and *b* in *bat*), words into individual sounds (phonemic awareness), and clusters (combinations of consonant sounds: *bl, str*) into individual sounds. Phonological awareness is best taught to small groups of students. Students operating on similar levels can work together, and the teacher can better monitor their performance.

Instruction in phonological awareness should be geared to the level of phonics students are learning and vice versa. When students can perceive beginning sounds, they should be taught the letters that represent those sounds, assuming that students know most of the letters of the alphabet. Speech sounds are connected to letters, which makes the sounds more concrete. This also enables children to read alphabet books. Phonological awareness is reciprocal.

Phonological awareness enables the teaching of phonics. The teaching of phonics, if sounds are emphasized, advances phonological awareness. Writing, especially when invented spelling is encouraged, also benefits from and extends phonological awareness. Because of the reciprocal relationship, phonological awareness and phonics should be taught in tandem. The best time to teach awareness of initial consonant sounds is when teaching initial consonant correspondences, such as s = /s/ or m = /m/; the best time to teach the separate sounds in clusters is when teaching cluster correspondences, such as st = /st/. Therefore, teaching students to segment clusters, such as noting the separate sounds in *str*, while they are still learning initial consonant correspondences is not a good use of time. However, when students are learning to decode clusters, it becomes an essential skill.

Some suggested phonological awareness activities include tasks such as deleting sounds and then saying the remaining word: Say *mice*; now say it without the /m/. Tasks of this type, which are not necessary for reading and spelling but which make heavy demands on working memory, should be replaced by activities more closely related to what students actually need to be able to do to read and spell words.

Helping Students Who Have Difficulty Developing Phonemic Awareness

Despite instruction, about one-third of all kindergarten graduates start first grade with little or no phonemic awareness (Seifert, 2004). The problem might be developmental. A number of five- and six-year-olds are simply unable to meet the cognitive demands of phonemic awareness. They are unable to think of words as words and as being composed of a series of sounds. An age-graded curriculum may be at fault (Seifert, 2004). It requires teaching certain skills when children reach a certain age rather than teaching skills when students are developmentally ready for them. One solution is to change the curriculum. The other is to change the task so that it becomes developmentally appropriate. If children are struggling with phonemic awareness, instead of requiring that they detect the sounds in words, children are taught to detect the articulatory movements necessary to form the sounds. Although students may be unable to hear the differences in the sounds, they can be taught to detect the differences in articulatory mechanics needed to form the sounds. For instance, have students say "mmm" and discuss how the lips are used to make this sound. Noting the separate movements can help students become more fully aware of the speech sounds they are making. This is a concrete way of experiencing phonemes. Realizing how phonemes are articulated helps lay a conceptual foundation for phonemic awareness (Lindamood & Lindamood, 1975, 1998). For instance, the three phonemes in *meat* can be seen in the three successive mouth movements needed to articulate *meat*. Lips are pressed together to form /m/, teeth are shown to form /ē/, and the tongue is used to articulate the final /t/ sound. Using articulatory movements to explore sounds may help students who have difficulty perceiving them auditorially (Torgesen, Morgan, & Davis, 1992). Other programs use colored chips or blocks to represent the sounds. As Seifert (2004) explains:

> Both techniques apparently work because they create concrete, non-auditory referents. In the articulation strategy, the child focuses on the shape of the mouth, the position of the tongue, the timing of voicing, and the like, that are associated with a phoneme. In the visual chip strategy, the child focuses attention on a permanent visual record of each phoneme available for inspection and reflection. . . . In either case, the teaching strategies render phonemes as objects of thought, and not merely as the vehicles of thought that they were before.

Activities for Developing Phonological Awareness

A natural way to foster overall phonological awareness is through listening to rhymes, riddles, puns, jokes, songs, and stories that call attention to words as words and sounds as sounds. When students play with language, instead of just listening to the meaning, they are drawn to words and sounds as abstract units of language. The most critical phonological awareness skills are rhyme, blending, detecting beginning sounds, and segmenting words into separate sounds.

Rhyme. To develop the concept of rhyme, read nursery rhymes and other rhyming tales to students. As students become familiar with rhyming pieces, stress the rhyming elements. As you develop a concept of rhyme, also build the language used to talk about rhyme: *same, sounds, rhyme, words,* and so forth. To extend the concept of rhyme, build rhymes with students. Using the element *at,* explain how a rhyme might be built. Say *at.* Have students say *at.* Tell students that you are going to make words that have *at* in them. Say *c-at,* emphasizing the *at* portion of the word. Ask students if they can hear the *at* in *c-at.* Holding up a picture of a *cat,* have students say *cat* and listen to the *at* in *c-at.* (By using pictures, you are reducing the burden on students' memories.) Hold up a picture of a *hat.* Have students tell what it is. Tell students that *h-at* has an *at* in it. Ask them if they can hear the *at* in *h-at.* Introduce *rat, bat,* and *sat* in the same way. Ask students if they can tell what sound is the same in *cat, hat, rat, bat,* and *sat.* Stress the *at* in each of these words. Explain that *cat, hat, rat, bat,* and *sat* rhyme because they all have *at* at the end. Invite students to suggest other words that rhyme with *cat: mat, pat, fat, that* (Gunning, 2002).

After students have a firm grasp of the concept of rhyme, have them sort rhyming pictures. Some pictures that might be used in sorting rhymes include *bat, cat, hat, rat; nail, pail, sail, snail; cake, rake, snake; bed, bread, sled; car, jar, star; king, ring, string.* Pictures are sorted in much the same way as objects. Select a picture to serve as a model for each rhyming pattern and have students place rhyming pictures underneath. Students can work individually, in pairs, or in small groups. After a sort has been completed, have students say the name of each picture in a category. If students are slow or hesitant, discuss any questions they might have and ask them to sort again. If students have completed a sort under your guidance, have them sort the items a second time for additional practice.

Blending.   Through blending, students reconstruct words by putting the word's sounds together. Blending builds on students' ability to rhyme and prepares them for noting beginning sounds and segmenting words into their component sounds. Students begin by blending onsets and rimes The onset is the consonant or consonant cluster preceding the rime: *f, pl, scr*. The rime is the pattern's vowel and any consonants that follow it: *o, at, ot, een*. As they master blending onsets and rimes, they move into blending individual sounds: /p/, /e/, /t/. To introduce blending, use a hand puppet and tell students that the puppet says its words in parts. Instead of saying *hat* the way we do, it says /h/, /at/, so we have to help him by putting the parts of the word together. Have students help put the following words together: *m-an, s-and, c-at, r-at, r-an*. Present the words in groups of four. In order to involve all students, provide each student with a set of pictures showing the four words. When you say the word to be blended, students choose the picture that shows the word and hold it up (Gunning, 2005). By observing students, you can tell who is catching on and who is struggling. Discuss the names of the pictures before beginning the activity so that students know them:

cat, hat, bat, rat
can, man, pan, fan
king, ring, wing, ball
lock, rock, sock, mop
pie, tie, tire, bus

After students have held up the picture for the word being blended, have them say the word. Affirm students' efforts but correct wrong responses. For a correct response, you might say, "*Hat*. That is correct. When you put /h/ and /at/ together, you get *hat*." For an incorrect response, you might say, "That was a good try. But when I put /f/ and /an/ together, I get *fan*. You say it, *f-an—fan*." After students have completed a group, go through it again. Encourage them to put the words together faster. If students have difficulty with the activity, provide assistance or go back to rhyming activities.

After students become proficient at blending onsets and rimes, supply the individual sounds of words and have students blend them. Using the same set of pictures and words, have students blend individual sounds: /c/, /a/, /t/; /h/, /a/, /t/.

Beginning Sounds.   Once students have mastered the concept of rhyme, introduce beginning sounds. A fun way to do this is through reading Dr. Seuss's *There's a Wocket in My Pocket* (Geisel, 1974), which combines rhymes and perception of beginning sounds. After reading the text, discuss the rhymes and the words that Dr. Seuss made up. Lead students to see that Dr. Seuss made up his silly words by changing the first sound of a real word: *pocket—wocket*. Supply real words and help students create silly words by changing the first sound. Also use names to convey the concept of beginning sounds. Ask students if you are Ms. anning. When they say no, and say you are Ms. Manning, ask them what was missing from *anning*. Lead them to see that the beginning sound was missing, that you are Ms. MMManning, drawing out the initial /m/. Go around the room and ask: Is this am? Is this alvatore? Is this ason? Have students add the beginning sound to each name. Repeat the child's name, stretching the initial sound as you do so, "SSSalvatore."

Also read alliterative verses and sing alliterative songs. Discuss the names of common objects that begin with /f/ and create a bulletin board of objects whose names begin like *feather*. Use naturally occurring opportunities to reinforce awareness of beginning sounds: If it is the ninth of November, discuss how *nine* and *November* begin with the same sound.

Sounds in Words: Segmentation.   To introduce the concept of sounds in words, try this activity. Pointing to a picture of a moose, ask, "Is this a /m/?" When the class says no, agree and explain, "That's right. I didn't say all of the word's sounds. I said, 'Is this a /m/?'" Then say, "Is this a /m/, /oo/?" (emphasize each sound). Explain that no, this is not a /moo/. It doesn't have enough sounds. Next ask, "Is this a moose?" Once again, carefully enunciate all three sounds, /m/, /oo/, /s/. When the class says yes, explain that they are right. "*Moose* has three sounds, and you said all three of them." Present *sun* and *hat* and other three-sound words in this same way.

If students have difficulty segmenting words into sounds, practice with words that have just two sounds: *go, no, me, he*. Also present two-sound words in which the vowel comes first: *ape, ate, eat, it*. Words that begin with a vowel are a little easier to segment than those that begin with a consonant (Uhry & Ehri, 1999). Avoid words like *on*, in which it is hard to separate the vowel from the consonant.

Elkonin Technique.   To reinforce and to extend the concept of sounds in words, use the Elkonin technique (Elkonin, 1973). Through the use of sound boxes, Elkonin sought to "materialize" the analysis of a word into its component sounds (phonemes). Children are given a picture of an object whose name contains two or three sounds. Underneath the picture appear boxes that match the number of sounds the picture's name contains. One block is drawn for each sound. For the word *hat*, three blocks are drawn, one each for /h/, /a/, /t/. Three boxes are also drawn for the word *goat*. Although *goat* has four letters, it has only three sounds: /g/, /ō/, /t/. Students indicate the number of sounds in a word by placing a marker in the box for each sound they hear. Figure 8.1 shows Elkonin boxes.

Phonological Awareness and Word Analysis

Phonemic awareness is most effective when it is integrated with phonics (Bus & van Ijzendoorn, 1999; Vandervelden & Siegel, 1997). Because the letters in a word

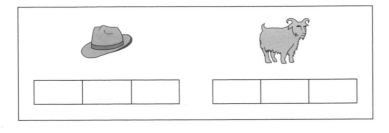

FIGURE 8.1 *Elkonin Boxes*

represent the word's sounds, working with letters is a way of marking sounds. "Learning to attend to letters in words and relating these to how words sound appeared to make explicit the underlying phonemic structure" (Vandervelden & Siegel, 1997, p. 78). A program that integrates phonemic awareness and phonics is speech-to-print phonics. Speech-to-print phonics provides a easy introduction to phonics because it requires students only to recognize the printed form of a word spoken by the teacher. The teacher presents a correspondence and then asks students to point to the word that contains that correspondence. After two correspondences are presented, the students are shown two words, one of which starts with the correspondence just taught. After introducing *s* = /s/ and *m* = /m/, the teacher shows cards containing the words *man* and *sun* and asks students to hold up the card that says *man*. After a third correspondence is taught, the teacher asks students to choose from all three correspondences. However, as additional correspondences are introduced, the teacher drops one so that students are not required to choose from more than three correspondences. At-risk students who take part in speech-to-print recognition activities of this type improve in phonemic awareness, letter-sound recognition, and the ability to learn new words (Vandervelden & Siegel, 1997). An adapted lesson is presented below.

Speech-to-Print Lesson

Step 1: Introducing the correspondence. Present the correspondence *m* = /m/. Emphasize the way that the lips are pressed together to form the sound /m/. Explain that the letter *m* stands for the sound /m/ heard at the beginning of *man* and *moon*.

Step 2: Guided practice. Assuming that the correspondences *s* = /s/ and *f* = /f/ have been introduced, present groups of word cards similar to the following. To make the activity more concrete, you might have students place a plastic letter on the word they have identified, placing an *m* on *man*, for example.

Which word says *man*?   man   sun   fish
Which word says *sun*?
Which word says *fish*?

Which word says *me*?	me	see	five
Which word says *five*?			
Which word says *see*?			
Which word says *mat*?	mat	sat	fat
Which word says *fat*?			
Which word says *sat*?			

Affirm students' responses: "Yes, that word says *man*. You can tell it says *man* because it begins with the letter *m*. The letter *m* makes the sound /m/ that you hear at the beginning of *man*."

After students have learned initial consonants, introduce them to final consonants and make matches based on both the initial and final consonants. For instance, give the students the word cards *cat, can, cap*, and say, "Which word spells *can*? Which word spells *cat*? Which word spells *cap*?" After vowels are introduced, choices are made on the basis of vowels. Give the word cards *bit, bet, but*, and ask, "Which word spells *but*? Which word spells *bet*? Which word spells *bit*?"

Step 3: Guided spelling. In guided spelling, you carefully articulate the words, and students spell them with a set of plastic letters. Initially, students might simply select from three plastic letters the one that spells the beginning sound. Later, as students learn to spell whole words, they might be asked to spell two- or three-letter words and might be given the letters in mixed-up order.

Step 4: Real-world words. Also use real-world materials. Holding up a milk carton, have students point to the word *milk*. Holding up a tub of margarine, have students point to the word *margarine*. (Gunning, 2002, p. 208).

Road to the Code

Another program that integrates phonemic awareness and initial phonics and works especially well with struggling readers is *Road to the Code* (Blachman, Ball, Black, & Tangel, 2000), a research-based program. It features a variety of hands-on phonological awareness activities and integrates phonological awareness and phonics by having students learn the short vowels *a* and *i* and the consonants *m, t, s, r, b, f*. The program uses these elements to build a series of words. Instructions are step by step in an easy-to-follow manual that contains blackline masters for all needed materials.

How Words Are Read

To teach phonics effectively, it is important to know how words are read. When students decode words, four processors are at work: orthographic, phonological, meaning, and context (Adams 1990, 1994). The orthographic processor is responsi-

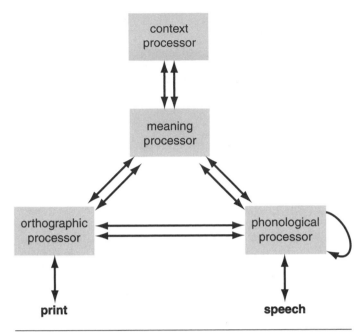

FIGURE 8.2 *How Words Are Read: Four Processors*

Source: Adams, M. J. (1990). *Beginning to read: Thinking and learning about print: A summary.* Prepared by S. A. Stahl, J. Osborne, & F. Lehr. Urbana-Champaign, IL: Center for the Study of Reading, University of Illinois.

ble for perceiving the sequences of letters in text. The phonological processor is responsible for mapping the letters into their spoken equivalents. The meaning processor contains one's knowledge of word meanings, and the context processor is in charge of constructing a continuing understanding of the text (Stahl, Osborne, & Lehr, 1990). The processors work simultaneously, both receiving information and sending it to the other processors; however, the orthographic and phonological processors are always essential participants. Context may speed and/or assist the interpretation of orthographic and phonological information but does not take its place (see Figure 8.2). When information from one processor is weak, another may be called on to give assistance. For instance, when a word like *lead* is encountered, the context processor provides extra help to the meaning and phonological processors in assigning the correct meaning and pronunciation.

Because of the nature of the way words are read, nonsense words should not be used to assess or teach phonics. Using nonsense words short-circuits the process. As students are decoding the sounds of a word, they are also assigning a meaning to it. If their recoding of the word doesn't result in a real word, they know they have to try again. If nonsense words are used in instruction or assessment, students don't have this feedback.

Another poor practice is to encourage students to merely guess at a word from context. Because the processors work simultaneously, students should be using both decoding and context at the same time. Context assists the process but does not replace the necessity of decoding the word (Adams, 1990).

Systematic, Functional, Contextual Phonics

There is an insidious relationship between phonics instruction and reading achievement. According to the National Reading Panel Report (National Reading Panel, 2000), beyond a certain point there is a negative relationship between amount of time spent on phonics and reading achievement. One explanation for this curious finding is that struggling readers are given more phonics instruction, so, of course, there would be a negative relationship between the two. Another interpretation is that excessive time spent on phonics steals time from more valuable instructional activities, such as reading.

Phonics is essential. It is especially important for struggling readers. However, phonics should be taught as a means to an end and not for its own sake. Instruction should be functional so that students are taught short vowel patterns, such as *at* or *et* when they are reading about a cat on a mat or a wet pet. Activities in which students read selections containing short vowel words are the best reinforcement. Exercises in which students note whether vowels are long or short do not foster use of short vowels as a decoding skills and so are inefficient uses of time.

Phonics instruction should be developmental. Often, intervention teachers will note that students are weak in phonics and decide to start over, from the beginning. This is a disastrous decision. It fails to give students credit for what they know and undermines them by giving them material that is too easy. Assess to find out where students are and begin instruction there, making adjustments as necessary. Similarly, whole-class instruction in phonics is a poor practice. In virtually all classes, there is range of phonics knowledge. Students have different levels of understanding of the alphabetical principal. Some are just beginning to grasp that letters represent sounds. Others have a concept that each sound in a word is represented by a letter, as in *hat*: /h/, /a/, /t/. On a more advanced level, some realize that not all words can be processed sound by sound. They have come to the understanding that some words have final *e* markers that indicate the preceding vowel is long as in *hate* or vowel digraphs that perform a similar function as in *wait*. Instruction should be geared to students' developmental level. Students who are just beginning to grasp that letters represent sounds are not ready for instruction in final *e* or digraph vowel patterns. Research clearly indicates that students make the most progress when they are grouped according to their developmental levels (Juel & Minden-Cupp, 2000).

Phonics is best taught in small groups to students who need the element being presented. Whole-class phonics is generally inefficient. It's too easy for the best readers and too hard for the poorest readers. In his observation of a whole-group phonics lesson taught by Karen, a first-grade teacher, Meyer (2002) noted that the most responsive group included children who could already read and so didn't need the lesson. There was also a group for whom the lesson was too advanced. They responded by echoing whatever other students said.

Phonics instruction should be functional, which means that it should prepare students to read or decode words that they're about to encounter. In fact, if students are not about to read a selection containing the element being taught, there is little reason for teaching that element. The best time to introduce the *oy* pattern is when students are reading about a boy who is enjoying a new toy. For that reason, phonics workbooks and supplementary phonics programs are not usually the best way to present phonics. They tend to introduce skills in isolation and don't provide useful application, which is reading selections containing the element that has been taught. One exception to this generalization is Ready Readers (Modern Curriculum Press). It features sets of up to fifty books that are decodable but that

TABLE 8.1 *Checklist for Word Analysis Lesson*

	Fully	Partially	Limited	Suggestions
New element is pretested. Students who know 90 percent go to next element.				
Element is one that is needed for upcoming reading.				
New element is carefully introduced. Teacher highlights the onset and the rime and also the individual sounds in the words.				
New element is placed on a model words chart so students can refer to it.				
Students apply element to words that were not introduced but that contain the element.				
Students are given prompts and feedback as they encounter difficult words.				
Students report and discuss instances of using the new element to decode words.				
Reinforcement activities include sorting and a reading selection that contains the element.				
Students are assessed on ability to read new element. Element is reviewed as necessary.				

do not have the sing-song language found in many decodable texts. (To achieve a more natural flow, some of the books contain a fairly large number of content words that need to be pretaught. Word Building [Phoenix Learning Resources] also uses decodable but natural sounding text.) When Mesmer (1999) substituted Ready Readers for predictable books, the struggling student she was working with began making encouraging progress. Students using Ready Readers also outperformed students using basal readers (Hiebert, Martin, & Menon, 2005; Menon & Hiebert, 2005). The reason they did better was because the students in Ready Readers read a greater variety of words than the students in the basal series. The students in the basal series read just one story a week. The students in the Ready Readers read a number of little books each week. Although both groups may have encountered the same number of words, students in the Ready Readers' group encountered a greater variety of words, whereas students in the basal program reread the same words over and over again.

It isn't necessary to use Ready Readers to get the results that were obtained in these two studies. You can achieve the same goal by selecting and sequencing children's books or well-written decodable texts that do the same thing. Lists of children's books that reinforce phonics patterns are found on the author's Web site at http://www.thomasgunning.org.

A checklist for assessing a word analysis lesson is presented in Table 8.1. You can use the checklist to evaluate your own lessons or, if you are assisting others, use it to evaluate their word analysis lessons.

Integrating Sound-by-Sound and Onset-Rime Approaches to Teaching Phonics

What is the best way to teach phonics? Phonics can be taught in variety of ways, but the two main approaches are sound by sound or in rime-onset patterns. In a sound-by-sound approach, students are typically taught initial consonants, final consonants, and vowels, and are then taught to blend all three. Reading the word *pet*, they would read it sound by sound; they would say /p/, /e/, /t/ and blend the sounds to form the word *pet*. In a rime-onset approach, students learn *at* in *hat*, *pat*, and *cat*, or *et* in *bet*, *wet*, and *set*. They learn to add onsets to rimes to form words. The onset-rime has two advantages: First, rimes are more predictable than single vowels. The vowel *a* can represent a variety of sounds, as in *at, ate, around*. However, when followed by a consonant or consonant combination, the *a* is almost always short, as in *hat* and *cap*. When followed by a consonant and final *e*, it is typically long, as in *hate* and *cape*. Second, rimes are easier to detect than single vowels. It is easier to detect the /at/ in *cat* than it is the /a/ in *cat*.

However, some beginning readers have difficulty processing rimes and seem to need to process individual sounds (Juel & Minden-Cupp, 2000). On the other hand, some students have difficulty blending individual sounds (Gaskins, Gaskins, Anderson, & Schommer, 1995). The best approach is to combine both approaches. In a study involving high-risk students in the four first grades in high-poverty schools, only the two groups of students taught with an onset-rime approach were reading close to grade level by year's end (Juel & Minden-Cupp, 2000). However, the group in which the students analyzed the individual sounds in the rimes did the best, by far, of all four groups. They were able to read an end-of-first-grade-level passage with an average of 91.3 percent accuracy. Many of the struggling readers had difficulty seeing patterns in words and so did better with a sound-by-sound approach. For some students, it might be necessary to build awareness of individual sounds before they can detect patterns.

Based on this and other research and extensive experience with struggling readers, it appears that the most efficient way to present phonics is through a word-building approach that uses rimes or patterns but segments the rimes into their individual sounds. A word-building approach helps children note the onset and the rime in each word (Gunning, 1995). Students are presented with a rime (*at*, *et*) and then add onsets or consonants (*c*, *h*, *s*) or consonant combinations to create words: *cat, hat, sat*. Next, students are provided with onsets to which they add rimes. Presented with *c*, *h*, and *s*, they add *at* to make *cat, hat*, and *sat*. Because some students have difficulty with rimes (Bruck, 1992; Juel & Minden-Cupp, 2000), rimes are broken down into their individual sounds after being presented as wholes. After introducing the rime *at* as a whole, the teacher would highlight its individual sounds: /a/ and /t/. This also fosters phonemic awareness.

Word-Building Lesson

Step 1: Fostering phonemic awareness and building the rime. Read a selection such as *The Cat in the Hat* (Geisel, 1957) or a rhyme in which there are a number of *at* words. Call the students' attention to the pattern words from the selection: *cat, hat, sat*. Stressing the rhyming element as you say each word, ask students to tell what is the same about the words. Lead students to see that they all have an /at/ sound, as in *cat*. Ask students to listen carefully so they can tell how many sounds the word *at* has. Articulate it slowly, stretching out the /a/ and repeating the /t/ as you do so: "aaattt." Tell the students to say the word *at* and stretch out the /a/ and repeat the /t/ as they do so. Discuss how many sounds the word *at* has. Then tell students that you are going to spell the word *at*. Ask students to tell what letter would be used to spell the sound /a/ in *at*. Write *a*, commenting as you do so that it makes an /a/ sound. Have students tell what sound they hear at the end of *at*. Ask them what letter would be needed to spell /t/. Add *t*, saying /t/ as you do so. Explain that now you have the word *at*. Run your hand under each letter as you say its sound. Have several students read *at*.

Patterns that end in the nasal consonants /n/ and /m/ may need special handling. Nasal consonants are partially absorbed by the preceding vowels and sometimes the consonant that follows it. Contrast the sound of /a/ in *at* and *an*. When introducing *an* and *am* patterns, present them as a unit. Do not ask students to say the sound of *a* and then the sound of *n* and blend them together.

(Adding onsets to rimes is a spelling approach. Some students may find it easier if a reading approach is used. In a reading approach, you add the rime, and students read the word. For instance, while adding *h* to *at* you would say, "What word do I get if I add *h* to *at*?". Adding *s* to *at*, you would ask, "What word do I get if I add *s* to *at*?" In introducing patterns, you might use a reading approach instead of a spelling approach or along with a spelling approach.)

Step 2: Adding the onset. Explain to students that you can use *at* to make other words. (Write a second *at* under the first one.) Ask students, "What do I need to add to *at* to make the word *cat*?" As you add *c* to *at*, carefully enunciate the *c*, the *a*, and the *t* and then the whole word. Have several students read the word. Then have students read *at* and *cat*. Then write *at* underneath *cat*. Ask students, "What do I need to add to *at* to make the word *sat*?" As you add *s* to *at*, carefully enunciate the *s* and the *at* and then the whole word. Have several students read the word. Then have students read *at*, *cat*, and *sat*. Introduce the words *hat* and *rat*. Then have students read all the words that have been formed. Lead students to see what is the same about the words—that they all end in *at*. Ask students if they know of any other words that rhyme with *cat*: *bat*, *mat*, *pat*. Write these on the board.

Step 3: Adding the rime. To make sure that students have a thorough grasp of both key parts of the word—the onset, which is the initial consonant or cluster, and the rime, which is the vowel and an ending consonant or cluster—present the onset or initial consonant and have students supply the rime or vowel-consonant element. Writing *c* on the board, have students tell what sound it usually stands for (if students say /s/, note that *c* spells two sounds and you are looking for the other sound). Then ask them to tell what you would add to /k/ to make the word *cat*. After adding *at* to *k*, say the word in parts, /k/, /a/, /t/, and then as a whole. Pointing to *c*, say /k/, pointing to *a*, say /a/, pointing to *t*, say /t/. Running your hand under the whole word, say "cat." Form *sat*, *hat*, *rat*, *bat*, *mat*, and *pat* in this way. After all words have been formed, have students read them. Then add onsets to *at* and have students read them. As you add *h* to *at*, ask, "What word will I make if I add *h* to *at*, *s* to *at*, etc.?"

Step 4: Providing mixed practice. Realizing that they are learning words that all end in the same way, students may focus on the initial letter and fail to take careful note of the rest of the word, the rime. After presenting a pattern, mix in words from previously presented patterns and have these read. For instance, after presenting the *at* pattern, present a list of mixed *at* and *an* words: *cat*, *can*, *ran*, *rat*, *pat*, *pan*, *man*, *mat*. (This assumes that *an* words have been introduced.) Besides being a good review, this trains students to use all the word's letters in their decoding processes. Otherwise, students might say the first word in a series of pattern words and then just use the initial consonant to say the rest. If students fail to use all the letters when reading on their own, they may misread *ran* for *rat* or *can* for *cat*.

Step 5: Introducing the model word. Choose one of the pattern words to be a model word. Select a word that has high frequency, is easy, and—if possible—can be depicted. For the *at* pattern, you might choose *cat*, which is easily illustrated. Create a model words chart for your class. After a pattern has been introduced, add its model word to the chart. If students forget the pattern, they can refer to the model words chart. Point out the model word *cat* and explain that it has a picture that shows the word. Tell students that if they forget how to say the model word, the picture will help them. As students encounter difficulty with *at* words, help them to look for a part of the word they can say (*at*) and, if that does not work, use the model word *cat* as an analogy word to help them decipher the unknown word. (Some students might not be able to perceive the rime of the word as a unit. They might need to decode the words sound by sound: /k/, /a/, /t/.) Also encourage the use of context. Students should use context to assist in the use of pronounceable word parts or other sounding-out strategies and especially when sounding-out strategies do not work. Context should also be used to make sure that the word decoded is a real word and fits the sense of the selection.

Step 6: Guided practice.

- Use functional reading materials to provide practice with the pattern. Holding up an advertisement for a cat food, ask students to tell which word says *cat*. Do the same with an advertisement for a baseball bat.
- Have students sort *an, at,* and *am* words (assuming that they have learned these patterns). They might complete a spelling sort as well as a card sort.
- Web sites such as http://www.starfall.com offer excellent practice with a range of phonics patterns.

Step 7: Application. To apply a correspondence that was just taught, choose a selection that contains a number of words that fit the target pattern. Walk students through the selection. Discuss the title and illustrations, clarify unfamiliar concepts, and point out and read to them difficult words (they should follow along with you in their books). Place particular emphasis on words that follow the pattern you just introduced. Note a sentence or caption that contains a pattern word and ask them to find the pattern word and point it out to you.

Step 8: Spelling. Learning to spell new pattern words is excellent reinforcement. Along with providing an opportunity for students to apply skills, it helps them to focus on vowel sounds and patterns within words. Choose pattern words for spelling that students will most likely use in their writing: *at, cat, hat, sat, pat.* To introduce the spelling lesson, explain to students that they will be learning how to spell words that use the pattern just presented. To introduce the words, give a pretest. Dictate the words and have students attempt to spell them. Say each word, use the word in a sentence, and then say each word. "At. I will see you at nine o'clock. At." "Cat. My cat is orange with white stripes. Cat." "Hat. A hat will keep your head warm. Hat." "Sat. I sat on the chair. Sat." "Pat. Do not pat the dog on the head. Pat." Have students say the word, enunciating it carefully before writing it. This will help them focus on the word's sounds. After the pretest, write the correct spellings on the board, and have students check their attempts, making any corrections necessary. They should focus their studying on words that were difficult for them.

Step 9: Writing. Students compose an illustrated piece telling about a hat they would like to have. To prepare them for this task, read aloud and discuss *Hats, Hats, Hats* (Morris, 1993) or *Do You Have a Hat?* (Spinelli, 2004). Encourage the use of developmental (invented) spelling. However, students are expected to spell pattern words correctly.

Syllabic Analysis as Part of Phonics Instruction

Don't neglect syllabic analysis. Even beginning reading materials contain multisyllabic words. An effective way to teach syllabic analysis is to incorporate it with single-syllable phonics (Wilson, 1997). As part of learning the *oy* pattern, students might learn the word *enjoy*. Also as part of presenting a pattern, teach students how to use the element to decode unfamiliar words. As students encounter an unfamiliar word, encourage them to use the pronounceable word part strategy. Encountering the word *destroy*, ask them if there is any part of that word they can say. Guide them as they identify the *oy* and use that to help them reconstruct the word.

Some students have difficulty learning single-syllable phonics even when it is presented systematically in step-by-step fashion. For these students, you might try speech-to-print phonics, as explained earlier in this chapter.

Helping Students Who Have Difficulty with Multisyllabic Words

Some students do well with single-syllable phonics, but have difficulty with multisyllabic words. For syllabic analysis, use the pattern approach. One advantage of this approach is that it reviews basic phonics as new elements are being introduced. For instance, when introducing the *aw* multisyllabic pattern, the teacher automatically reviews the *aw* element, as in *law*. This is helpful to struggling readers, who often have gaps in their skills. Shefelbine (1990) found that 15 percent to

20 percent of the students in the fourth- and eighth-grade classes that he tested had difficulty with multisyllabic words, and some students were still experiencing problems with single-syllable phonics, especially vowel elements.

The traditional way of teaching multisyllabic words doesn't work very well. A pattern approach and sorting are two approaches that seem to work better.

Pattern Approach

In a pattern approach, students use their knowledge of single-syllable words to learn multisyllabic words. For instance, when presenting the long *o* open syllable, multisyllabic pattern, relate it to a known single-syllable word that ends in long *o*. Present *so* and have it read, and then present *soda*. Have students read *soda* by comparing the two words and seeing the *so* in *soda*. Present other open *o* multisyllabic words as shown below:

so
soda
total
local
vocal
motel
hotel
notice

Sorting

Sorting also provides an excellent way to explore and reinforce multisyllabic words. Students might sort open and closed syllables so that they can discover that syllables that end in a consonant are usually short and those that end in a vowel are usually long. They might sort words, such as the following: *pepper, pebble, fever, female, pedal, elbow, helmet, shelter, evil, lettuce, seven, legal, cedar, prefix,* as in Figure 8.3. (note that *pedal* and *seven* are exception words). Through sorting, stu-

fever	pepper	pedal
female	pebble	seven
legal	elbow	
evil	helmet	
cedar	shelter	
prefix	lettuce	

FIGURE 8.3 *Sorting of Multisyllabic Words*

dents form their own generalizations and so come to a deeper understanding of the patterns of English. For additional suggestions for working with multisyllabic words and sorting, see *Building Words* (Gunning, 2001) and *Words Their Way* (Bear, Invernizzi, Templeton, & Johnston, 2004). Sample sorts are found at the *Words Their Way* Web site at http://cwx.prenhall.com/bookbind/pubbooks/bear/chapter1/deluxe.html.

The Importance of Teaching Needed Skills

Some older struggling readers are seriously deficient in phonics. Teachers need to go back as far as necessary. If, for example, a fifth-grader does not know short vowel patterns, it is essential that he be taught them, even those that are typically learned in first grade. However, the skills should be taught in a mature fashion.

Helpful Activities for Struggling Readers

Activities that are especially helpful for struggling readers are writing for sounds and sorting (Juel & Minden-Cupp, 2000). Writing for sounds is an activity in which students use spelling to help them become aware of the separate sounds in a word. To spell the word *sad*, they would emphasize the first sound /s/ and represent it with a letter, stretch out the word so they could hear the /a/ and represent it with a letter, and emphasize the last sound /d/ and represent it with a letter. (Note that sounds such as /s/, /m/, and /h/ can be elongated, but other sounds such as /t/, /b/, and /d/ cannot. However, these sounds can be repeated or "bounced": /b/-/b/-/b/.) Sorting, on the other hand, seems to help students to become more aware of onsets and rimes. Sorting forces students to compare and contrast words, noting similarities and differences. Both writing for sounds and sorting are activity-oriented and engage students' attention.

Creating a Word Wall

Instead of using a model words chart, you might put newly learned pattern words on a word wall. Place pattern words on the word wall in alphabetical order by pattern rather than by first letter: *a* pattern words, followed by *e* pattern words, followed by *i* pattern words, and so on. As new patterns are studied, add them to the word wall. As the word wall becomes full, eliminate some of the patterns learned earlier. Star the model words so that they stand out (Lapp, Flood, Frey, Begley, & Moore, 2004). High-frequency, nonpattern words should be placed in a separate section of the word wall. The model words chart and/or the word wall can be used along with prompts to help students learn to use decoding strategies.

Teaching Decoding Strategies

Along with the content of phonics, students should be taught strategies for decoding unfamiliar words. The most effective strategies are phonological. Students recode a word in the following ways.

- By processing it sound by sound (seeing *hat*, they say /h/, /a/, /t/ and then blend the sounds to say *hat*)
- By using the initial consonant and the word's rime
- By decoding a part that they recognize and using that to reconstruct the word (note the *an* in *stand*, say it, and add *d* and *st*; If the student noted the *and*, he would say it and just add the *st*)
- By using an analogy (realize that the unknown word *bent* is like the known word *sent*, and use that knowledge to decode *bent*)

Prompting Strategy Use

When students encounter a difficult word, do not tell them the word. Instead, use a pause, prompt, praise approach (Tunmer & Chapman, 1999). Pause and give students a chance to note the problem and work out the word. If they are unable to do so, provide a prompt. Unless the word is *of* or *off* or another word that doesn't lend itself to decoding, provide a decoding prompt. Although some programs advise starting off with a context prompt, it's better to begin with a decoding prompt. Decoding is more direct and more effective (Greaney, Tunmer, & Chapman, 1997). A decoding prompt also gives students the message that most words are worked out phonologically. Because it is direct and easy to implement, prompt the pronounceable word part strategy first. Ask, "Is there any part of that word that you can say?" If the student doesn't respond, but you believe that there is a part of the word that she knows, cover up all but that part of the word. For the word *wheat*, you might cover up all but the *eat*. After the student pronounces it, uncover the *wh* and prompt the student to say the sound represented by *wh* and put the two parts of the word together. Some students, especially those who are struggling to learn to read, have difficulty seeing patterns in words (Juel & Minden-Cupp, 2000). For these students, the pronounceable word part might be the initial consonant. You might need to prompt these students through the word sound by sound.

If students don't respond to the pronounceable word part strategy, prompt the analogy strategy. Ask, "Is that word like any word you know?" If students are unable to respond, direct them to the model words chart or word wall: "Is that word like any word on the model words chart (or the word wall)?" If students are unable to locate an analogy word, write the word above the problem word. Have them read the analogy word, note how the analogy and problem word are the same, and use the analogy word to read the problem word. For example, if students are unable to read the word *vest*, write the known word *best* above it. Have them read *best* and then *vest*.

To read a hard word, ask:

- Is there any part of this word that I can say?
- Is this word like any word I know?
- Is this word like a word on the model words chart or the word wall?
- What word would make sense here?

After you figure out a hard word, ask:

Is the word I made a real word?
Does it make sense in the sentence?

FIGURE 8.4 *Word Reading Chart*

Students need to be taught to be flexible in their strategy use, especially when they encounter vowel digraphs. For instance, the digraph *ow* can represent long /ō/ as in *snow* or /ow/ as in *cow*. Students need to be prepared to try more than one pronunciation. If the first pronunciation doesn't result in a real word that fits the context of the sentence, they need to try an alternate pronunciation.

If the word is not decodable but is in a context that lends itself to the use of context clues, prompt the use of context clues: "What word would make sense here?" If nothing else works, provide students with two possibilities, one of which is the correct answer. "Do you think the word is *toy* or *top*?" After students respond, follow up with a question that requires them to justify their response by using their decoding skills: "What makes you think that the word is *toy*?" (Clay, 1993b).

After students have worked out a word, affirm their efforts with specific praise: "I like the way you all used a part of the word you knew to figure out that word." Specific praise encourages students to try to work out words and also lets them know what they did right so that they will continue to use that strategy.

Teaching students to use decoding strategies is easy. The hard part is getting them to use the strategies. To foster application of word identification strategies, Success for All, a reform literacy program, provides frequent opportunities for students to apply skills. Working in pairs, students practice reading new words and sentences virtually every day. Students are also given laminated cards that highlight key strategies. You might use the strategy reminders in Figure 8.4 as a basis for constructing a strategy reminder card for your students.

Using Context

When decoding words, context is always a factor. After students decode a word, they must make sure that it is a real word and that it makes sense in the context in which it is being used. At times, phonological strategies can't be used or don't work. At that point, context should be used. At the very beginning stages, students might use picture clues. Coming across an unfamiliar word, they might note that it is shown in a picture. Picture clues should not be emphasized and are of very limited value. As students gain decoding skills, picture clues should be phased out. Through processing words phonologically, students practice and apply their skills and also create bonds between spellings and sounds. When these bonds become strong enough, the words are recognized immediately and are sometimes known as sight words. Overusing pictures clues can hinder students' reading progress.

The Importance of Coaching

Spending large amounts of time on phonics in grades 2–3 has a negative impact on students (National Reading Panel, 2000). This time is better spent reading self-selected or assigned materials or on other profitable activities. This assumes that these second- and third-graders didn't need the phonics they were being taught. However, the practice of coaching in word recognition strategies during reading has a positive payoff for older students. "Coaching in the application of phonics strategies is very different from explicit instruction focused on the letter-sound correspondences and rules, and is inherently more metacognitive and strategic in nature" (Taylor, Peterson, Rodriguez, & Pearson, 2002, p. 45).

Balancing Instruction and Application

Phonics instruction should be balanced with extended opportunities to apply the skills being taught. Baumann and Ivey (1997) had a 20-80 rule: 20 minutes of instruction was accompanied by 80 minutes of application. However, as noted in the Juel and Minden-Cupp (2000) study, time spent on phonics instruction will vary depending on the nature of the learner and the stage that the learner is in. Struggling readers need more instruction. More instruction is also called for in the early stages of learning to read. For struggling readers in the early stages, a one-third ratio is a sensible rule of thumb: in a 90-minute block of time, no more than 30 minutes should be spent on phonics instruction.

Decodable Text

The best application for phonics is for students to encounter newly taught elements in their reading. To provide practice, some states have demanded and publishers have created what is known as decodable text. Decodable text is text in which students have been taught the phonics elements needed to read the text and content or high-frequency words that don't lend themselves to phonics. In principle, this is a good idea. Students do best when they read material in which they apply what they have learned (Juel & Roper-Schneider, 1985; Mesmer, 1999). But in some decodable texts, phonics are overemphasized so that the text has a singsong sound and might use words like *drat* or *vat* that follow a decoding pattern but might not be in the students' listening vocabulary. This short-circuits the meaning processor, so that students are unable to use phonics and meaning in tandem.

On the other hand, there are books known as predictable books in which patterned sentences are used and pictures depict any words not part of the pattern, so that students can read the books by using the patterns and pictures to assist them. This shortchanges the use of phonics. The best books are those that reinforce patterns taught but have a natural sound to them. They strike a balance between being decodable and predictable. Mesmer (1999) found that a struggling reader that she was working with did not make progress with predictable books but did so with books that were decodable but had a natural sound. However, predictable books do have some valid uses. For students who are struggling in the beginning stages of reading, predictable books can give them the feel of what it's like to be a reader.

Building Fluency

Because they are still learning the code, beginning readers may read in slow, halting fashion. If labored reading persists, comprehension will suffer. Students will expend so much mental effort decoding that they won't be able to devote energy to understanding what they read. Students need to become fluent as well as accurate readers. Fluency has been defined as "freedom from word identification problems that might hinder comprehension in silent reading or the expression of ideas in oral reading; automaticity" (Harris & Hodges, 1995, p. 85). Fluency is composed of accuracy and automaticity. Students are accurate if they can recognize the words.

BOX 8.1

Predictable Books: Personal Perspective

While working with a group of five first-graders who were making very slow progress, I introduced some predictable books to them and arranged for them to practice reading the books until they could read them fairly smoothly. Although it was important that they learn basic phonics patterns, it was also important that they see themselves as readers. Up to this point, we had been working primarily with decodable text, but I sensed that the children weren't having much fun reading. They were still having a difficult time with short *a* and short *i* patterns. The predictable texts, with their repeated language and heavy picture support, were easier to read. Learning to read these books boosted the children's self-confidence. They were quite pleased that they could take books home and read to mom, dad, grandma, grandpa, or other family members. Among the predictable books that I used with the five struggling readers, there was one that depicted a number of things that the main character could do: "I can read; I can sing; I can run." The book reinforced the *an* pattern, a pattern that the children were still slow in recognizing. Another predictable book had a number of *it* words, a pattern that was recently introduced. A judicious use of predictable books can foster both confidence and skill.

They have automaticity if they recognize the words rapidly. Students can be accurate but slow decoders. Oral reading is most often used to assess fluency. If students misread a number of words, this indicates that accuracy is a problem. It also may be an indication that the material is beyond their instructional level. If they read word by word and need to sound out an excessive number of words, or read at a slow rate, then automaticity is an issue. Fluency should also be assessed by noting students' rate of silent reading and their comprehension. If they can read at a reasonable pace, then they probably are able to recognize the words rapidly. If they can answer questions about what they read, their word recognition is probably accurate.

The foundation for fluency is to build solid word analysis skills (Wolf & Katzir-Cohen, 2001). Wide reading of books at the students' independent level is the best way to build fluency. The reading should be silent. If students continue to read in a labored, halting fashion, the material might be too difficult. Try material that is easier, and gradually move up to more difficult selections. Students, especially if they are younger, might also be encouraged to read the same selections a second, a third, or even a fourth time. However, extensive reading seems to work just as well, if not better, than repeated reading. Extensive reading has the added benefit of building background. Instead of reading a selection three or four times, students read three or four different selections. In a study comparing repeated reading of a selected number of texts and wider reading of a variety of texts, Van Bon, Bokesbeld, Font Freide, and Van den Hurk (1991) found that reading a variety of texts worked just as well as reading the same text over and over. However, repeated reading did not improve performance in reading new words or new texts or even reading lists of words. "What children learn by rereading the same text over and over is apparently highly context-specific and is not transferred to new situations—not even to reading the same words outside the original text" (Van Bon et al., 1991, p. 475). Although silent reading should be emphasized, you might do some oral reading as long as the reading is purposeful. Students might read aloud to younger students, read poetry and plays, read selections chorally, and engage in reader's theater. During your read-alouds to students, model oral reading so that students understand about phrasing and intonation and reading with expression. Above all, encourage students to read, read, read, and then read some more.

High-Frequency Words

A small number of words, such as *of* and *once*, and, to a lesser extent, *where* and *come*, are said to be irregular. There is not a close match between their spellings and their sounds. Because these words are not spelled the way they sound, at one time it was believed that the best way to learn them was through visual memory so they became known as "sight words." They were put on cards and studied. However, a solid body of two decades or more of research demonstrates that even irregular words are learned phonologically. A better term for these words is "high-fre-

TABLE 8.2 *High-Frequency Words*

1. the	35. when	69. see	103. through	137. such	171. under
2. of	36. we	70. no	104. back	138. here	172. last
3. and	37. there	71. could	105. much	139. take	173. read
4. a	38. can	72. make	106. good	140. why	174. never
5. to	39. an	73. than	107. before	141. things	175. am
6. in	40. your	74. first	108. go	142. great	176. us
7. is	41. which	75. been	109. man	143. help	177. left
8. you	42. their	76. its	110. our	144. put	178. end
9. that	43. said	77. who	111. want	145. years	179. along
10. it	44. if	78. now	112. sat	146. different	180. while
11. he	45. will	79. people	113. me	147. number	181. sound
12. for	46. do	80. my	114. day	148. away	182. house
13. was	47. each	81. made	115. too	149. again	183. might
14. on	48. about	82. over	116. any	150. off	184. next
15. are	49. how	83. did	117. same	151. went	185. below
16. as	50. up	84. down	118. right	152. tell	186. saw
17. with	51. out	85. way	119. look	153. men	187. something
18. his	52. then	86. only	120. think	154. say	188. thought
19. they	53. them	87. may	121. also	155. small	189. both
20. at	54. she	88. find	122. around	156. every	190. few
21. be	55. many	89. use	123. another	157. found	191. those
22. this	56. some	90. water	124. came	158. still	192. school
23. from	57. so	91. little	125. three	159. big	193. show
24. I	58. these	92. long	126. high	160. between	194. always
25. have	59. would	93. very	127. come	161. name	195. until
26. not	60. other	94. after	128. work	162. should	196. large
27. or	61. into	95. word	129. must	163. home	197. often
28. by	62. has	96. called	130. part	164. give	198. together
29. one	63. more	97. just	131. because	165. air	199. ask
30. had	64. two	98. new	132. does	166. line	200. write
31. but	65. her	99. where	133. even	167. mother	
32. what	66. like	100. most	134. place	168. set	
33. all	67. him	101. know	135. old	169. world	
34. were	68. time	102. get	136. well	170. own	

Adapted from *The Educator's Word Frequency Guide* by S. M. Zeno, S. H. Ivens, R. T. Millard, & R. Duvvuri, 1995. Brewster, NY: Touchstone Applied Science Associates.

quency words" since they are the most frequently occurring words in English. Table 8.2 lists two hundred high-frequency words in order of their frequency of appearance. These words make up about 60 percent of the words in continuous text. Except for highly irregular words such as *of* and *one*, most of the words contain some letter-sound regularities. Many of the high-frequency words, such as *and*, *that*, *he*, and *with*, are totally predictable. When teaching high-frequency words, take advantage of any phonic regularities that are present. For instance, present *at* and *that* when presenting the *at* pattern. For a word like *what*, point out that *wh* makes a /w/ sound as in *when* and ends with a /t/ sound as in *hat*. Since the *a* is irregular, students would need to use visual memory to recall that element. Have students focus on the spelling of the word. Also plan practice reading so that they meet the word many times and thereby form a visual image of the word in addition to making phonological connections.

As students are learning irregular words such as *they* or *where*, point to the regular as well as the distinguishing parts of the words. Because high-frequency words are such a prominent element in students' reading, it is essential that they learn to recognize them rapidly. Novice readers need to develop automaticity, the ability to process words effortlessly and automatically (Laberge & Samuels, 1974). Ultimately, because they have met them many times in print, most of the words that skilled readers encounter, although learned through phonics, are processed as rapid recognition words because strong bonds have been formed between the printed words and their spoken equivalents and meanings.

Importance of Phonological Processing

It is no secret that the main cause of reading difficulty is a weakness in phonological processing that shows up as students experience difficulty acquiring phonological awareness and, later, phonics. Some researchers have attempted to bypass a weak phonological system by teaching students words using their visual memory (Olson, 1985). Unfortunately, there is no getting around a weak phonological system. Words are learned and stored phonologically. Students who have a weakened phonological system need extra instruction. Actually, orthographic awareness, which is an awareness of the appearance of words, is built on phonological awareness (Share, 1995). Students weak in phonological awareness tend to be weak in orthographic awareness. For instance, when assessed in spelling, a group of older struggling readers had particular difficulty with adding final *e* to words and doubling consonants: *trip* was misspelled as *tripe*; *dinner* was misspelled as *diner* (Bourassa & Treiman, 2003). Difficulty with final *e* and doubling consonants indicates a lack of understanding of key orthographic features. However, proficient phonological awareness does not automatically result in proficient orthographic awareness. Some good readers are poor spellers. Frequently this is a result of poor orthographic awareness.

Providing Guidance in Word Learning Skills

Students should also be guided in the use of key word learning strategies. Instruction will vary depending on whether students know the words but cannot read them or whether students don't know the words because they are not in their listening vocabularies. If students know the words, instruction will take the form of teaching phonics and syllabic analysis. If students don't know the meanings of the words, instruction will use word learning skills, such as use of the dictionary (print and electronic), contextual analysis, and morphemic analysis (roots, prefixes, and suffixes). What makes instruction especially effective is having all teachers explain how to use word learning strategies in their subject areas. Science, for instance, offers a rich source of prefixes and suffixes, and roots should be taught. Along with explaining technical terms such as *ecosystem* and *geosynchronous,* the teacher might also discuss the morphemic elements in the words.

Morphemic Analysis

A powerful but underused word learning skill, morphemic analysis is the ability to determine a word's meaning through examination of its prefix, root, and/or suffix. A morpheme is the smallest unit of meaning. It may be a word, a prefix, a suffix, or a root. The word *pass* has a single morpheme; however, *impassable* has three: *im-pass-able.* Whereas syllabic analysis involves chunks of sounds, morphemic analysis is concerned with chunks of meaning.

Based on their research, White, Power, and White (1989) estimated that average fourth-graders double their ability to use morphemic analysis after just ten hours of instruction. To be effective, instruction in morphemic analysis should be generative and conceptual rather than mechanical and isolated. For example, students can use their knowledge of the familiar words *thermostat* and *thermometer* to figure out what *therm* means and to apply that knowledge to *thermoplastic, geothermal,* and *hypothermia.* By considering known words, they can generate an understanding of *therm* and apply it to unknown words, which, in turn, enriches that concept (Dale & O'Rourke, 1971). The key to teaching morphemic analysis is to help students note prefixes, suffixes, and roots and discover their meanings. It is also essential that elements having a high transfer value be taught and that students be trained in transferring knowledge (Dale & O'Rourke, 1971).

Instruction in morphemic analysis can be initiated as early as grade 3. Greek roots are generally taught before Latin roots (Edwards, Font, Baumann, & Boland, 2004). After students have been taught prefixes, suffixes, and root words, these might be displayed on the word wall. One way to teach prefixes is to group them by families of meaning (Baumann et al., 2002). Possible groupings include the following.

- Number: mono-, bi-, di, tri-
- Negative: un-, im-, in-, il-, ir-
- Below or part: sub-, under-
- Again and remove: re-, de-
- Before and after: pre-, post-
- Against: anti-, counter-

- Excess: over-, super-, out-
- Bad: mis-, mal-

Because their structures differ, morphological elements differ in difficulty level. Base words are easier than root words. Base words can stand alone as words: *help* as in *helpful.* Roots cannot stand alone: *spect.* They must have affixes added to function as a word: *inspect, spectacle* (Templeton, 2004). The easiest elements are those containing a base word in which the base word is not changed when an affix is added: *excitement.* More difficult are words containing roots and words in which the pronunciation changes when an affix is added: *sign, signature* (the long *i* of *sign* become a short *i* in *signature*). A basic principle in English orthography is that meaning dominates pronunciation. The spelling of a word will stay the same even if the pronunciation changes so that the relationship of the derived word to its base is maintained, as in *bomb* and *bombard.*

Contextual Analysis

Note how the meaning of the word *solstice* is developed in Figure 8.5. The word *solstice* is explained in context; and then, in a sidebar, the morphological compo-

---

Circle of Our Four Seasons

Hear a Music Clip

Lyrics to Song

Get the most out of these pages with the *Weather Dude*Music CD

Solstice: This comes from two words, *sol,* meaning "sun," and *sistere,* meaning "to stand." In the Northern Hemisphere, the summer solstice is when the sun "stands" at its most northern position in the sky. The winter solstice is when the sun "stands" at its most southern position.

Summer in the City

Heat

It's summer and the heat is on. The summer solstice in the Northern Hemisphere, or top half of Earth, is around June 21. That's when the sun reaches its most northern point over our planet. The days around June 20 are the longest of the year, and the rays from the sun beat almost directly down on use and warm us up.

Longest, Not Hottest

You might think that the longest days of the year would be the hottest. But they are not. The hottest weather, on average, comes about a month after the summer solstice. This is because the amount of heat from the sun continues to accumulate during the long hot days, and the short nights don't allow as much heat to leave. The days start to cool down only after the days grow short enough to allow more heat to leave Earth's surface than arrives.

FIGURE 8.5 *Context for the Word* **Solstice**

Source: Nick Walker, The Wea ther Dude," Summer in the City. Available at http://www.wxdude.com/summer.html. Copyright Nick Walker.

nents of the word are supplied. This gives students additional retrieval clues. At this point, you might discuss with them other words containing the word part *sol,* meaning "sun": *solar, solarium.*

Not all contexts are helpful. An informal survey of difficult words in children's periodicals, textbooks, and trade books indicates that definitions or usable context clues are supplied about one-third of the time (Gunning, 1990). Overall, the probability of deriving a word from context is .15 (Swanborn & de Glopper, 1999). Out of one hundred hard words, a typical reader is able to derive a suitable meaning for fifteen of those words. However, the ability to use context develops over the years and is higher for achieving readers than it is for struggling readers. Grade 4 students have a .08 probability of learning a word from context; Grade 11 students have a probability of .33. When performance is averaged across grades, struggling readers have a .075 probability of learning a word from context, average-ability readers .12, and high-ability readers .19. Even when the passage contains excellent contextual clues, struggling readers frequently fail to use them (Bonacci, 1993).

The difficulty of the passage being read also has an impact on the probability of successfully using context clues. If there are very few unknown words, the probability of learning a word is about .30. But if there is a large proportion of unknown words—if, for example, 10 percent of the words are unknown—the probability plummets to .07. At this point, there are so many unknown words that students are overwhelmed. This is just one more reason for giving students books on the appropriate level.

Even when context clues are fairly obvious, students may fail to take advantage of them. Fortunately, with practice, students do become more proficient at using context clues. Simply directing students to use context to get the meaning of an unfamiliar word is not effective. The directive has to be accompanied by practice and feedback to let them know if their contextual guesses are correct (Carnine, Kame'enui, & Coyle, 1984). Provide students with opportunities to apply context clues and to discuss the effectiveness of that application. The ability to use context depends on the ability and grade level of the readers and the complexity of the text (Swanborn & de Glopper, 1999).

Deriving the Meaning of a Word from Context

Deriving the meaning of an unfamiliar word requires the following steps.

- Recognizing that a word is unknown (Nation, 2001).
- Deciding to use context to derive the meaning of the unknown word. Many readers skip unknown words. Even when not skipped, most use of context is incidental (Rapaport, 2004). Readers are often barely aware of using context. A more deliberate use of context is not initiated until readers note a disruption in meaning and decide to use context (Kibby & Wieland, 2004).

- Selecting clues to the word's meaning. These clues constrain the meaning of the word. They might limit possible meanings to nouns or verbs, for instance. They may suggest a negative rather than a positive meaning.
- Using the clues to compose a general meaning of the word. Readers use clues and background experiences to create hypotheses as to the word's meaning. Although the passage is used to provide clues, readers' background knowledge is probably more of a factor than context. Context leads to the making of inferences based on the readers' background knowledge. Readers also revise their hypotheses based on subsequent encounters with the word. The basis for making inferences about the word's meaning then becomes a combination of context clues and reader background (Rapaport, 2004). In a sense, context is in readers' heads rather than on the page. One way to increase the effectiveness of students' use of context clues is to show students how to make inferences based on background knowledge. In one experiment, although all the students had the necessary background to infer that a rachet is a small hound, only half were able to use background knowledge to make this inference. The other half could not guess that the rachet was a small animal until asked what happened when the knight picked up the rachet (Rapaport, 2004). They figured the rachet must be small if the knight could pick it up.
- Testing the meaning of the word and changing or refining the meaning if necessary. Readers try out the hypothesized meaning to see if it fits. If it doesn't fit, readers repeat the process. Good readers revise when they find the hypothesized definition is not working out. Poor readers start all over again with a new hypothesis. In one study, readers required five or six encounters with a word before they could derive an accurate meaning (Kibby & Wieland, 2004).
- Using the newly learned word. When the newly learned word is encountered again, readers recognize it and assign it a meaning.

When modeling how to use context, try it with words whose meanings you don't really know. This will make the think-aloud much more realistic. It's easy to pick out context clues when you know the meaning of the word (Kibby & Wieland, 2004).

When students are attempting to use context, use prompts to guide their efforts. Because struggling readers may not be using their understanding of the text as a context clue, it is important when providing them prompts to first ask them to tell what the target section is about.

Struggling readers have a more difficult time deriving meaning from context (McKeown, 1985). They have difficulty selecting clues, using information provided by the clues, and testing the derived meaning. As McKeown and Beck (2004) conclude, "For many students the most difficult part of deriving word meaning from context is the process of reasoning about how to put information together from the context and what kind of conclusions are valid to draw" (p. 24). Using think-alouds, demonstrate for students the kind of reasoning that is required to derive the meaning of an unknown word. During guided practice sessions, have students use context clues to derive the meanings of difficult words. Use prompts to guide them in the use of the necessary reasoning processes.

Glossary and Dictionary Usage

Context, especially when combined with phonics and morphemic and syllabic analysis, is a powerful word-attack strategy, but some words defy even these four strategies. When all else fails, it is time for students to consult a glossary or dictionary. Although students might not use a real dictionary in first and second grades, preparation begins early. In first grade and, in some cases, kindergarten, students compile word books and picture dictionaries. They also learn alphabetical order, a prerequisite skill for locating words, and phonics, which is necessary for using the pronunciation key.

Using Glossaries

Glossaries are easier to use than dictionaries. They contain only words that have been highlighted in a text. Glossaries can be found in reading programs beginning in first grade and in many informational books. An especially useful type of glossary is the eGlossary, which can be found on the Internet or in computer software. With its speech component, an eGlossary says the target word, says its definition, and reads an example sentence. The eGlossary is especially helpful for students who are unable to pronounce the word. Because it reads the word, its meaning, and an example sentence, the eGlossary is a helpful study aid. Hearing the word spoken fosters retention. The eGlossary also helps students to independently go over hard words before reading a selection. For an example of an eGlossary, go to http://www.eduplace.com/kids/ and click on School Books.

Using Dictionaries

By third grade, students with average reading achievement are ready to use real dictionaries. Instruction in dictionary use is most effective when it is functional. Avoid isolated drills on dictionary skills. Concentrate on building dictionary skills through functional use—that is, show students how to use the dictionary and encourage them to incorporate it as a tool for understanding language. For instance, when they have questions about word meaning, pronunciation, spelling, or usage, encourage them to seek help in the dictionary.

One word of caution is in order: For word recognition, the dictionary should generally be used as a last resort. Looking up a word while reading a story interrupts the flow of the story and disturbs comprehension. Students should try context, phonics, and morphemic or syllabic analysis before going to the dictionary. Moreover, unless the word is crucial to understanding the story, they should wait until they have read the selection to look up the word. The dictionary is also a good check on definitions derived from context clues. After reading a story in which they used context clues, students should check their educated guesses against the dictionary's definitions.

Assessing the Word Analysis Component of Your Program

Word analysis skills, ranging from phonics and phonological awareness to contextual analysis and dictionary skills, are an essential element in an effective literacy program. Inadequate word analysis skills are a prime cause of below-level reading. Use the checklist in Table 8.3 to determine strengths and weaknesses of the word analysis component of your program.

TABLE 8.3 *Assessment Checklist for Word Analysis Program*

Action	Fully	Partially	Limited	Suggestions
Phonological awareness is taught as needed.				
Phonological awareness instruction is integrated with phonics instruction.				
Word analysis skills are taught systematically and directly.				
Word analysis skills are taught in functional fashion. Instruction focuses on using word analysis as a tool.				
Skills taught are ones that are needed.				
Instruction builds on what students know.				
There is a balance between instruction and application, with the emphasis on application.				
Skills are applied to reading materials.				
Students are grouped according to needs.				
Key strategies are taught and reinforced so that eventually they are applied independently.				
Fluent reading, both oral and silent, is modeled and fostered.				
Elements are applied in a variety of contexts, in the rereading of previously read materials, and/or in easy selections so that students' fluency is fostered.				

9

The Effectiveness of Affective Factors

To be effective, a program of school improvement needs to have a can-do, we're-all-in-this-together spirit. Previous chapters have explored technical aspects of an effective beat-the-odds program. They have delved into the how-to factors. This chapter considers the can-do spirit necessary for a successful program. An effective program begins with an affective component: high expectations.

High Expectations

Having high expectations is an essential element in closing the literacy gap. If our expectations are high, we tend to try harder and do better. The staff at Rockcastle County Middle School attributed having high expectations as one of the reasons for their success in this low-income, high-performance school. A staff member explains the school's philosophy this way: "not accepting failure from our students, having high expectations, and being able to vocalize those expectations to our students   I would credit as [some] of the major things [that improved student performance]." (Picucci, Brownson, Kahlert, & Sobel, 2002, p. 21)

Most 90/90/90 schools also stress having high expectations, but those expectations are based on where students started and how much progress they make (Reeves, 2000). Instead of emphasizing how high students' scores are, they emphasize how much students have improved. Their attitude is "It's not how you start here that matters, but how you finish." Imperfectly completed assignments are seen not as an occasion for chastisement and a low grade but as an opportunity for improvement. Teachers in 90/90/90 schools don't focus on how badly the student has done but rather on ways that he could improve. The expectation is that students, if given the help they need, will be successful. The 90/90/90 schools also demonstrate that it is the teacher and not the program that matters most. A wide variety of programs are used. Some are commercially produced; some are school created; however, all have a singular focus on building students' skills.

Basing Expectations on Progress

As is demonstrated by 90/90/90 schools, students should be assessed on how much they have gained. Some struggling readers might be two or three years behind. However, if they work hard and make substantial gains, they should be given credit for their progress, even if they are still below the standard that has been set. Sociologists from Johns Hopkins University found that even when impoverished and middle-class students make similar gains in reading, the impoverished students are given low grades (Entwisle, Alexander, & Olson, 2001). Because the impoverished students are behind at the start of the school year, their reading achievement scores are lower than those of the more affluent students, even though both groups make equivalent progress during the school year. In one school where 88 percent of the students received subsidized lunches, all of the first-graders were given failing marks at the end of the first quarter. In other words, poor children were not being marked in terms of how much they advanced during the school year but in terms of where they started and where they finished—even though, judged by the gains they made on standardized tests, they improved as much as the youngsters from more affluent families. Report cards indicated that many of these children were failures. Seeing their children's low grades, parents lowered their expectations, as did the teachers. Their expectations were lowered when they should have been raised.

When expectations are lowered, students are given fewer opportunities. Low grades also harm students' sense of efficacy. It is very discouraging to work hard and do as well as more privileged students and then to be marked as failures. Judging students on the basis of level of performance rather than amount of growth also is discouraging to the schools. Schools in impoverished areas are unfairly blamed for not being effective even when they are doing just as well as schools in more affluent areas.

The Importance of Caring

Closely tied in to having high expectations is an attitude of genuine caring. A teacher at Memorial Junior High School explains how the faculty understood that this belief served as an important motivator for students:

> If they know that we care about them and that we want them to succeed and that we're going to be right there, they try harder. I mean, teachers will do whatever it takes to make learning fun and to motivate the kids. The kids wonder why, and the only thing we can come up with is because we care. And I think that has really been the magic behind everything here. (Picucci, Brownson, Kahlert, & Sobel, 2002, p. 23)

To students, quality instruction means a caring teacher who accepts no excuses and refuses to let students fail. These teachers provide three essential elements: caring relationships, high expectations, and opportunities for participation and contribution (Benard, 2003).

> If teachers are caring and respectful, if they never give up on their students, if they help them discover and use their strengths, if they give them ongoing responsibilities as active decision makers—the students will learn empathy, respect, the wise use of power, self-control, responsibility, persistence, and hope. Moreover, when teachers model this invitational behavior, they create a classroom climate in which caring, respect, and responsibility are the behavioral norms. (Benard, 2003, p. 125)

Without caring relationships, high expectations, and opportunities for growth, even the best instructional practices won't work. As Wilson and Corbett (2001) state, "Even if a teacher tried to adhere to current thinking about instructional practices, students in these schools would still fall through the cracks unless the teacher believes it is his or her responsibility to construct a supportive net to catch them" (pp. 120–121).

Caring expectations also apply to the staff. Teachers, paraprofessionals, and other staff members must feel that they are valued. They must also sense that the administration has high expectations for them: that they will be successful. Teaching struggling readers and writers can be stressful and discouraging. Both teachers and students need to experience success. For teachers to be effective, they must believe that all students can learn and that they are the teachers who can teach them (Benard, 2003).

Using Motivation to Overcome the Gap

Having high expectations and a caring attitude set the stage for a program that is motivational. At Loma Terrace, a National Title 1 School, in addition to having a demanding academic curriculum, the school also has a motivational curriculum (Picucci, Brownson, Kahlert, & Sobel, 2002). The purpose of the curriculum is to instill in students attitudes, habits, and strategies that will enable them to be successful. At every grade level, students are taught how to set and work toward goals. Students develop a plan of action to meet their goals. Work ethic is stressed.

All too often, struggling readers fail to realize the importance of hard work and perseverance in achieving academic success. Students attribute success to ability, effort, luck, or other people. Attributing success to ability, luck, or other people can have a negative effect. If students don't believe they have the ability to complete a task, then they don't try. If they attribute success to other people, they may become overly reliant on others and might not develop the skills needed. Luck is random. There is nothing to be done to increase one's luck. The attribution that has a payoff in increased achievement is the belief in effort. Students who were persuaded to put forth more effort made substantial gains (Marzano, Gaddy, & Dean, 2000). One way to help students understand the connection between effort and success is to give them real-life examples of people who have met the challenge, including yourself (Marzano et al., 2000). Explain how you and others have successfully met difficult challenges. Also encourage students to tell about times when they completed tasks that they didn't think they could do.

When students are undertaking a difficult task, make sure that they have the needed skills. Then affirm their efforts. Be very specific with your affirmations. General praise such as "Good job!" doesn't provide adequate feedback and may sound insincere. The affirmation, "You did a good job by adding specific details to make your true story come alive," is much more convincing and highlights the

TABLE 9.1 *Guidelines for Effective Praise*

Effective Praise	*Ineffective Praise*
1. Is delivered contingently	1. Is delivered randomly or unsystematically
2. Specifies the particulars of the accomplishment	2. Is restricted to global positive reactions
3. Shows spontaneity, variety, and other signs of credibility; suggests clear attention to the student's accomplishment	3. Shows a bland uniformity, which suggests a conditioned response made with minimal attention
4. Rewards attainment of specified performance criteria (which can include effort criteria, however)	4. Rewards mere participation, without consideration of performance processes or outcomes
5. Provides information to students about their competence or the value of their accomplishments	5. Provides no information at all or gives students information about their status
6. Orients students toward better appreciation of their own task-related behavior and thinking about problem solving	6. Orients students toward comparing themselves with others and thinking about competing
7. Uses students' own prior accomplishments as the context for describing present accomplishments	7. Uses the accomplishments of peers as the context for describing students' present accomplishments
8. Is given in recognition of noteworthy effort or success at difficult tasks (for this student)	8. Is given without regard to the effort expended or the meaning of the accomplishment (for this student)
9. Attributes success to effort and ability, implying that similar successes can be expected in the future	9. Attributes success to ability alone or to external factors such as luck or easy task
10. Fosters endogenous attributions (students believe that they expend effort on the task because they enjoy the task and/or want to develop task-relevant skills)	10. Fosters exogenous attributions (students believe that they expend effort on the task for external reasons — to please the teacher, win a competition or reward, etc.)
11. Focuses students' attention on their own task-relevant behavior	11. Focuses students' attention on the teacher as an external authority who is manipulating them
12. Fosters appreciation of and desirable attributions about task-relevant behavior after the process is completed	12. Intrudes into the ongoing process, distracting attention from task-relevant behavior

Source: "Teacher Praise: A Functional Analysis," by J. Brophy, 1981, *Review of Educational Research, 51*(1), p. 26. Copyright 1981 by the American Educational Research Association. Reproduced with permission of the publisher.

importance of using details to flesh out a written piece. However, don't overemphasize effort. Also affirm students' ability. Students might get the idea that they have to work extra hard because they are lacking in ability. Guidelines for effective praise are presented in Table 9.1.

Tasks Must Be Doable

Tasks must also be doable. If students are just learning to summarize, give them well-structured paragraphs that contain a clearly stated main idea and details that are clearly signaled as being supportive. If initiating self-selected reading, begin with brief periods of reading. If working on vocabulary, present just five new vocabulary words rather than ten. The task should be challenging but not overly so.

Overcoming Roadblocks

At the Benchmark School, the staff has identified five roadblocks that interfere with students' learning: passivity, inattention, nonpersistence, impulsivity, and inflexibility (Gaskins, 2003). To help students overcome these roadblocks, the staff implemented a cognitive behavior approach (Gaskins & Baron, 1985). The goal of the program, which has been successful over the years, is to help students become aware of these blocks to learning and to take steps to overcome them.

Active Involvement

To help students overcome their passivity, the staff members build awareness of the need to be an active learner. They demonstrate and discuss the advantages and results of being an active learner. A teacher might describe a time when she read a whole page but had no idea what she was reading because she wasn't paying attention or got lost on a trip because she hadn't read the road map carefully. The teachers demonstrate ways of being active learners, such as summarizing and imaging while reading or questioning while listening.

Attention

If they are not paying attention, students are losing an opportunity to learn. Attention can be fostered indirectly by making the work interesting and challenging. It also helps if the work is on the right level. Struggling readers' attending behavior improves dramatically when texts that are too hard for them are replaced with texts that are closer to their level (Anderson, 1990). However, attention can't be at the whim of interest or engagement. Students need to develop habits of attention, even when the topic might not be one that they are particularly interested in. To foster attending behavior, the teacher might tell about a time when she didn't really "hear" what someone said because she was watching a TV program. The teacher also shares tips for paying attention, such as sitting up front, focusing on the speaker, or taking notes. Active purposeful listening is the best antidote to inattention.

Persistence

Persistence is also an essential ingredient in learning. The staff provides examples of the benefits of persistence. They might talk about famous people who were persistent, but they are sure to mention Murphy's (1996) study. Murphy studied Benchmark graduates and found that students with the highest persistence ratings at the time they graduated from Benchmark were the most successful of the school's graduates. The teacher gives tips on being persistent: breaking up the assignment into smaller subtasks, focusing on the here and now, picturing what it will be like to complete the assignment. One way to build persistence is to have students tackle short-term tasks first and gradually work up to longer ones.

Reflectivity

When students rush through their reading, comprehension suffers. To overcome this habit, teachers at Benchmark ask students to assess their comprehension. They might ask them to compose an oral summary of the selection. Not being able to do so is an indicator that students did not read in reflective fashion. The teacher asks the students to tell what things are getting in the way of comprehension and helps students plan ways for overcoming the obstacles.

Flexibility

Having a history of failure, struggling readers have a need to be right and might hang onto a response even though the evidence points elsewhere. To lessen the threat of providing an incorrect answer, teachers focus on the reasoning behind the response rather than its rightness or wrongness.

Attribution

If students are labeled as being dyslexic or learning disabled, they might live up to the labels and give up trying because they believe that they can't learn. However, if students believe that they are capable but just learn in different ways, then they will be encouraged to put forth effort. According to Irene Gaskins (2004), founder of the Benchmark School, students engage in a lot of avoidance behavior to protect their egos when faced with tasks that they believe might be too difficult because they are lacking in ability. These students need to have their beliefs changed. To help students overcome their dysfunctional beliefs, teachers discuss successful people identified as being dyslexic or learning disabled. At the Benchmark School, graduates who have beaten the odds come back and discuss how they became successful despite having difficulty with reading and writing.

Motivating Students to Put Forth Needed Effort

Summarizing, questioning, imaging, and other reading strategies take more effort than simply glancing over the page. As Gaskins (2003) comments, "Implementing strategies almost always entails more effort than students are accustomed to putting forth when they read" (p. 149). Therefore, it is essential that students see the payoff for the extra effort. Explain to students that their grades are almost sure to improve if they use appropriate strategies. Tell them that research studies show that students move up one or two grade levels after learning strategies. A more direct approach is to teach one-half of the class a strategy and then give a quiz to the whole class and compare how students do.

Taking Responsibility

At the Benchmark School, teachers explain that they will do their part: They will supply materials on the proper level and teach whatever strategies, vocabulary, or background knowledge is needed, but students must do their parts. Teachers have found that when the staff members deliver on their promises, then the students apply themselves. Students also need to learn how to overcome obstacles such as not having a quiet place to study or assignments that are too hard for them.

Students also need to learn to use resources so they get the help they need. If an assignment is too difficult, they need to get help from the teacher or classmates. If an explanation is not clear, they need to seek clarification. If they need extra help, they should know how to ask for it. As Gaskins (2003) says, " Encouraging and guiding students to be self-advocates is one of the greatest gifts a teacher can give" (p. 161).

Using Engagement to Close the Gap

A key element in closing the literacy gap is engagement. Engaged readers are proficient readers. On the 1998 NAEP, nine-year-old participants answered questions that suggested whether they were engaged readers. Degree of engagement turned out to be more important than poverty, gender, or parents' education. Highly engaged readers who lived in poverty and whose parents had limited educations outperformed less engaged students who lived in affluence and had highly educated parents. As Guthrie (2003) concludes, "Based on a massive sample, this finding suggests the stunning conclusion that engaged reading can overcome traditional barriers to reading achievement, including gender, parental education, and income."

What is an engaged reader? Guthrie (2004) provides the following contrast.

> Joaquin's behavior reveals that he is an engaged reader. He reads intently without being distracted for a sustained period of time. Joaquin is an active reader. He thinks about what he is reading and monitors for meaning. If the passage fails to make sense, he reads or applies another fixup strategy. During discussions, Joaquin is able to provide an overview of what he has read and also to analyze the text. He

has a lot to contribute during discussions because he constructed a deep under-standing of what he read. Although he has a particular interest in football and snakes, he reads his social studies and science texts with focus and concentration.

Joaquin has a novel with him that he reads when the teacher announces that it is time for free reading. He also reads at home for enjoyment for 30 minutes or more. All tolled, Joaquin spends about two hours a day in engaged reading.

Savannah, who is also in fourth grade, is a disengaged reader. Savannah is easily distracted and takes a while to settle into her reading. Often she doesn't begin reading until the teacher urges her to do so. Her purpose to read is to com-plete the assignment. She has no question in mind as she reads and does not moni-tor for meaning. Unable to answer a question during a postreading discussion, she goes back over the selection until she finds the needed information. Because her comprehension was limited, she has little to add to the group discussion.

Because she is unengaged during much of the reading time, she only spends about 20 minutes during a school day in actual reading. She doesn't read at home on her own. As a result of her limited time engaged in reading, she is reading below grade level.

An engaged reader reads intently (Guthrie, 2004). An engaged reader is focused and involved. Engaged readers are intrinsically motivated. They're not reading to gain points or pass a quiz, but are reading for pleasure or because they are curious about a subject. Engaged readers also apply strategies as they read, such as predicting, summarizing, or evaluating. They enjoy discussing their read-ing. A hallmark of engaged readers is they read because they want to.

Engaged readers display four key qualities: cognitive competence, motiva-tion, quest for knowledge, and social interactivity. Cognitive competence means that students are able to use background knowledge, pose questions, search for information, summarize, organize their information, and monitor their compre-hension.

Motivation is intrinsic and entails wanting to learn. It also means that readers have a sense of self-efficacy. Given their motivation and sense of self-efficacy, they persist when the going gets tough and are able to see their goals through to com-pletion. For engaged readers, motivation and cognition are integrated.

Quest for knowledge means that engaged readers seek out the big ideas as they relate new information to what they already know. "They expand their con-ceptual structures deliberately" (Guthrie, 2003).

Being socially interactive means that engaged readers work with others to gather and share knowledge. They work together on projects, exchange ideas, and learn from each other. Knowing that they will be sharing with others impels engaged readers to read more carefully and more thoughtfully so they can explain what they learned to their peers.

Disengaged readers may lack necessary cognitive strategies. They lack the desire to master new concepts in books. "Often they are not confident nor do they possess strong self-efficacy as readers. Many believe that if new information does not come immediately from texts, it is not possible to understand the material" (Guthrie, 2003). Because of a lack of competence or confidence, they might be reluctant to work with others on projects.

A program known as CORI (Concept-Oriented Reading Instruction) is designed to turn all students into engaged readers or, at least, to increase the degree of engagement. A first step is to teach students the needed cognitive strategies. However, mastery of the strategies will be of little benefit if students don't want to apply them. Both motivation and cognitive strategies must be taught at the same time. When the concept of engagement is applied to science, students begin with a hands-on experience. It might entail examining birds' feathers, life in an aquarium, a recycling plant, leaves from different trees, or a similar phenomenon. The hands-on activities spur questions. Students want to know why different birds have different feathers or how feathers function or whether all the feathers on a bird are the same. Since students have posed their own questions, they are more motivated to seek answers. Key cognitive strategies that are introduced are activating background knowledge and asking questions.

In the second phase, students seek resources to answer their questions. They learn how to use books, periodicals, recordings, videos and CD-ROMs, the Internet, observations, and interviews. They learn how to use search tools as well as the table of contents and indices.

In a third overlapping phase, students comprehend and integrate information. They locate answers to their questions, summarize what they have read, organize information, monitor comprehension, and apply fix-up strategies. In the fourth phase, students communicate their knowledge. They can write a conventional report, prepare a PowerPoint presentation, compose a booklet, create a poster, create a video clip, or add to their group's Web site.

CORI provides struggling readers with more time to learn a complex skill such as summarizing. One group needed nine days before they could summarize

BOX
9.1

Model Teaching: Integrating Motivation and Strategy Instruction

After her students discussed owls, dissected and analyzed owl pellets, and took notes on their findings, Sally Trent distributed trade books on owls (Guthrie, 2003). Students leafed through the books and were fascinated by the colorful illustrations. Because the students had limited experience with informational books, Trent showed them how to navigate the books. She explained the table of contents and the index. She also explained headings and pointed out illustrations, captions, charts, and sidebars. Students were invited to pose one good question that the whole class would work together on. After listing a number of questions, the class chose its favorite: What enemies do owls have?

Trent then asked the students to tell where they might find the answer. The students replied "in the books," at which point Trent explained how the index might help. The students started searching through their books. Because of the diversity of reading levels, books were on a 2 to 5 level. (An important feature of CORI is that all students are provided with materials on their level.) Students located answers and volunteered responses. Responses were recorded on the board. Students documented their answers by reading passages from the text.

just one page. "By the end of this time, the students had gained competence in writing short summaries of a single page of the book. They had gained a beginning sense of self-efficacy as strategy users in reading. Frequent opportunities for learning under the conditions of support for fluency, strategy simplification, and the availability of a bridge are needed" (Guthrie, 2003).

Assessing the Affective Component of Your Program

The affective component is the heart of your program. Bridging the gap will take both commitment and hard work. Motivation and confidence will provide the impetus and persistence necessary to enable students to beat the odds. Use the checklist in Table 9.2 to determine strengths and weaknesses of the affective component of your program.

TABLE 9.2 *Assessment Checklist for Affective Component of a Literacy Program*

Action	Fully	Partially	Limited	Suggestions
Students are given interesting and challenging materials and tasks.				
Students are given only tasks and materials that are within their capabilities.				
Students are given choice when possible.				
Students see the connection between what they are learning and their lives.				
Students have input in class planning and assessment.				
Students work cooperatively.				
Students are taught how to make the best use of their abilities.				
Students are provided with strategies needed to overcome difficulties and to be persistent.				
Students learn to attribute success to their efforts.				
Students' efforts are affirmed.				
Instruction builds on what students know.				
Key strategies are taught and reinforced so that eventually they are applied independently.				

10

Using Added Resources to Close the Gap

To close the literacy gap, students who are behind need to make average progress and then some. As a practical matter, this means getting extra help and putting in extra time. One way of getting extra help is through tutoring.

Tutoring

Trained Professionals

Because it provides one-on-one instruction, tutoring can be tailored to the students' needs in a way that no group approach can. Tutoring is potentially the most effective approach of all. Bloom (1984) believes that tutoring provides insight into how much students could learn and that highly effective tutoring could raise students' achievement by 2 standard deviations. In other words, if students taught in a group achieved at the 50th percentile, they could achieve at the 98th percentile if taught individually. Indeed, supplementary intervention programs that include instruction in phonics and high-frequency words, include reading and spelling the words in isolation, and include reading the words in context can result in large gains. In one study, first-graders taking part in a supplementary tutoring programs jumped from the 6th to the 50th percentile (Jenkins, Payton, Sanders, & Vadasay, 2004). This means that they moved from being virtual nonreaders to being average readers. They made significant gains that far exceeded the progress made by students who were just taking part in the school's core program. The program was extensive. It consisted of four sessions per week for twenty-five weeks. Students read at least between 7,100 and 8,000 words. Students were instructed by paraprofessionals who were provided with training and were supervised.

However, not all tutoring is equal. Tutoring by trained professionals is most effective (Wasik & Slavin, 1993). Having knowledge of how children learn and what constitutes effective literacy instruction and having the experience to be able to use judgment to plan and modify instruction enables trained professionals to be more effective. The most effective tutoring programs are those such as Reading Recovery and Early Steps, which use trained professionals. Reading Recovery accelerates the progress of low-achieving first-graders by providing intensive one-on-one instruction, 30 minutes a day, five days a week, for a period of twelve to twenty weeks by highly trained teachers. Key activities include rereading familiar books, reading a new book, applying decoding strategies, and writing a sentence, which is cut up and then reassembled. See Clay (1993a, 1993b) for a full description of the program. Early Steps is based on Reading Recovery but adds a sorting component to systematically introduce and reinforce phonics patterns. Detailed instructions for implementing Early Steps are found in Santa and Høien (1999). The key activities—reading a number of books, reassembling cut-up sentences, and sorting word patterns—provide high-payoff practice and should be a part of any program.

Volunteer Tutors

One of the most successful of the volunteer tutoring programs is Book Buddies. Created by University of Virginia faculty in 1991 in collaboration with the Charlottesville City Schools and the Charlottesville community, Book Buddies is being successfully used in a number of communities. The tutoring is provided by community volunteers who teach from a lesson plan prepared by reading specialists. The key to Book Buddies effectiveness is the training and supervision provided by the reading specialists. An initial two-hour training class includes video lessons of tutorial sessions. On-site coordinators provide tutors with ongoing training and support by writing lesson plans, gathering materials, and providing feedback regarding specific activities, techniques, and pacing. Each on-site coordinator supervises fifteen volunteer tutors and their students. Tutors instruct children twice weekly for 45 minutes per session. For a complete description of the program, see Johnston, Invernizzi, and Juel (1998) or the Book Buddies Web site at http://curry.edschool.virginia.edu/reading/projects/bookbuddies/what.html. The Howard Street Tutoring program (Morris, 1999), which is similar to the Book Buddies program, also uses community volunteers. However, because it is more extensive than the Book Buddies program, the Howard Street program is frequently used to train teachers.

Characteristics of Effective Tutoring Programs

The effectiveness of tutoring programs depends on the quality of the program. Tutoring programs should incorporate the following elements, most of which are based on Wasik's (1998) recommendations.

- Coordination and supervision by a knowledgeable professional. Since volunteers don't have the background to plan lessons, it is important that a knowledgeable professional, preferably a certified reading specialist, plan the program and the tutoring lessons. The professional should also supervise the sessions, answer questions, and provide feedback. In addition, the specialist gathers whatever materials are necessary. Usually, tutoring materials and lessons are housed in some sort of tutoring box. The professional should also provide ongoing training and regularly hold conferences with tutors to see how things are going and provide any necessary help.
- Sessions should be structured and focused on high-payoff activities and geared to the needs of the students. Sessions typically include review of previously taught materials, perhaps a rereading of a previously read text; introduction or extension of a key word recognition or comprehension skill; introduction of a new text that provides application of the newly taught or reviewed skill; discussion of the text; and a brief writing activity related to the skill taught.
- Tutoring should be substantial. At a minimum, tutoring should consist of at least two 30-minute sessions a week. Daily sessions, of course, are even more effective. For best results, tutoring should be additive. It should be in addition to the regular school program. At Baskins, a high-performing elementary school, students can take part in an Aim High after-school tutoring program in which small groups of students meet for two 45-minute sessions each week (Rivkin, Hanushek, & Kain, 1998). Kindergarten children at Baskins who are struggling meet with tutors during center time and also are tutored for 20 extra minutes each day.
- Appropriate materials should be available. The tutor should have access to interesting materials on the student's reading level. White boards, games, writing paper, and writing instruments should also be available.
- Ongoing monitoring should be a part of the program. The tutor should conduct a brief assessment to see if the student has learned the skills taught during the sessions. Ongoing monitoring also helps the tutor and the supervisor make necessary adaptations, plan future lessons, and make sure the student is making adequate progress.
- Tutoring should be aligned with the classroom program. The tutor should use the same approach that the classroom teacher uses. The tutor might be providing added reinforcement for skills presented in the regular class or added practice. It would be confusing if the classroom teacher emphasized the use of decoding prompts to help the students read difficult words but the tutor stressed contextual clues.

Peer Tutoring

Peer tutoring typically has a double payoff: Both students learn. Peer tutoring can be set up on an informal basis so that achieving or more knowledgeable students help students who are struggling or lacking in information on a topic or a certain skill. Or you can make use of structured peer tutoring programs, such as Class Wide Peer Tutoring (CWPT), which has been validated in several scientific studies (Juniper Gardens Children's Project, 2004).

In CWPT, participants follow a schedule. Each Monday, students are pretested on upcoming material. It might be the week's spelling words or a set of vocabulary words or a set of fluency passages. Students are assigned to one of two teams. They are taught different aspects of new material and then take turns tutoring each other on the material they were taught. After 10 minutes of tutoring, the tutor tests the tutee. The tutee is awarded two points for each correct response. If the tutee gives a wrong answer, the tutor corrects it and then records it on a tutoring sheet. This earns the tutor one point. The partners switch roles. At the end of the session, they turn in their points. The team with the most points wins. Tutoring sessions are held every day for 30 minutes, with 10 minutes being allocated to presentation of the material and 20 minutes to tutoring. On Fridays, students are tested on the material.

More than thirty evaluations of the program have been conducted. Results were positive. Not only did CWPT students outscore the control group by 11 percentile points, they also had better behavior, spent more time on task, and were more fully engaged in their learning. The program has been used with regular education; learning disabled, autistic, and educable mentally disabled students; and economically disadvantaged students. Regardless of population, there were large gains.

PALS Overview

Peer-Assisted Learning Strategies (PALS) is a version of classwide peer tutoring (PALS, 2004). Teachers identify which children need help on specific skills and which children are the most appropriate choices to help them learn those skills. Teachers then pair up students. Pairs are changed regularly so that all students have the opportunity to be "coaches" and "players." The teacher circulates in the class, observes students, and provides help as needed. PALS, which is designed to complement the core reading program, is a 25- to 35-minute activity implemented two to four times a week. In Kindergarten PALS, children practice letter-sound correspondences and phonological awareness. First-grade PALS emphasizes decoding and reading fluently. In grades 2–6, there are three PALS activities that promote reading fluency and reading comprehension: partner reading, paragraph shrinking, and relay predicting. In partner reading, pairs of students read to each other and prompt for corrections when a word is misread. In paragraph shrinking, the reader reads a paragraph and the coach asks the reader to tell the *who* and the *what* of the paragraph and to tell the most important thing about the *who* or the *what*. If the responses are too wordy or contain irrelevant details, the coach asks the reader to shrink it. In relay predicting, the coach asks the reader to make a prediction, read the paragraph or section about which the prediction has been made, evaluate the prediction, and summarize.

High School PALS is similar to PALS at grades 2–6 but uses different motivational and helping strategies. Additional information is available at the PALS Web site at http://kc.vanderbilt.edu/kennedy/pals/.

Cross-Age Tutoring

In cross-age tutoring, older students help younger ones. Typically both the older and the younger students benefit. The younger students benefit because they are getting one-on-one help, and the older students benefit because they engage in additional reading and writing as they prepare their lessons. Helping younger children is also motivating and builds the older students' self-confidence and self-esteem.

NCLB Mandated Tutoring

If you are in a school that fails to make adequate yearly progress under NCLB, you may be required to offer parents the opportunity to have their children tutored by a qualified provider. Although the provision may seem punitive to the schools designated, it is a way to obtain extra services for students who need it. To optimize the benefits of this service, explore the available programs and determine the relative advantages of each. Make sure that the programs and procedures for participating in them are fully explained to parents. In addition to letters and notices sent home, you might also arrange for meetings for groups of parents and conduct individual conversations with parents of children who would seem to derive the most benefit from the program.

Having selected a provider, parents should sit down with the provider, mutually set goals, and then monitor their child's progress toward meeting those goals. Since this might be a new role for many parents, hold information sessions to discuss possible goals and ways of monitoring progress toward meeting literacy goals. Just as with regular schools, parents should make sure their child attends regularly, is on time, and has the necessary materials. Parents should also make sure their child completes assignments.

At this point, the program is underutilized. Fewer than 50 percent of eligible students have signed up for these programs. For resources and suggestions for setting up and maintaining a supplemental tutoring program, including descriptions of model programs, refer to Tutors for Kids at www.tutorsforkids.org.

The benefit of effective tutoring often goes well beyond what is learned in the sessions. The attention provided by a caring adult, the building of confidence and academic self-efficacy, and the learning of key skills often give students a boost that sets them on the road to academic success.

Providing Extra Time

To help students catch up, it is necessary to add instructional and practice time. All nine of the high-poverty schools cited for outstanding achievement in a U.S. Department of Education study found ways to provide added time for literacy instruction (Johnson, 2002). Programs can be offered before school, after school, on Saturdays, and during the summer. In one high-performing school, tutoring sessions were offered during lunch time. In many school districts, students who perform poorly on benchmark assessments or state tests are required to take off-hours classes. Students are surprisingly enthusiastic about well-run supplementary programs. In an after-school program that I participated in, struggling readers in a dual language school were provided with two hours of intervention instruction twice a week by teachers who were learning to become reading specialists. Although they were required to teach basic skills and strategies to the students, the teachers created programs that built on students' interests. More important was the attention and affirmation that the teachers provided. When that program ended, many students begged for more sessions.

Used well, a minimum of added instructional time can result in maximum improvement. The town of Henrietta, New York, added an hour to its half-day kindergarten to provide extra instruction for students who scored low on phonological awareness, letter knowledge, and other prereading indicators (Fredette, 2003). The extra hour was sandwiched between the departure of the morning kindergarten class and the arrival of the afternoon class. Results were remarkable.

Extending half-day kindergartens to a full day would be even more effective, of course, than adding an hour. In a study of poor children in Baltimore, first-graders who attended full-day kindergarten were absent fewer days in first grade, were retained less often, and had higher grades and test scores than children who attended for just half a day (Entwisle, Alexander, & Olson, 2001).

Summer School

Cooper (2003) found that students lost the equivalent of a month of instruction during their summer break from school. Learning losses are greater for math facts and for spelling than for reading comprehension and problem solving (Cooper, 2003). Although children from lower-income families tend to lose ground on reading, children from middle-class families actually progress in reading during the summer (Cooper, Charlton, Valentine, & Muhlenbruck, 2000). The U.S. Department of Education explains the pattern this way:

> Children of the middle-class appear to rely on school for only a portion of their academic learning. Their proficiency in basic and advanced academic subjects is boosted by parents' instruction, extracurricular activities (e.g., private lessons, vol-

untary associations such as scouting or sports), and family activities that reinforce education even when they are construed as entertainment. Children in poor families, on the other hand, rely primarily on school for academic learning. (U.S. Department of Education, 1993, p. 2)

Entwisle, Alexander, and Olson (2001) found that low socioeconomic status (SES) and middle-class SES made the same amount of progress during the school year, but that the low SES students lost ground during the summer months.

> When school was in session, the resource faucet was turned on for all children, and all gained equally; when school was not in session, the school resource faucet was turned off. In summers, poor families could not make up for the resources the school had been providing, and so their children's achievement reached a plateau or even fell back. Middle-class families could make up for the school's resources to a considerable extent. (Entwisle, Alexander, & Olson, 2001, p. 12)

One way of preventing the loss by low SES students is to offer summer school programs for students. The programs that work best are those that are designed for small groups, provide individual attention, and last for a significant period of time. In her review of studies, Karweit (1985) suggested that an additional thirty-five days of instruction would be needed to make a significant difference. However, a key factor is how that time is used. Programs are most effective that focus on math and reading, are coordinated with the regular program, and involve parents and community (Borman, 2000; Funkhouser, Fiester, O'Brien, & Weiner, 1995). Programs should begin in the early grades, be offered over multiple summers, and focus on prevention and development (Borman, 2000).

Summer school can also be a means for ameliorating reading and writing deficiencies. "Summer school may be the primary intervention through which educators prevent the cumulative widening of the reading achievement gap" (Borman, 2000, p. 124). If possible, summer schools should be staffed with certified teachers and teachers should be provided with time for collaborative planning. The Minneapolis Public Schools (2002) draws on its experience to recommend the following strategies for building a successful summer program.

- Clearly communicate summer session goals and student responsibilities
- Provide a rigorous curriculum that helps students meet individualized learning goals and state standards
- Provide meaningful, ongoing home communication regarding student attendance, behavior, and progress (Minneapolis Public Schools, 2002)

It is also important to involve parents. They are the ones who will make sure that their children sign up for programs, attend the programs, and complete their assignments. As a practical matter, remove all obstacles that might prevent students from attending. Provide transportation and meals for those students who need them. Although the program will be fostering reading and writing skills and so should be coordinated with the school's program, it need not have the same structure or activities. Since this is summer and the students' peers may be off at the ball field or town swimming pool, the program should have activities that are imaginative and engaging but effective for fostering literacy. While planning summer school, include students and parents in your sessions.

Alternatives to Summer School

If summer school is not available to students, urge them to take part in programs offered by the community. A number of organizations offer free or low-cost high-quality programs and may provide reduced rates or scholarships for families that can't afford to pay. Alert families to possibilities. Also provide take-home activities, such as booklists and reading records and journals, that might help students maintain and possibly improve their skills. Promoting summer reading is especially important if students are to maintain the gains they made during the school year.

Summer reading pays off. In a classic study of summertime reading, Heyns (1978) studied nearly three thousand sixth- and seventh-graders in the Atlanta public schools for two years. She found a close relationship between the amount of reading students did during the summer and academic gains. In fact, reading had a greater impact than attending summer school. Regardless of economic status, children who read six or more books over the summer made significant gains. As Heyns (1978) concludes:

> More than any other public institution, including the schools, the public library contributed to the intellectual growth of children during the summer. Moreover, unlike summer school programs, the library was used by over half the sample and attracted children from diverse backgrounds. (p. 77)

Students were more likely to read during the summer if they used the public library and if they lived close to the public library.

Many public libraries have a variety of summer programs for students. Find out what's available in your school's area and encourage students and parents to make use of appropriate programs.

Some cites and states have summer reading programs. Minneapolis kicked off its Summer Reading Achievers Program by explaining the program, providing each student with a Summer Reading Achievers Log, and starting the whole process by giving each student a book to read (Minneapolis Public Library, 2004). The public schools partnered with local libraries. The libraries offered reading incentive programs and, of course, access to books. Corporations and community organizations provided financial support and prizes. As part of the program, participants set their own goals; were given fun activity sheets; could take part in contests; and could attend demonstrations, shows, and celebrations held at the libraries. At the end of the summer, students were awarded certificates and prizes if they met their goals. Connecticut has a Governor's Summer Reading Challenge (Connecticut State Department of Education, 2004). Letters explaining the program are distributed to students and parents. Schools signing up for the program record the number of students participating and the total number of books read. Top performing schools are recognized at a statewide assembly and are awarded certificates by the governor.

Unfortunately, many children living in poverty do not have access to a library and have few or no books in the home. One solution is to send books home for the summer. Students in a fairly typical urban school were found to have an average of .2 books in their homes (S. Goodison, personal communication, March 16, 2004). Although the neighborhood had a library, it was in a high-crime area, so many parents were reluctant to make the trip. To provide the students with reading materials, the school collected books and distributed them to the children. Each child was able to take home at least three books for the summer.

Role of Retention

Accompanying the institution of standards and high-stakes testing is increased retention of students. Many states and school systems specify that students be retained if they do not reach proficiency on designated state or national tests. In California, for instance, state law mandates that students be retained who fail to meet proficiency standards on the basis of scores on state tests or grades and other indicators of academic achievement designated by the district (California State Department of Education, 2004). The teacher may state in writing that retention is not the proper intervention and may specify summer school or some other intervention. At the end of the remediation period, the pupil's status is reassessed.

Because of polices such as these, the retention rate in the nation's schools has hit 15 percent (National Association of School Psychologists, 2003). It is estimated that 30 percent or more of students are retained at least once before ninth grade. Despite the widespread use of retention, it is not an effective tool for closing the literacy gap and, in fact, contributes to it. Although students who have been retained may do somewhat better, those gains fade after two or three years. Underachieving students who have been promoted do just as well as compared to underachieving students who have been held back. Moreover, students who have been retained are more likely to have social and emotional problems and to drop out of school. In fact, retention is the best predictor of future dropout.

Social Promotion

Concerned about the emotional impact of retention, social promotion was initiated in the 1930s (Steiner, 1986). Students were promoted on the basis of age and other social considerations rather than on achievement. The standards movement has reinstated the concept of promotion on the basis of proficiency, the idea being that motivation to learn and achieve high standards is undermined if students are promoted on the basis of social factors, rather than on the basis of what they know and can do (Steiner, 1986).

Social promotion is not an effective learning tool. Social promotion has been criticized because it "frustrates promoted students by placing them in grades where they cannot do the work, sends the message to all students that they can get by without working hard, forces teachers to deal with under-prepared students while trying to teach the prepared, gives parents a false sense of their children's progress, leads employers to conclude that diplomas are meaningless, and dumps poorly educated students into a society where they cannot perform" (Thompson & Cunningham, 2000). Students who are lacking needed skills or knowledge need intervention.

Limiting Retention

Some groups of children are more likely to be retained than others (National Association of School Psychologists, 2003). Boys are more likely to be retained than girls. African American or Latino students are more likely to be retained, as are students who are living in poverty, have a late birthday, have delayed development, or experience attention problems. Students whose parents are single parents, have limited education, or are uninvolved in their children's education are more likely to be retained, as are children who change schools frequently. Children who have behavior problems are also more likely to be retained. Key candidates for retention are struggling readers.

To counter retention, a strong program of intervention and ongoing follow-up is recommended. The National Association of School Psychologists (2003) recommends the following.

- Encourage parents' involvement in their children's schools and education through frequent contact with teachers, supervision of homework, and so on.
- Adopt age-appropriate and culturally sensitive instructional strategies that accelerate progress in all classrooms.
- Emphasize the importance of early developmental programs and preschool programs to enhance language and social skills.
- Incorporate systematic assessment strategies, including continuous progress monitoring and formative evaluation, to enable ongoing modification of instructional efforts.
- Provide effective early reading programs.
- Implement effective school-based mental health programs.
- Use student support teams to assess and identify specific learning or behavior problems, design interventions to address those problems, and evaluate the efficacy of those interventions.
- Use effective behavior management and cognitive behavior modification strategies to reduce classroom behavior problems.

- Provide appropriate education services for children with educational disabilities, including collaboration between regular, remedial, and special education professionals.
- Offer extended year, extended day, and summer school programs that focus on facilitating the development of academic skills.
- Implement tutoring and mentoring programs with peer, cross-age, or adult tutors.
- Incorporate comprehensive schoolwide programs to promote the psychosocial and academic skills of all students.
- Establish full-service schools to provide a community-based vehicle for the organization and delivery of educational, social, and health services to meet the diverse needs of at-risk students. (pp. 2-3)

In addition to academic needs, the recommendations target social, emotional, and motivational factors. These recommendations are appropriate for all students, not just those who are at risk for retention.

Some Alternatives to Retention

A number of districts have adopted absolute standards for promotion. The most common standards are to retain students if they aren't reading on grade level or if they don't achieve a certain score on a high-stakes test. Setting absolute standards penalizes students who are making good progress but might be so far behind that they are unable to reach the absolute standard. Along with the absolute standards, consider how much progress students are making. Students who are making a year's progress in a year's time are making average progress. If students are significantly behind, plan a program that will help them to make better-than-average progress. Set long-term goals. It would be extremely difficult, if not impossible, for students who are three years behind to make three years of progress in a year's time. However, a student might be able to catch up if given extra help over a period of four years or so.

Alternatives to retaining students should be considered. Maybe they would benefit from an after-school, Saturday, or summer program. Maybe they need a more intensive intervention program, one that consists of one-to-one tutoring. Retention is a drastic step. Before students are forced to spend an extra year in a grade, every attempt should be made to bolster the students' achievement or make an alternate plan so that retention is not necessary.

Students should not be retained on the basis of performance on a single test, especially a group test. If students are failing because they did not make the cutoff in reading but are doing satisfactory work in other areas, analyze their status in reading. Since group tests can be misleading, administer an informal reading inventory. Based on the student's performance, note whether he would be able to read on-level texts if provided with assistance or he would fit into a below-grade level group in the next grade. Note, too, the difference between where the student is and where he should be. Calculate what he would need to learn to reach the benchmark. Based on your analysis, plan a program of intervention or compensation. Provide help during the school year. If possible, provide 30 to 45 minutes of additional assistance before or after school on a daily basis for a significant period of time, for the entire year if necessary. Also enlist the aid of the home. Make sure that the student is reading on his own for at least 20 to 30 minutes a night. Schedule the student for a summer program that builds skills and an incentive program in which the students reads five to ten books during the summer. Monitor progress and make adjustments as necessary. If the student fails to make progress, schedule a thorough diagnostic assessment. The student might have a serious learning problem that requires specialized instruction. Before being retained students should be given a diagnostic assessment. Their instructional program should also be examined. Examine students' opportunity to learn. Analyze the benchmark that the students failed to meet. Note whether it reflects skills, strategies, and content taught in the students' program. If, for instance, the test assesses map skills, but map skills weren't taught, then the students were unfairly penalized. Note how well the students did in those areas that were taught. Perhaps there are barriers to their progress that might be removed. There might not be a match between their needs and the program in which they have been placed.

Getting an Early Start: Kindergarten and Preschool

One way of gaining more gap-closing time is to start early. Both kindergarten, especially if it is a full-day one, and preK programs can get students off to a more equitable start.

Kindergarten

Kindergarten children vary greatly in their literacy knowledge. In the fall of 1998, 22,000 kindergartners were assessed to determine their basic literacy skills (West, Denton, & Germino-Hausken, 2000). Print familiarity skills such as knowing that print reads left to right, knowing where to go when a line of print ends, and knowing where the story ends were assessed. Some 82 percent of kindergartners exhibited knowledge of at least one of these three skills. About two-thirds of kindergartners can name the letters of the alphabet. However, only 29 percent can point to letters representing sounds at the beginning of words, and only 17 percent can recognize final consonant sounds. Only about two children out of a hundred can read high-frequency words. And only about one in a hundred can read simple sentences. However, children raised in poverty are less proficient. Only 68 percent of children whose parents have received welfare evidenced some print familiarity. Only 41 percent of children whose caregivers are receiving welfare benefits can identify the letters of the alphabet. A greater percentage of children raised in poverty are also judged to have more difficulty forming friendships and accepting the ideas of their peers. They are also seen as being less eager to learn, less attentive, and less persistent.

Although some kindergarten children raised in poverty have the same level of literacy skills and the same level of social skills and motivation as do children from the most privileged families, a greater percentage of children whose caregivers are receiving welfare have limited literacy, social skills, and command of behaviors necessary for learning. Obviously, these students require a more intensive and extensive program in kindergarten. More attention will have to be paid to social and work skills as well as to literacy skills.

Unfortunately, based on an examination of a large number of schools that participated in DIBELS, which is a continuous progress monitoring system that assesses letter knowledge and phonological awareness in kindergarten, Good and associates (2002) concluded that most schools have shortcomings in their kindergarten programs. Based on students' performance on letter knowledge and phonological awareness, the researchers concluded that overall about 15 percent of kindergarten students will need intensive intervention. About 17 percent of students will need some added instruction. However, these percentages vary from school to school. Schools with large numbers of at-risk students might have a larger percentage of students who need intensive intervention or extra help. The researchers also concluded that most kindergartens do not have an adequate program for phonological awareness. The schools may not spend enough time on phonological awareness, may not provide enough instruction for at-risk learners, and may not key in on the most essential skills.

The degree of successful intervention varied widely. On average about 26 percent of students receiving intervention reached the program's goals, which is the ability to segment words into their component sounds by the end of kindergarten. However, in schools that had well-planned, systematic programs, nearly all the intervention students reached the program's goals (Good et al., 2002). Effective programs focus on the most important skills. The most important skills in phonological awareness are detecting initial consonants (Stahl & McKenna, 2002), blending, and segmenting (National Reading Panel, 2000). The most effective programs also integrate instruction in phonemic awareness with instruction in letter-sound relationships. Conversely, the programs might move into blending and segmenting too soon (Good et al., 2002). At-risk students might need to build a firmer foundation by spending more time with rhyming and detecting initial sounds.

Preschool Programs

Based on a survey of four hundred kindergarten teachers working in impoverished areas who assessed the development of their children, researchers concluded that preK attendance made a dramatic difference in children's progress in kindergarten (Benson, 2003). Children with two years of preschool were judged as being twice as likely to be proficient in language and literacy and one and a half times as likely to have the social and emotional skills and fine motor skills needed for success in kindergarten. Parents of children who attended preschool were more heavily involved with their children's education. English as a second language (ELL) students who attended preschool for two years performed significantly better in language and literacy, math, social/emotional, and fine motor skills than ELL children with one year of preschool.

Despite the dramatic difference that two years of preschool made, it wasn't adequate. Only 65 percent of students who completed two years of preschool were judged to be ready for the demands of kindergarten. Adherence to quality standards, implementation of a systematic program of cognitive, language, and literacy development, and better training for preschool providers were recommended for preschool along with improved transition between preschool and kindergarten.

Quality of Preschool Varies

High-quality preschool programs can be highly effective. For instance, the Perry Preschool project, which was conducted in Michigan from 1962 and 1967, and the Abcedarian project, which was implemented in North Carolina from 1972 to 1985, had dramatic long-term effects. At age twenty-one, children from the Abcederian Project had higher tests scores and were twice as likely to have stayed in school or to have ever attended a four-year college than children who did not. As of age forty, graduates of the Perry Preschool projects had higher test scores, had spent more years in school, were less likely to be on welfare, earned more money, and were less likely to have been incarcerated (Schweinhart, 2004). Because of the preschool program, graduates were more highly motivated, were better prepared cognitively, and were better behaved. As a result, they did better in school and were less likely to engage in antisocial behavior. Information about setting up a program using Perry Preschool High/Scope principles is available at http://www.highscope.org/Educational Programs/Early Childhood/preschoolkeyexp.htm. *Teaching Our Youngest: Guide for Preschool Teachers and Child Care and Family Providers* (Early Childhood-Head Start Task Force, 2002) is a downloadable booklet published by the Department of Education that provides a good overview of approaches for building preliteracy and language skills in preschoolers.

A series of ten standards for programs for early childhood programs have been established by the National Association for the Education of Young Children (NAEYC). The six standards that apply most directly to literacy include the following.

- The program promotes positive relationships among all children and adults to encourage each child's sense of individual worth and belonging as part of a community and to foster each child's ability to contribute as a responsible community member.

- The program implements a curriculum that is consistent with its goals for children and promotes learning and development in each of the following domains: aesthetic, cognitive, emotional, language, physical, and social.
- The program uses developmentally, culturally, and linguistically appropriate and effective teaching approaches that enhance each child's learning and development in the context of the program's curriculum goals.
- The program is informed by ongoing systematic, formal, and informal assessment approaches to provide information on children's learning and development. These assessments occur within the context of reciprocal communications with families and with sensitivity to the cultural contexts in which children develop. Assessment results are used to benefit children by informing sound decisions about children, teaching, and program improvement.
- The program employs and supports a teaching staff that has the educational qualifications, knowledge, and professional commitment necessary to promote children's learning and development and to support families' diverse needs and interests.
- The program establishes and maintains collaborative relationships with each child's family to foster children's development in all settings. These relationships are sensitive to family composition, language, and culture (National Association for the Education of Young Children, 2002).

Head Start Programs

Unfortunately, Head Start programs vary in quality and so may not match the achievement of the Perry Preschool High/Scope and Abcederian projects. However, Head Start programs are generally more effective than privately run preschools. Although originally emphasizing social, emotional, and health factors, Head Start programs are now attempting to provide a better balance of social-emotional health and cognitive factors. Many Head Start programs use some or a portion of the High/Scope curriculum. Head Start programs have also begun devoting more time to early literacy activities. On graduating from Head Start, children are expected to "know that the letters of the alphabet are a special category of visual graphics that can be individually named; recognize a word as a unit of print; identify at least ten letters of the alphabet; and associate sounds with written words" (Taylor, 2001, p. 2). Participation in Head Start was found to reduce the Latino-white score gap in vocabulary, math, and reading between one-quarter and one-third (Walker-James, Jurich, & Estes, 2001). Head Start now serves approximately 800,000 children. However, this is only about one-third of those eligible.

Importance of Extended Support

Although getting off to a good start is important, it is not sufficient. Unfortunately, some programs have a fade-out effect. Initial gains gradually disappear. This is less likely to happen if there is adequate follow-up. When given two or more years of extended support after participating in a preschool program, poor children in Chicago maintained higher reading achievement, experienced fewer retentions, and were less likely to be placed in a special education program. These results were maintained up through seventh grade (Reynolds & Temple, 1998).

Longer-lasting and involving more children is a program known as Chicago's Child-Parent Centers (CPC). Graduates of CPC were much more likely to finish high school and less likely to be held back a grade, drop out, or get arrested (Reynolds & Temple, 1998). They also had higher achievement in reading. A distinguishing feature of the program was that it was continued beyond pre-school. Chicago youngsters participate in CPC for up to six years. CPC is designed for three-, four- and five-year-olds living in impoverished neighborhoods. How-ever, the sites also offer an in-school component that reduces class size and pro-vides one-on-one tutoring and a staffed parent room for children in grades 1–3. CPC has a better trained staff than most preschools. CPC teachers are more experi-enced and more highly trained, on average, than Head Start teachers. And, per-haps most important, CPC is much more focused than Head Start on getting children ready to learn to read.

Chicago's public schools also sponsor an interactive Web site, Virtual Prek (https://www.virtualpre-k.org/), that is designed for preschool parents as well as teachers. A series of short video lessons and Web site sessions provide demonstra-tions and activities for preK children. The program's resources are available in both English and Spanish.

Need for Transitioning

Despite the obvious value of preschool, many schools fail to proved a transition between preschool and kindergarten. Currie (2001) found that only 38 percent of the kindergarten teachers had policies or guidelines for transitioning the children into their classes. Nearly all the teachers agreed on the importance of working with preschools to foster success in kindergarten. They even suggested specific strategies to improve transitions, such as record sharing, shared curriculum, meet-ings with preschool teachers, and shared professional development trainings. However, only 20 percent of kindergarten teachers met with children, parents, or preschool teachers.

Assessing the Use of Extra Resources Component of Your Program

To close the literacy gap, students who are behind need extra time and extra help. A close-the-gap program needs to offer extra resources. Use the checklist in Table 10.1 to determine strengths and weaknesses of the extra resources component of your program.

BOX

10.1

Exemplary PreK Program: Bright Beginnings

The Charlotte-Mecklenburg Pre-Kindergarten Program, Bright Beginnings, is designed to provide a preparatory program for four-year-olds judged to be at greatest risk for having difficulty in kindergarten and beyond (Smith, Pellin, & Agruso, 2003). The overall objective is to ensure that all children in Mecklenburg County (North Carolina) enter kindergarten ready to learn. Bright Beginnings currently serves approximately three thousand students in 157 classrooms. In addition to promoting social and personal objectives, the program seeks to develop oral language and literacy skills. General literacy skills include being able to listen to and comprehend stories read aloud and acquiring concepts of print. Specific literacy skills include beginning to hear rhyming words, beginning to identify words that begin with the same sound, identifying and naming letters, being able to identify own name in print, and exploring writing.

The curriculum is a balanced one, with an emphasis on concrete real-life experiences and exploration. The curriculum is aligned with the kindergarten program of the Charlotte-Mecklenburg schools. Each spring, kindergarten teachers and principals are invited to visit Bright Beginnings classes to meet the students who will be coming to their schools. In addition, extensive assessment data is sent to the schools. Lists of children who have participated in Bright Beginnings are sent to principals so that the principals can see to it that their schools build on the concepts and skills that the Bright Beginnings graduates have acquired.

Parents are active partners in the program and are asked to read one hundred books to their children. Books are supplied by the centers. Teachers visit homes during the week before schools start to explain the program to parents, to get additional information about the children, and to provide parents with some tips for working with their children. Each of the program's units has a Family Connection Activity. This is a description of things that parents might do to reinforce and extend the unit's key concepts and skills. Surveys are also sent to parents to find out about their hopes and dreams for their children and their ideas for activities. Workshops for parents are held frequently.

Bright Beginnings makes extended use of community resources. Both public and private agencies and volunteers provide health, tutoring, and other services and materials. Students who complete the Bright Beginnings program are better prepared for kindergarten than those who haven't participated in it. Bright Beginnings graduates also do better in reading and are less likely to be retained. The program narrows the gap between Bright Beginnings children and children who are not educationally disadvantaged. The gain is most pronounced at the end of grade 1, but fades somewhat at the end of grades 2 and 3. Evaluators of the program conclude that more effort needs to be put into K–3 programs so as to capitalize on the gains that Bright Beginnings children made:

> Most educationally needy four-year-old children continue to live in educationally needy environments; thus, it is important that intense, literacy-focused attention and learning resources be provided for these children and their families at least through

continued

BOX
10.1 *Exemplary PreK Program: Bright Beginnings* (continued)

Grade 3 in order to close the literacy gap. Results of the follow-up studies of Bright Beginnings participants indicate the need in grades K–3 for more effective literacy interventions, more learning resources for educationally needy children, more effective teaching, smaller classes, and increased family involvement similar to that in Bright Beginnings in order to sustain the initial momentum provided by the Bright Beginnings experience. (Smith, Pellin, & Agruso, 2003, p. 103)

TABLE 10.1 *Assessment Checklist for the Use of Extra Resources in a Literacy Program*

Action	*Fully*	*Partially*	*Limited*	*Suggestions*
Students who need it are provided with tutoring.				
Tutors are well trained, provided with necessary materials, and supervised.				
If used, student tutors are well prepared and supervised.				
Students who need it are given extra help outside of school hours.				
Extensive, carefully planned summer school sessions are offered.				
Special programs are set up to encourage students to read during the summer months.				
In lieu of being retained, students not making adequate progress are provided with extra help.				
Children are encouraged to attend preschool and kindergarten.				
Kindergarten and preK programs offer developmentally appropriate literacy activities.				
Transition is provided between preK and kindergarten and between kindergarten and first grade.				
Skills learned in intervention programs are built on in the classroom.				
Parental support is enlisted.				

11

Organizing to Close the Gap

Closing the gap requires optimizing the literacy program. It requires making the best possible use of time and resources. It takes the concentrated efforts of the total school staff to beat the odds. It also requires the wholehearted cooperation of parents and the community at large. A first step toward bringing everyone together is to set up a literacy committee.

Literacy Committee

The literacy committee should include parents as well as teachers, administrators, and specialists. The literacy committee sets up literacy goals for the schools. Based on the goals, the committee creates a program. The program includes specific

BOX

11.1

Model Program: Literacy Committee Fosters Cooperation

Realizing that pullout intervention programs can be disruptive to class schedules, the literacy committee in Alleman's (2003) school set up block schedules so that students participating in pullout programs would lose the least amount of time. The committee set up criteria for intervention, enlisted the PTO in obtaining "gently used" books and in leveling books. The committee also put out an easy-to-understand description of tests administered to students. But perhaps the committee's biggest achievement was to create a sense of mission and solidarity. Instead of categorizing students as being the responsibility of the ESL teacher or the special education teacher or the reading specialist, they adopted a "these are our kids" attitude with everybody pitching in for the common purpose of helping the children become the best readers and writers they could be. The committee met twice a month for an hour before school.

objectives, materials, teaching approaches, an evaluation component, and group-ing patterns. In addition to a core program, there should be intervention programs for those who fail to make adequate progress in the core program. Other areas of concern include the following.

- Guidelines for intervening
- Guidelines for diagnosis
- Program for involving parents
- Program for involving the community
- Monitoring of school's progress
- Plans for improvement
- Program of professional development
- Program of voluntary reading

Grade-Level Meetings

Schools are most effective when teachers work together. Along with a literacy committee, there should also be grade-level groups. Meeting on a regular basis gives teachers the opportunity to share their expertise and to learn from others. Possible topics include an analysis of screening data, discussion of program imple-mentation, discussion of students who are having difficulty, discussion of success-ful practices, consideration of possible improvements, and discussion of factors that are hindering progress in closing the gap. Grade-level meetings work best when they are held on a regular basis and have an agreed-on format and agenda. An ongoing item on the agenda is whether the actions formulated at previous meetings have been carried out. At Urban Public, grade-level meetings became more productive when attendees began filling out a form summarizing topics cov-ered and listing actions planned or taken. Without planning, grade-level meetings run the risk of becoming a forum for registering complaints.

Grade-level meetings should be complemented with cross-grade level meet-ings. This provides an opportunity to discuss broader concerns and to plan a pro-gram that is articulated across grade levels. In addition, it promotes teamwork and a whole-school spirit.

Organizational Factors That Help Close the Gap

There are a number of organizational factors that can help close the gap. These are generally factors that add to the amount of instructional time and to the effective-ness of the way that time is used.

Smaller Class Sizes

Smaller class sizes can result in increased achievement. In a four-year study con-ducted in Tennessee, students in small classes (thirteen to seventeen students) outperformed students in larger classes (Finn, Gerber, Achilles, & Boyd-Zaharias, 2001). In the STAR (Student/Teacher Achievement Ratio) study, minority students benefited the most, and the results were long lasting. Two years after having been in smaller classes, fifth-graders, on average, were five months ahead of students who had been in regular-sized classes. Students in smaller classes behaved better, responded more, and were more fully engaged in classroom activities. Teachers believed that smaller classes also made it easier to individualize instruction. In a more extensive study, teachers in California report increased individualization when class sizes were reduced (Bohrnstedt & Stechter, 2000). Teachers in smaller classes reported spending more time with small groups and more time working with individuals.

Time

In a sense, time is the great enemy of closing the gap. Closing the gap means that students must not only make average progress but also must make progress over and above average so that they can catch up. There are two issues involved: arranging for more time and using time well. Schools need to set aside additional time for literacy instruction. Time set aside might range from one and a half to two and a half hours. However, that time should be protected. No announcements, no specials, no interruptions. In some schools, pullout programs are not held at that time so children aren't leaving their literacy block to attend a reading intervention or other special programs. Literacy intervention should be additive to optimize its impact.

As important as how much time is set aside for instruction is how that time is used. The ideal is a 100/100 class: 100 percent of the students are on task 100 percent of the time. Even the best teachers fail to achieve that standard, but they do hit 90/90 (Taylor, Pearson, Clark, & Walpole, 2002). Through carefully planned routines and transitions, they're able to make the most of time.

However, using time efficiently isn't the same thing as using it well. Teaching students what they already know is a waste of time, and it's boring. For example, several studies have demonstrated that most of the words slated for introduction in reading programs are already known (Ryder & Graves, 1994). By examining the words listed for introduction, you can eliminate those that students probably know. Or you could simply list the words on the chalkboard and ask the students which ones seem difficult and focus on those. Follow similar procedures with phonics elements and other skills.

Grouping

Students do better when taught in small groups and when they are grouped according to common needs (Foorman & Torgesen, 2001; Juel & Minden-Cupp, 2000; National Reading Panel, 2000). In small groups, students' needs can be met more easily, they have more opportunity to respond, and the teacher is better able to assess their progress and adjust instruction accordingly. Groups, however, should be flexible. Students should be moved to higher-performing groups when their progress warrants it.

High-Payoff Activities

To optimize the use of time, you need to look at each activity and make sure that it has a high payoff. Putting together a diorama, for instance, might not justify the time involved, especially if there is little or no reading and writing involved. A good way to assess your use of time would be to videotape or audiotape a lesson and then calculate how much time was spent on instruction, how much on explaining directions, how much on transitions, and how much on interruptions and discipline. A checklist for assessing time use is presented in Table 11.1.

Providing Extra Practice

Practice is a crucial part of learning to read and write, especially when it's guided so that mistakes and missteps are corrected. Practice fosters fluency. However, practice can also foster accuracy. One result of practice, especially in the early stages of learning, is that it provides students with the opportunity to adapt the skill so that can apply it properly. As they practice summarizing, for instance, students might become aware that they are including too many nonessential details. Through practice they can modify their strategy application so that they become better at focusing on essential details. During initial practice sessions, the focus should be on looking at a few samples in depth, rather than looking at a large number of examples. For instance, when practicing locating the main idea, students might focus on a few selections and take time to discuss their responses so

TABLE 11.1 *Checklist for Use of Time*

Activities	Time	Comments	Activities	Time	Comments
Instruction			Writing		
Guided Practice/ Application			Seatwork		
			Centers		
Silent reading			Computer		
Oral reading			Discussion Group		
Writing			Other		
Seatwork					
Centers			*Management*		
Computer			Directions		
Discussion Group			Transitions		
Other			Discipline		
			Interruptions		
Independent Practice/ Application					
Silent reading					
Oral reading					

that they can modify their concept of what a main idea is or how to find or construct one. It would be better to focus on three passages in depth rather than complete a series of five or more passages (Marzano, Gaddy, & Dean, 2000).

Homework

One traditional means of providing additional practice is homework. A controversial subject, homework is an important part of closing the gap. Well-planned homework assignments provide students with much-needed independent practice. Because homework is completed on the students' time, it adds to the total amount of time on task without using up valuable instructional minutes. However, for homework to be effective, it is important that assignments be valuable and not just a form of busy work. Homework assignments should provide independent practice, and students should clearly understand what they are to do. Homework should not be so difficult that students require parents' help to complete it. However, parents' help should be enlisted in seeing to it that their children do take the assignments seriously and do complete them. It is helpful if schools have a homework policy that specifies the student's role as well as the parents' role and places limitations on the amount of homework given.

Homework is also more effective when the school emphasizes its importance. Homework that is graded or has comments has more than twice the payoff than homework that is not graded or has not been commented on (Marzano, Gaddy, & Dean, 2000). In addition, homework has greater payoffs for older students than it does for younger students. One reason might be that older students typically have more homework.

Challenging Work: Standards in Practice

It isn't just the quantity of work that leads to higher achievement; it's also the quality. Students should be given challenging assignments for which they have been prepared. If students can't meet the challenge, their work will show it, and the teacher will be alerted that some preparatory instruction is needed. In standards in practice meetings, teachers discuss whether assignments are aligned with standards, whether assignments are rigorous enough, what instruction students might need to reach the standards, and how all students might be helped to meet the standards (Education Trust, 2004). Where this has been implemented, teachers have begun to give students more challenging assignments and achievement has improved.

The Role of Paraeducators

Paraeducators can play a vital role in helping to close the gap if they are well trained and used wisely. (Under recently passed regulations, paraprofessionals paid with Title 1 funds and who have an instructional role must have a high school diploma or equivalent and two years of higher education and an associate's degree or must pass a formal assessment demonstrating knowledge of and the ability to assist with instruction in reading, writing, and math.) Currently there are more than 600,000 paraeducators working in the nation's schools (Northwest Regional Educational Laboratory, 2002). About 75 percent of paraeducators work in elementary schools. They are concentrated in Title 1 programs and bilingual programs and special education classes. Unfortunately, the role of the paraeducator is ill-defined, and teachers are given little instruction in the supervision of paraprofessionals. Often, paraeducators are omitted from professional development activities. Often, too, there is a lack of planning time so that teachers and paraprofessionals can talk over mutual concerns.

Duties performed by paraeducators vary. Some key duties include the following.

- Providing tutoring or other instruction if supervised by a teacher
- Organizing instructional materials
- Assisting with classroom management
- Obtaining data on pupil performance and keeping records
- Conducting parent involvement activities
- Assisting in a computer laboratory
- Assisting in a library or media center
- Acting as a translator

In general, paraeducators' instruction is delivered under the supervision of the teacher. It is important to clarify the role of the paraprofessional so the paraeducator is not over- or underutilized and conflicts don't arise. "Clearly differentiating between the role of teacher and paraeducator is important because they differ significantly, even though paraeducators and teachers often work side-by-side, appearing to perform similar tasks. . . . A guiding principle is this: Teachers provide leadership and clarify roles for paraeducators; paraeducators assist teachers in meeting their instructional goals. Various factors may affect the responsibilities assigned to paraeducators, such as their level of expertise in content areas and instruction" (Pickett, Vasa, & Steckelberg, 1993, p. 26). Paras should be prepared for the roles they perform. They should also be provided with feedback and professional development so that they can undertake increasingly more responsible, but appropriate, roles.

Paras should be made to feel that they are part of the instructional team. Paras might have a different working relationship with students and so might have a different perspective. Paras should be encouraged to supply feedback on the students they work with as well as suggestions. Often paraeducators are hired from the community and so would have specialized insight into the community. Paras should be encouraged to share their knowledge. Although paras should be provided with lessons plans, as they become more experienced and knowledgeable, they should be encouraged to adapt the plans.

Since teachers might not have worked with paras before, they should receive some training in this area. They should receive instruction in working collaboratively, supervision, communication, and delegation. They need to see how paras might make an optimal contribution. Teachers and their paras should have at least a half-hour each week to plan together.

The Role of Test Preparation

When students read more, instruction and assessment are aligned, and teaching is more focused, students' achievement improves and test scores go up. It isn't necessary to institute an extensive program of test practice. In fact, implementing extensive programs of test preparation may actually limit students' progress. However, there are steps that can be taken to make sure that test results reflect the genuine gains that your students have made. The most effective step is to integrate key content and skills that are tested into your curriculum (see Chapter 5 for more information on test preparation). For instance, in Connecticut, the state competency test has a large number of questions that require students to give evidence for judgments that they make about a selection. Instead of having students complete test-prep passages in which they justify responses, it is more effective and more authentic if, as part of your discussions and assignments, you ask students to quote passages from the selection that prove that the main character is kind or that prove the statement, "Hard work pays off in the end," is the theme of the story. Justifying responses is a legitimate reading skill and should be a part of the curriculum.

If a rubric is used to assess test essays or open-ended responses to test questions, use the same type of rubric to judge students' work. Discuss the rubric so that students understand it. If appropriate, use the same formats in your tests and quizzes that are used in the high-stakes assessments that your students will be taking.

High-stakes tests sometimes ask questions or assess areas that wouldn't normally be a part of your instruction. For instance, in the assessment of the main idea on one state's proficiency test, students are asked to supply an alternate title and justify their response. In the real world, we aren't asked to suggest new titles and explain why. As a practical matter, spend some time, but not too much, asking students to supply new titles. They have a right to be prepared for the kinds of tests they will be required to complete.

In her study of high-performing versus low-performing schools, Langer (2004) found that schools in which teachers incorporated test skills into the curriculum outperformed schools that focused on test preparation. Higher-performing schools used tests to examine their language arts programs. They analyzed the tests so as to note which skills and strategies were being assessed and then revised their programs to include assessed skills. Some time, but not an excessive amount, was spent instructing students in test-taking skills and in familiarizing them with the test format (Langer, 2004).

> Overall, higher-performing schools seemed to focus on students' overall literacy learning, using the tests to be certain skills and knowledge that are tested are related to and being learned within the framework of improved language arts instruction. They regarded tests as one of many literacy activities students needed to learn to do well and believed that the underlying skills and knowledge to do

well in coursework thus needed to be encompassed within the ongoing curriculum. In contrast, the more typical schools viewed test performance as a separate goal, apart from the regular curriculum. Therefore, they saw test preparation as requiring a focus on the tests themselves, with raising test scores, rather than improving students' literacy learning, as the primary goal. (Langer, 2004, p. 1066)

At Foshay Middle School, teachers met and used the high-stakes test to identify areas of need (Langer, 2004). Uncovering difficulties in vocabulary, reading comprehension, and spelling, they planned lessons that would integrate instruction in these areas into the curriculum. They also developed a series of model lessons that showed how these areas might be fostered within the regular curriculum. In Dade County, teachers and administrators met and, after analyzing the new writing assessment, created a curriculum that stresses the kinds of writing skills and strategies that would enable students to write well-developed, polished pieces. The writing curriculum was enriched. At Springfield High School, teachers enhanced vocabulary and writing instruction to meet test demands. Although the staff of high-performing schools had varying ways of preparing their students for the demands of high-stakes testing, all had a sense of efficacy. They believed that their students could do well on the tests and that they could prepare them for the tests by providing a program that integrates assessed skills into the regular curriculum.

In higher-performing schools, teachers used standards and assessment to improve their programs. As high school teacher Celeste Rotundi explains:

> Standards, as much as they're a kind of pain . . . when we have these meetings and align the standards and all that stuff, it has helped me. . . . My curriculum is strong. But once I started looking at the standards I realized I didn't have a lot of oral writing activities, and so it kind of helped me to conceptualize that a little better and forced me to incorporate that. (Langer, 2004, p. 1068)

In many locales where students are required to take a high-stakes writing assessment that involves writing a piece, an inordinate amount of time is spent writing to practice prompts. As Fletcher and Portalupi (2001) note, a testing environment differs dramatically from a workshop environment. However, writing workshops properly implemented should prepare students for whatever writing assessment they encounter.

> Your students need time to write their hearts out; to explore many different subjects; to write deeply about a single one. They need to write for the fun of it, and at times they need coaches by their sides stretching them to write with more precision and craft.
>   It boils down to this: Your students will perform fine on these tests as long as you provide them with regular opportunities for writing in the workshop. (Fletcher & Portalupi, 2001, p. 110)

However, the writing program should include some instruction in composing on-demand responses and writing to test prompts, as discussed in Chapter 5.

Danger of Excessive Test Preparation

One danger of excessive test preparation is that it takes the enjoyment out of learning. Instead of being intrigued by reading interesting stories or writing about topics that they care about, students become bogged down in reading test-type selections and writing to prompts. Perhaps, as a result of the increasing pressure of high-stakes tests and widespread test preparation, students are less engaged in learning. The percentage of children who are highly engaged in school has declined. Children's engagement in school was measured by asking parents questions such as whether their child "cares about doing well in school," "only works on schoolwork when forced to," "does just enough schoolwork to get by," and "always does homework." The percentage of six- to eleven-year-olds who had a high level of engagement in school dropped from 43.1 in 1997 to 34.7 in 2002. For twelve- to seventeen-year-olds, the percentage dropped from 38.2 to 30.9 (Vandivere, Gallagher, & Moore, 2004).

Using Technology to Close the Gap

Technology is motivational and provides another means of learning. Students who lack access to hardcopy reference sources or homework help can find a wealth of materials on the Web. Sources of high-quality sites include the following.

Awesome Library
http://www.awesomelibrary.org/
Awesome Library has 22,000 carefully reviewed resources and browses in fourteen languages. Awesome Library also has detailed suggestions for conducting searches. Students can search by keyword, subject, or index. Awesome Library also has a link to a child-safe version of the Google search engine.

Awesome Talkster
http://www.awesomelibrary.org/Awesome_Talking_Library.html
Combines a browser, a directory, a search engine, and text-to-voice technology. Students can have whole pages read to them or they can select the text they wish to have spoken. Awesome Library is accessible to all computers. Awesome Talkster is only accessible to PCs.

Enchanted Learning
http://www.EnchantedLearning.com
Enchanted Learning is probably the richest source of free educational materials on the Web. The site has hundreds of informational articles on a wide range of topics; a vast variety of activity sheets and games designed to foster literacy; a number of posters, calendars, and craft projects; and an extensive picture dictionary. Materials are available in eight languages. Materials are free, but for a nominal fee subscribers can obtain materials that do not contain announcements or other extraneous information.

Great Web Sites for Kids
http://www.ala.org/ala/alsc/greatwebsites/greatwebsiteskids.htm
Sponsored by the American Library Association and the Association for Library Service to Children, it is probably the best source of suitable sites. Sites have been assessed by professional librarians and judged to meet strict criteria for quality and usefulness. Sites, which are designed for students from ages four through fourteen, are designated as being appropriate for preK, elementary, or middle school.

School Resources Library
http://www.schoolresources.com
School Resources Library contains four thousand classic texts including the *Adventures of Pinocchio, Aesop's Fables, Grimms' Fairy Tales,* and *Rebecca of Sunnybrook Farm.* They can be read online or downloaded. The site also contains the World Factbook Web Edition. The Factbook features thousands of full-color pages containing information about every country in the world. Reading level is middle school or beyond.

Using e-books

Some students might be motivated by the novelty of e-books. Because they are in a digital format, e-books have a number of advantages. For one thing, they can be read by a screen reader, such as Awesome Talkster, or a talking word-processing program, such as Co:Writer (Don Johnston). This makes them accessible to struggling readers. To make them even more accessible, e-books can be linked to a dictionary so that students can readily get help with difficult words. A third advantage is that the text can be added to or altered. Teachers might add explanatory notes or illustrations or even rewrite difficult portions. E-books are readily available on the Web from a number of sources. The International Children's Digital Library (ICDL) features a collection of multicultural e-books in dozens of languages for children ages three to thirteen. Guided tours explain to students how to locate books by topic, genre, author, title, or country where the book was written.

Other extensive sources of digital books include Project Gutenburg (http://www.promo.net/pg/) and the University of Virginia (http://etext.lib.virginia.edu/). The University of Virginia has a Young Readers collection of public domain texts. Texts can be downloaded using commercial readers such as the Microsoft Reader or the Palm Pilot Reader or HTML. Some e-books incorporate study skills such as electronic note taking, underlining, and bookmarking. Digital materials can also be used when materials are in short supply but funds are limited. In addition to free e-books, there are a number of commercially produced e-books available.

Free and Inexpensive SourceS of Materials

Many government agencies, such as NASA, educational institutions, libraries, museums, professional organizations, and commercial groups offer a variety of activities and downloadable materials. In addition, there are a number of Web sites that offer materials for a small subscription fee. Reading A-Z (http://www. readinga-z.com) offers extensive reading materials and lesson plans for a small subscription fee. Included are decodable books, leveled readers for guided reading, worksheets, and lesson plans. Another site, Mighty Book (http://www. mightybook.com), offers read-alouds, sing-alongs, and brief videos.

Learning Aids

Technology provides a number of learning aids that can compensate for reading and writing difficulties and also build literacy skills. Key aids include spell checkers, built-in dictionaries, and thesauruses, editing functions, and text-to-speech capability. Most word-processing programs now incorporate spell checkers, dictionaries, and editing functions.

Text-to-Speech Software

Text-to-speech software reads printed text. Most computers have text-to-speech software built in. Commercial programs typically include a highlighting function so that the text is highlighted as it is being read. This helps students follow along and match what they hear with what they see. Reading along with text is an effective easy way to build fluency. Text-to-speech programs include the following.

- Write:OutLoud. Easy-to-use talking word processor. Voice and rate of speech can be adjusted. Has a number of writing aids. Can be combined with Co:Writer.
- Cast ereader (http://www.cast.org). Reads aloud and highlights text from the Internet or word-processing programs.
- WYNN Reader (Freedom Scientific). Highlights text and reads it aloud. Also has word prediction, outlining, and note-taking features.

As noted above, text-to-speech software is also available at Awesome Talkster (http://www.awesomelibrary.org/Awesome_Talking_Library.html).

Behavior Management

It goes without saying that schools need an orderly environment where students feel safe and teachers are free to teach. One characteristic of schools that beat the odds is that they have created an environment conducive to learning. In all of the schools that beat the odds, clear rules were set down, often in consultation with students. A sense of responsibility was fostered by linking consequences to behavior. With clear, consistent rules and predictable consequences, students found it easier to take responsibility for their behavior. Positive behavior was affirmed. Several schools adopted behavior management systems. Teachers also worked together to support positive behavior. Personal relationships were established. The principal and other

BOX 11.2   *Exemplary Programs: Materials for Students with Disabilities*

For students who have physical limitations such as blindness, periodicals and books are available in Braille, large print, and recordings from the National Library Services for the Blind and Physically Handicapped (http://lcweb.loc.gov/nls/). No fees are charged for any reading materials or playback devices. Students with severe reading problems are eligible for services. However, they must provide proof from a medical professional that the root cause of their reading difficulty is physical.

Recorded textbooks are available for students with reading disabilities, regardless of cause, from Recording for the Blind and Dyslexic (RFB&D) (http://www.rfbd.org). RFB&D is a private organization, so there are fees involved, and playback equipment must be purchased. In an experiment comparing students who read a ninth-grade social studies textbook in a normal way with students who read recorded versions, those using the recorded versions learned nearly twice as much (Boyle et al.,

school administrators were highly visible. Principals knew students by name and also their families. Teachers and administrators listened to the concerns of students. Counseling was supplied when needed. Being listened to, students felt respected and valued. Mutual respect was at the core of the behavior management program. Students came to realize that teachers cared about them and were working hard to teach them. As Johnson (2002) comments:

> Ultimately, student behavior was also improved by the improvement of academic instruction in classrooms. Students were more likely to be actively engaged in learning. They were more likely to be excited about the level of challenge and rigor in their curriculum. They were more likely to be positive about their chances to succeed academically. Thus, there was less of a need for students to seek attention through negative behavior. Improved instruction led to improved discipline, which led to even better instruction. (p. 103)

Responsive Classroom

The responsive classroom is based on the idea that positive learning behavior can be taught (Charney, 2002). It is nonpunitive and uses the concept of natural consequences. A student who wastes time and doesn't get work done must do it during his own free time. A student who knocks over another's display must help the other student restore it. Responsive classroom is also based on the concept of choices. Students have a choice of obeying the class's rules or going to time-out, of talking in soft voices during center time or of not being able to talk at all. The responsive classroom also conveys a positive message: I care about you; it's not that I am correcting you as a person; it's your behavior. There is no sarcasm, personal attacks, or threats.

Routines

In the responsive classroom, the teacher takes time to teach routines. Routines are demonstrated and practiced until they are virtually automatic. Any activity that could be a source of disruption—including carrying chairs to a guided reading table—is taught.

Key Management Strategies

Three key classroom management strategies are reinforcing, reminding, and redirecting.

- Reinforcing: Affirms positive behavior. "You got right to work this morning. You remembered to bring your book from home. You tried to spell the hard words on your own."
- Reminding: Students are reminded of expected behaviors to prevent undesirable behaviors from occurring. "What do you do when someone else is trying to figure out a hard word or is thinking about an answer? What do you do when you go to the Word Study Center?"
- Redirecting: Students' off-task or disruptive behavior is redirected. "Keep your ears on me so you know what I'm saying." If a student is disruptive during class time—talking to a neighbor, for instance—start redirecting her behavior in low-key fashion but increase the intensity as necessary. Ways to redirect include the following.
    - A glance or gesture
    - A longer look
    - Words: "You need to pay attention."
    - Removal (students usually are given two warnings before being removed to time-out)

Logical Consequences

Logical consequences help students take responsibility for acting in a positive fashion. They lead students to reflect on their behavior rather than humiliating or embarrassing them. Using logical consequences, teachers work with rather than challenge students. Types of logical consequences include the following.

- Reparations: Student makes up for the damage or loss. Student fixes something he broke, apologizes for laughing at a classmate, or makes up for wasted time.
- Breach of contract: Student breaks rules and so loses privileges. "You haven't been taking care of the Writing Center. We must close it down until you learn to put things away."
- Time-out: Students take time to rethink their behavior.

Time-Out

Time-out is a choice. Students are given a choice of following the rules or directions or taking a time-out. For time-outs to be effective, students must believe that the teacher understands why they are not following the rules. They must also believe that the teacher cares for them and that time-out is an opportunity for them to reflect, settle down, or just get themselves calmed down so that they are able to rejoin the class. Time-outs are explained in matter-of-fact but caring fashion. "Samantha, I see that you aren't quite ready to work quietly. Take a time-out for a few minutes. Let me know when you are ready to get down to work." After a time-out, arrange for a check-in, which could be after class. Talk to the student about her behavior. Ask her what's going on. Ask if there is anything that you can help with. Note that time-out does not work for all students. About 5 percent of students are so difficult to handle that a team approach that includes parents is necessary.

Freeze

Freeze is an emergency signal. You can say "freeze," ring a bell, or simply use a nonverbal signal such as raising both hands in the air. When the freeze signal is given, students must give their immediate attention.

Other Responsive Classroom Elements

Other elements of the responsive classroom include guided discovery in which students discover in step-by-step fashion how to use a new set of materials, new device, or new literacy center; morning messages in which students learn to care about each other; academic choices in which students are provided with choices in their learning activities; classroom organizational style that maximizes learning; and a parent-school component. For more information about responsive classroom, see http://www.responsiveclassroom.org/.

The Role of Special Education

In high-performing schools, special education placement is viewed as a last resort. One-on-one tutoring, placement in intervention reading programs, providing extra help, and other measures are attempted before students are referred for special education testing. Special education placement is regarded as being temporary with the ultimate goal being to help the students return to full-time regular education. Special education teachers attend grade-level meetings and share their expertise with regular education teachers. Regular and special education teachers meet regularly to talk over such things as curriculum alignment and progress of students. Teachers at schools in which there is high achievement despite poverty and in which special education students are successful avoid the use of labels that might place limitations on students. They set high goals for all students.

Concept of Response to Intervention

In the latest version of the Individuals with Disabilities Education Act (IDEA), it is not necessary to show a discrepancy between a student's aptitude and achievement to establish a learning disability (LD). Response to intervention may be used to identify students with LD. A response to intervention means that the student has been provided with high-quality instruction but has failed to make adequate progress. In some schools, this is a three-tier process. In the first tier, the student is provided with high-quality instruction in the regular general education program. If the student falls behind, he is given supplementary instruction. This might be in small group or one-to-one. If the student stills fails to make progress, the student is provided with a more intensive program. Progress is carefully monitored. If the student still fails to make adequate progress, he is assessed for possible placement in special education.

The advantage of the response to instruction approach is that the focus is on prevention and intervention rather than on waiting for the student to fail. Because students are provided with high-quality classroom instruction, then with supplementary instruction, and finally with intensive instruction, most children will make progress. Response to intervention should greatly limit overidentification. If careful observations are made of the students' responses, this procedure should shed light on students' difficulties and also provide information on which interventions are effective for which students.

Using Effective Reading Programs to Close the Gap

Programs that have been effective in beating the odds take a number of forms. Some, such as the Calvert Program and Success for All, are highly structured, even scripted. Others, such as Bookshop (Mondo), which has been used successfully in a number of urban areas (Crèvola & Vineis, 2004), are more flexible. Bookshop is a commercial version of a teacher-directed guided reading program.

Guided Reading

Guided reading is a framework within which the teacher supplies whatever assistance or guidance students need for them to read successfully (Fountas & Pinnell, 1996). Guided reading is used with individuals or groups who are on approximately the same level of reading development. Reading materials are provided that match the students' level of development. The amount of guidance provided varies depending on the students' abilities and the complexity of the selection to be read. For beginning readers, the guidance might consist of conducting a text or picture walk, which consists of going through the text page by page, discussing the selection, and highlighting unfamiliar expressions, unknown concepts, and difficult words. For more advanced readers, guided reading includes making predictions and building needed background before students read a selection, silent reading, and a discussion of the selection after it has been read. "Although designed for all students, guided reading is a way of ensuring that struggling readers are given materials and instruction that is on their level" (Gunning, 2002, p. 529). Basal/anthologies include provision for guided reading but also advocate whole-class reading of selections.

Basal/Anthology Approach

Most teachers use a basal/anthology approach. Today's basal/anthology programs are more similar than different. All have strong synthetic phonics programs with decodable text (a switch is typically made from decodable to natural text about midway through first grade). However, the typical basal probably introduces too many phonics elements at one time, moves too fast, and doesn't provide enough reinforcement. The programs also fail to spend enough time explaining and reinforcing the use strategies such as the pronounceable word part. If you're using a basal, modify the program to adjust the pace, add reinforcement (basals have supplementary readers that can be used for this), and add strategy instruction as needed.

Optimizing Basal Instruction

Basals present an overwhelming number of teaching suggestions. If you're using a basal/anthology approach, select the activities that have the best payoffs. Reading always has a high payoff. Matching, filling in the blanks, and other workbook-type activities typically don't. In most instances, students are better off engaged in reading rather than completing workbook-type activities.

Basals also recommend whole-class teaching of the anthology's main selections so that everybody reads the same selection. The best readers read the target independently, average readers get help, and struggling readers have the selection read to them or read along with a recorded version. You don't have to be a rocket scientist to see who is being shortchanged. The poorest readers are reading the least. The research is clear on this point. Students get to be better readers by reading material that is on their level but with a little challenge (but not so much that they become frustrated). This fosters improvement of skills. The solution? Use materials that are on the students' level rather than the selection in the basal if it is too difficult for them.

Most basals provide suitable materials for struggling readers and may even provide a parallel program written on a lower level or that has easy-to-read alternatives for the anthology selections. The parallel selection is on the same topic as the main text selection but is easier to read and has activities designed to foster prerequisite skills. Because the program for struggling readers parallels the main program, some of the preparation and extension activities can be conducted with the whole class. In their intervention programs for students for whom the main text is too difficult, most basal publishers provides a summary of each of the selections in the main program. The summaries are written on a easy level so that there is a greater possibility that struggling readers will be able to read them. The purpose of the summaries is to enable struggling readers to have an opportunity to experience and discuss the main selection. Also provided are leveled readers that are written below grade level. Houghton Mifflin has a component known as Reader's Library, which is written below grade level. Stories follow the same themes and reinforce the same skills as those contained in the main anthology. In addition, there are libraries of leveled books on average, above-average, and below-average levels. The other basals have a similar component. One program, Harcourt, introduces the same vocabulary in its lower-level selections as is introduced in the core selection. Thus, the teacher is able to conduct a whole-class vocabulary lesson that helps prepare all students, even though they will be reading different selections.

Although the basals provide supplementary leveled readers for struggling students, these leveled readers are generally written to reinforce specific skills in the program and may not be of the same quality as leveled children's books. Insofar as possible, leveled readers supplied by the basal programs should be supplemented with children's books that are of higher quality and so do a better job of acquainting students with more fully developed characters and plot or a greater depth of information.

Basals also fail to adequately provide differentiated instruction in phonics and spelling. Whole-class lessons in spelling and phonics are suggested even though in virtually all classes, students are at different levels (Maslin, 2003). In his study of spelling achievement in grades 1 to 6, Schlagal (1982) found a range of at least three grade levels in each class. Although the basals suggest using assessment to determine where students are and to base instruction on assessment, "most of the programs suggested that students move through the program at the same pace, and suggestions for whole class instruction were the norm" (Invernizzi & Hayes, 2004, p. 223).

Another fault with basal readers is that they typically spend three days or more with the anthology's main selection. This is not the way to close the gap. Two days or even one day should be sufficient for a selection. Complete extension activities, if helpful, and move on. You can move on to the next selection or have students read from children's books. Basal teachers' manuals offer ample suggestions for additional reading and also have available libraries of children's books. In a study comparing students who read a variety of materials in supplementary readers to students who read the same basal anthology selection over and over again for a full week, the students who read a number of selections outperformed the students who read the same basal selection for a full week (Menon & Hiebert, 2005). After fifteen weeks, the low readers in the experimental group were reading as well as the average readers in the control group, and the average readers in the experimental group were reading just about as well as the higher achievers in the experimental group. By May, all but 10 percent of the students in the supplementary readers were reading at least at the primer or mid-first level. In the anthology group, a third of the students were reading below the primer level.

Alternatives to Basal Programs

One alternative to the use of basals is the use of guided reading with sets of trade books. In a teacher-directed guided reading approach, teachers obtain sets of trade books, both fiction and nonfiction, on a variety of levels and have students read these instead of basal anthologies. Bookshop is a commercial version of the guided reading/trade book approach that has been used successfully with struggling readers in Australia and the United States (Crèvola & Vineis, 2004). In the typical teacher-created guided reading program, the teacher must provide an assessment component, lesson plans, activities for skills development, and materials. These are provided for in Bookshop. One disadvantage of Bookshop is that the materials have been specifically produced for the program and don't include authentic literature, although the program does have a varied selection of high-quality informational texts. However, for teachers who want more control over their program but aren't quite ready to create their own guided reading program, Bookshop might be a good way to get started. As teachers become familiar with the approach, they can adapt it to suit their situation by adding other books and activities.

Reading Workshop (Individualized Reading)

In some ways, a program such as reader's workshop works better for struggling readers because all students read books on the appropriate level. (As originally used by Atwell, the term *reading workshop* was used to designate a type of program in which students choose their own books. *Reading workshop* is sometimes used to include guided reading, individualized reading, and voluntary reading. In this text, *reading workshop* is used to mean individualized reading.) Reading workshop is designed to give students choices in what they read. The session begins with a minilesson followed by self-selected reading. Each student chooses her own reading material and has periodic conferences with the teacher to discuss it. Conferences can be individual or group or both. As students are reading, the teacher can hold conferences or conduct guided reading or strategy lessons. Students might also meet with partners or small groups to discuss their reading (Calkins, 2004). The session ends with a brief sharing. Because students select their own reading, there is a better chance that they will read more. One disadvantage of reading workshop is that it is more difficult to manage. Another shortcoming is that skills instruction might be shortchanged. Lacking the structure of the basal program, reading workshop is potentially more rewarding but takes more planning if necessary skills are to be covered.

Reading workshop is similar to independent reading discussed in Chapter 7. However, the main purpose of independent reading is to foster voluntary reading. The main purpose of reading workshop is to improve skills.

Of the approaches to reading, reading workshop is probably the most effective. In addition to allowing choice of materials, it does a better job of providing for individual differences. Students are guided to select books that are on their level. However, even if you have a basal program, you can complement it with a reading workshop approach. This would then combine structure and choice.

More than any other approach to teaching reading, reading workshop fosters wide reading. One way of increasing reading among younger students is to have them read with partners (Calkins, 2004). In a partner read, each student meets with another student who is reading on a similar level. It also helps if both students have similar interests. These students introduce their books to each other and then read their books to each other. As a result, students experience two rather than one book in a sitting. In some versions of the activity, only one student introduces his book and reads it to his partner. Arranging for students to have conversations with partners has the potential to deepen understanding and to prepare them to participate in literature discussion groups.

Teaching children to read well has a great deal to do with teaching children to talk well about books, "because the conversations children have in the air between one another become the conversations they have in their own minds as they read. Children who've talked in small groups about the role of the suitcase in Christopher Paul Curtis's book, *Bud, Not Buddy*, will be far more apt to pause as they read another book, asking, 'Might this object play a significant role in this book, like the suitcase did in *Bud, Not Buddy*?'" (Calkins, 2004).

Initially students' independent reading is brief, but gradually it lengthens. Beginning readers spend only 10 to 15 minutes reading independently but confer with partners for about 20 minutes. By second grade, students read about 20 minutes independently and confer for about 10 minutes. At that point, it is no longer profitable for them to be reading aloud to a partner, so the conferring time is spent discussing books. As students move up through the grades, independent reading time increases to 30 or even 40 minutes, but conferring time with partners remains at 10 minutes.

A source of structure for a workshop program is A Field Guide to the Classroom Library at http://fieldguides.heinemann.com/how/libraries/b.asp. A Field Guide to the Classroom Library contains leveled lists of suggested titles for classroom libraries, general suggestions for holding conferences with most of the listed books, and suggestions for setting up a workshop program. The lists have been compiled by teachers working in the Teachers College Reading and Writing Project.

Effective Techniques

Effective reading programs require effective teaching techniques. A listing of major effective techniques is provided in Table 11.2. For a description of these and other instructional techniques, refer to *Reading Strategies and Practices: A Compendium* (6th ed.) by Tierney and Readence (2005) or *Improving Reading Strategies & Resources* (3rd ed.) by Johns and Lenski (2002).

Intervention/Prevention Programs

The best way to prevent reading problems is to have in place a strong core program. However, with even the best of programs, there are students who will expe-

TABLE 11.2 *Essential Techniques for Teaching Literacy*

Technique	Description	Benefit
Reading to students	Teacher reads for 10 minutes or more.	Builds background, vocabulary.
Shared or assisted reading	Using a big book, teacher reads to class, but they follow along and join in for a second reading.	Builds emergent literacy.
Buddy/partner reading	Students read together.	Builds fluency.
Paired reading	Proficient reader reads, and other student joins in when he can.	Builds fluency.
Echo reading	The teacher reads and the students follow.	Builds fluency.
Independent reading	Students read on their own.	Builds background, vocabulary, fluency, and satisfaction.
Word study	Time is devoted each day to studying the structure of words.	Builds decoding and vocabulary.
Phonological awareness	Students become aware of the sounds of words.	Builds skills needed for phonics.
Inductive phonics lesson	Based on an examination of examples, students draw generalizations about correspondences and patterns.	Students are actively involved in drawing conclusions based on their observations.
Word building	Students build words starting with vowel or rime and are also made aware of all the sounds in the words.	Students learn about the internal structure of words and build on what they know.
Pattern approach to syllabication	Students learn to analyze multisyllabic words based on syllable patterns rather than rules.	Learning syllable patterns is easier and more effective than learning syllabication generalizations.
Sorting	Students sort words according to sound, spelling, and meaning.	Students note differences in words and draw conclusions about these differences.
Morphemic analysis	Students use roots and affixes to derive the meanings of unfamiliar words.	Provides students with a tool for learning and remembering unfamiliar words.
Dictionary/glossary	Students learn how to obtain meanings and pronunciations of new words.	Provides another word learning tool and source of information about words.
Direct instructional lesson for skills and strategies	Students are taught strategies step by step.	Walks students through use of strategies so that they are able to use them independently.

continued

TABLE 11.2 *Essential Techniques for Teaching Literacy (continued)*

Technique	Description	Benefit
Modeling	Teacher shows how she would apply strategy.	Demonstrations are often more understandable than explanations alone.
Think-aloud lesson	Teacher tells what she is thinking as she applies a strategy or reads or writes.	Provides students with an insight about processes that otherwise are internal.
Guided reading	Students are prepared for reading text on their level.	Students receive instruction geared to their needs and are reading books on appropriate level.
Directed Reading Activity (DRA)	Similar to guided reading but preparation phase is more extensive.	Provides more guidance with reading. Good for use when students have limited background on a topic.
Directed Reading-Thinking Activity (DR–TA)	Students preview and set own purposes based on preview.	Causes students to be more active and more thoughtful readers.
Text walk/picture walk	Teacher walks students through text page by page going over words, expressions, or concepts that might interfere with understanding.	Provides maximum preparation for reading a selection. Most often used with novice readers.
Book discussion group/book club/literature circle	Students read book and discuss it.	Motivational. Builds discussion skills. Makes students more responsible for their own learning.
ReQuest	Teacher and students take turns asking each other questions about text until a purpose is set and students read on their own.	Excellent technique for building a basic level of comprehension. Very easy to implement. Motivational.
Reciprocal teaching	Students apply four key comprehension strategies as they read and discuss texts.	Acting as coach, teacher builds reading strategies and discussions skills.
KWL (Know, Want to Know, Learn) Plus	Students brainstorm what they know about a topic, decide what they would like to know, record what they actually learned, and what they still might like to learn.	Active technique that builds on what students know.

continued

TABLE 11.2 *Essential Techniques for Teaching Literacy (continued)*

Technique	Description	Benefit
Questioning the Author	Students read text part by part and respond to general queries in such a way that teacher and students are collaborators in constructing meaning.	Because they process brief segments of text, helps students understand difficult content-area text. Builds their confidence in constructing meaning.
GO! Chart	Under the teacher's guidance, class completes a chart that integrates major strategies used before, during, and after reading. Key steps include previewing and predicting, vocabulary, understanding, interpreting, connecting, and (retelling) organizing.	Provides students with a step-by-step graphic for strategies they use before reading, during reading, and after reading. Because it includes interpreting, making connections, and retelling (organizing), it is an effective approach for building deeper comprehension.
Language experience/shared writing	Class discusses an experience they have had and teacher helps them organize the information and scribes the experience for them.	Leads students to a higher level of writing. Models the acts of reading and writing.
Interactive writing	Similar to shared writing but students write some of the words or parts of the words.	Builds beginning writing and reading skills.
Guided writing	Students are grouped according to common needs and instructed in small groups.	Students' instructional needs are met.
Writing workshop	Time set aside for minilessons, writing, conferences, and sharing.	Students are given group guidance and individual help with their writing.
Independent writing	Students write on their own.	Students apply skills.

rience difficulties. All of today's basals have suggestions for helping struggling readers. They list books and other materials that might be used with struggling readers. They also have programs that can be used along with the core basal. In addition, there are a number of programs designed for struggling readers. These programs vary in approach and in emphasis. Most focus on decoding skills, since this is an area that most struggling readers have difficulty with. Others stress comprehension, and some emphasize language development. Major intervention programs are summarized in Table 11.3. Word Detectives Word Identification Program was created by the staff of the Benchmark School and is highly regarded as an effective program for students who have decoding and spelling difficulties. Produced on a variety of levels, Word Detectives can be used with students in grades 1 through 5 and beyond. Word Building is also designed for students struggling with decoding and spelling. Both Reading Mastery and Corrective Reading are examples of Direct Instruction. These highly structured scripted programs emphasize decoding. Fast Track, which is designed for students in grades 4–8, stresses the use of high-interest materials but also provides structured skill work. For students with serious decoding problems, Fast Track has a Word Work component. Word Work moves rapidly—all the short vowel patterns are introduced in the first lesson—and relies on text that is highly decodable but somewhat artificial. With its focus on language development, High Point works well with ELLs. A balanced approach, High Point has strong decoding, comprehension, and writing components. Using a highly effective comprehension building technique known as reciprocal teaching along with graphic organizers, Soar to Success has proven to be an effective comprehension builder for struggling readers.

A checklist for assessing intervention programs is presented in Table 11.4. You can use the checklist to evaluate your own intervention program or, if you are assisting others, use it to evaluate their intervention program. For a full description of a number of intervention programs, refer to FCCR Reports at http://www.fcrr.org.FCRRReports/reportlist.htm, which is maintained by the Florida Center for Reading Research. Since the site was set up to respond to requests for information from Florida teachers about specific programs, not all available programs are described.

Helping Students Who Fail to Make Progress Despite Intervention

Most struggling readers and writers will respond to well-planned instruction provided by caring teachers. Struggling readers need instruction in the same basic areas as achieving readers do. However, they may need instruction that is more explicit, comprehensive, intensive, and supportive in small-group or one-on-one formats (Foorman & Torgesen, 2001). Some of these students may have difficulty learning and so may need more repetition and added scaffolding in the form of coaching. A few may have such serious learning difficulties that they need extended one-on-one instruction by a reading specialist or special education teacher.

Schools sometimes underestimate the amount of help that severely disabled readers and writers need. Sometimes struggling readers are continued in programs even though they're not experiencing success. One advantage of continuous monitoring of all students is that it highlights students who are not making progress. Programs must be flexible. If students are not succeeding in one program, then you need to try another. Even people who have created highly effective intervention programs warn that their programs do not work with all students. If students continue to fail even though they have been placed in an intensive intervention program, they should be referred to the school's pupil planning team and be given a diagnostic evaluation. The team should include the classroom teacher,

TABLE 11.3 *Commercial Intervention Programs*

Title	Publisher	Interest Level	Grade Level	Main Areas
Bookshop	Mondo	K–3	K–3	Phonological awareness, decoding, comprehension, oral and written language
Corrective Reading	SRA	4–12	1–5+	Decoding and comprehension; scripted program
Earobics Literacy Launch	Cognitive Concepts	K–3	K–3+	Phonological awareness, decoding, comprehension; computer-based
Fast Track	McGraw-Hill	4–8	1–5+	Decoding and comprehension
High Noon	High Noon	3–12	1–4+	Decoding and comprehension
High Point	Hampton Brown	1–8	6–12	Decoding, comprehension, oral and written language; especially appropriate for ELLs
Language!	Sopris West	1–12	1–9	Decoding, comprehension, spelling, oral language, writing
Learning System 100	Harcourt	9–12	1–10	Decoding, comprehension, vocabulary, oral language, writing; computer-based
Lightspan Early Reading Program	Lightspan	K–3	K–3	Phonological awareness, decoding, comprehension; computer-based program
Reading 180	Scholastic	4–12	1–9	Decoding, comprehension, vocabulary, written and oral English; computer-based
Reading Advantage	Great Source	5–10	2–8	Comprehension, word analysis, vocabulary, and fluency
Reading Mastery	SRA	K–6	K–6	Decoding and comprehension; scripted program.
Reading Milestones	Pro-ed	1–12	K–5	Decoding, comprehension, spelling; designed for students with hearing impairments or language delays
Soar to Success	Houghton Mifflin	3–8	2–8	Comprehension
Success for All	Success for All	K–8	K–8	Phonological awareness, decoding, comprehension, oral and written language
Voyager Reading Intervention	Voyager	K–8	K–8	Phonological awareness, decoding, comprehension, and writing; has an extended day and summer program
Wildcats	Wright Group	2–8	1–6	Decoding and comprehension
Wilson	Wilson	K–12	K–5	Decoding and spelling
Word Building	Phoenix Learning Resources	K–4	K–5	Decoding and spelling
Word Detectives	Benchmark School	1–5+	1–5+	Decoding and spelling

TABLE 11.4 *Intervention Assessment Checklist*

Action	Fully	Partially	Limited	Suggestions
Students are selected on basis of assessment.				
Objectives are clearly stated.				
Focus is on needed high-payoff skills and strategies.				
Program builds on what students know.				
Direct, systematic instruction is provided.				
Pacing is brisk.				
Ample time is provided for reading and writing.				
Higher-level skills are included.				
Progress is continuously monitored.				
Intervention program is coordinated with class program.				
Intervention program is additive. It adds to instructional time.				
Students are placed at appropriate levels.				
Parents and community are involved.				

reading specialist, special education teacher, school psychologist, parents, and anyone else who might be able to shed light on the students' difficulty. If intervention programs have failed, the students might need a one-to-one approach taught by a highly trained specialist. Specialized techniques that use multisensory methods include the following:

- Fernald Tracing Technique (VAKT) (Fernald, 1943; Gunning, 2006)
- Orton-Gillingham Approach (McIntyre & Pickering, 1995)
- *Recipe for Reading* (Traub & Bloom, 2000)

Assessing the Organizational Components of Your Program

Closing the gap requires careful organization. Effective programs must be chosen, students must be carefully grouped, time and other resources must be used well. Use the checklist in Table 11.5 to determine strengths and weaknesses of the organizational component of your program.

TABLE 11.5 *Assessment Checklist for Organizational Factors in a Literacy Program*

Action	Fully	Partially	Limited	Suggestions
Literacy committee composed of administrators, teachers, parents, and community members plans and monitors the school's program.				
Teachers meet by grade level on a weekly basis to discuss program and progress of students.				
Class and group size are kept small.				
From 90 to 150 minutes of time is set aside for literacy instruction and protected.				
Students are on task 80 to 90 percent of time.				
Students are grouped according to needs.				
High-payoff activities are emphasized.				
Effective practice is provided.				
School has a homework policy. Homework is used to provide extra practice and/or extend learning.				
Students are provided with challenging assignments. Teachers meet to discuss quality of assignments.				
Test preparation is integrated into the curriculum but is not excessive.				
Parental support is enlisted.				
Technology is used to extend learning and provide assistance for those who need it.				
Technology is integrated into the curriculum.				
A behavior management program is implemented school-wide.				
Effective literacy programs are implemented.				
Literacy programs are adapted so, as to provide optimal benefit.				
Special education services are provided for students who need them.				
Special education and regular education are closely coordinated.				
Students are closely monitored. Those who fail to make progress are provided with effective intervention programs.				

12

Creating a Literacy Improvement Plan

In previous chapters, vision statements, goals, objectives, assessment, and various ways of improving instruction were discussed. Now it is time to put all the elements together to plan a program of improvement for students and a program of professional development for the staff.

Assembling the Elements of a Literacy Improvement Program

The process of creating a literacy improvement program begins with a creation of a mission statement. Based on the mission statement, goals for the program are created. The goals are then translated into specific objectives. A needs assessment is undertaken. This is done by examining the program's objectives and deciding to what extent they are being met. Unmet or partially met objectives become needs. Placement and screening tests and other sources of information are used to determine whether needs are being met. Once the needs assessment has highlighted objectives that aren't being met, a plan to meet those objectives is drawn up. You need to say how the objectives listed on the needs assessment will be met. What activities will be planned that will enable students to achieve the objectives?

Activities might include introducing and reinforcing twelve new vocabulary words a week, encouraging students to read 20 minutes a night, conducting guided reading lessons, starting a writer's workshop program, starting an intervention program, or holding tutoring classes after school.

These activities and the progress students make needs to be monitored. You need to collect data that indicates whether students are making reasonable progress. The program as a whole needs to be monitored, but individual students also need to be checked. The monitoring can be both formal and informal. You can formally monitor the program with a specific assessment, such as benchmark passages or informal reading invenories (IRIs), three to four times a year. You can informally monitor on an ongoing basis. Once a month or once a week, you might administer a running record. More frequent monitoring is recommended for students who have more serious difficulties. If students are not meeting objectives, you can then decide how you might revise their program so that they are on the road to success. Some changes might be made in the overall program. You might decide to institute a stronger phonics program or a new technique, such as sorting. Or changes can be geared to individual students. A student not meeting success might be given one-on-one lessons instead of being instructed in a group.

The school improvement plan must also provide for professional development. It must state how teachers will acquire the skills needed to implement the plan for improving students' performance. This is explored in the second half of this chapter. The school's literacy committee is responsible for drawing up the school's improvement program. A portion of a sample plan shown in Table 12.1 lists baseline data to show where students were, projected data to show where students should be at the end of the year, activities designed to accomplish the objectives, results of monitoring, ongoing revisions, and final outcomes. The plan is implemented and, based on ongoing monitoring, revised. The plan is based on one that was drawn up and implemented at Urban Public.

Drawing up an improvement plan is recursive. As you assess and instruct students, you might determine that certain objectives are not being addressed. You might note that there is a need for study skills or writing informational pieces or using research skills. Goals, objectives, and teaching methods can and should be revised. The unifying factor is the continuing quest for improving the progress of students.

Implementing the Literacy Improvement Program

Some of the literacy improvement needs at Urban Public were addressed on an ongoing basis. Others required more time and planning. Since there were so many needs to be addressed, the literacy committee had to set priorities. Beefing up classroom libraries and improving vocabulary and comprehension instruction were implemented on an ongoing basis. Guided reading and other approaches to differentiating instruction were also implemented on an ongoing basis. A new reading program was introduced in September. A new writing program was introduced the following January. A new spelling program was put into place in February. With all those changes, extensive professional development was required. Professional development sessions were conducted for two weeks during the summer. Professional development sessions were also conducted monthly along with weekly grade-level meetings. In addition, two coaches were hired. The professional development was based on the needs assessment and priorities set by the literacy committee.

Professional development was altered as needs changed. Because students were doing poorly on end-of-theme tests, professional development in teaching higher-level thinking skills and responding in writing to higher-level questions was instituted.

TABLE 12.1 *Literacy Improvement Plan (Partial)*

Objectives	Plans	Revisions	Initial Achievement	Target Achievement	Monitoring	Outcomes (May)
Read at grade level.	New reading program. Intensive instruction. Wide reading. Extra help.	After-school program.	1/2 in 1-2 at level	1-2 80% at level	Oct. 50% Dec. 60% Mar. 75%	80%
			1/3 3-6 at level.	3-6 60% at level	Oct. 33% Dec. 40% Mar. 60%	70%
Year's growth in reading for all.	New reading program. Intensive instruction. Wide reading. Extra help.	After-school program.			Oct. 80% Dec. 90% Mar. 90%	90%
1 1/2 yr's growth for those behind.	New reading program. Intensive instruction. Wide reading. Extra help	Summer program. More intensive tutoring.			Oct. 30% Dec. 40% Mar. 40%	50%
Obtain at least a 3 on scoring rubric.	New writing program. Writing every day. Writing in every class.		1/3 at level 3	2/3 at level 3	Mar. 50%	60%
Read a total of two hours a day.	Add to classroom libraries. Improve SSR. Involve home. Voluntary reading. Read in every class. Acquire trade books to go along with content texts.	Voluntary reading campaign. Home contact. Coaching for teachers. Discussions with students. Make voluntary reading part of grade.	50%	100%	Dec. 60% Mar. 90%	95%

Professional Development

The aim of professional development is to increase capabilities, to foster increased capacity. You need to ask: What is it that I want to be able to do as a result of professional development? What new skills do I need to enhance the learning of my students?

Data-Based Professional Development

The most effective professional development is based on data. Data provides evidence of a need for change and also shows where change should occur. In addition, monitoring data guides the professional development efforts (Joyce & Calhoun, 1996). It shows whether professional development is being successful or whether additional changes are needed. For faculty who have doubts about students' ability to achieve on high levels, data can be both convincing and encouraging.

Professional development must be intensive with a focus on application and follow-up. Otherwise, implementation is sparse (Showers, Murphy, & Joyce, 1996). Even when providing a theoretical base for instructional techniques, multiple demonstrations of techniques, and the opportunity to practice them in a work-

BOX
12.1

Model Program: Data-Based Professional Development

When teachers expressed a concern about the effectiveness of their spelling program, Gill and Scharer (1996) conducted a program of professional development that began with a developmental assessment of students' spelling. Examining the test results, teachers were surprised at the range of spelling levels in their classes. Test results quickly convinced them that the single weekly spelling list was not appropriate. As they examined the kinds of errors students made, they gained insight into the development of spelling abilities and got to know their students better as spellers. Having acquired insight into the spelling system and the development of spelling abilities, they were eager to attempt new methods of organizing their spelling program and instructing their students. Realizing that students were on varied levels, they began grouping students for spelling instruction. Seeing that the rote memory techniques they had taught their students had not been very effective, at the suggestion of Gill and Scharer (1996), they took a more cognitive approach to spelling and began using sorting techniques that would allow students to compare and contrast the features of words and make discoveries about their spellings. Change wasn't easy. It was a lot more work to plan instruction for several groups rather than just conduct a whole-class spelling lesson revolving around a single list. However, seeing their students' growth motivated the teachers. As one first-grade teacher comments:

> I am glad I had the opportunity to change because I would have done it like it had always been done. I would have felt in my heart it wasn't right. This is so much more pleasant. You can see growth. What more could you ask for? (Gill & Scharer, 1996, pp. 94–95)

shop setting, only 10 percent of teachers actually implemented the techniques. However, when these elements were augmented with extensive support, nearly 90 percent of the teachers implemented the techniques.

Teachers were urged to try out the techniques in their classrooms on a long-term basis and to continue using them regularly. Study groups were formed so that teachers could discuss their efforts, observe each other, and coach each other in the use of the techniques. The researchers found that it takes twenty to thirty trials before new techniques are integrated into teachers' repertoire of techniques (Showers, Murphy, & Joyce, 1996). Ultimately, the integration of the new techniques resulted in improved student performance. The results were notable. In one middle school, promotion rates soared, while the average achievement test score jumped from the 25th to the 42nd percentile. In addition, disciplinary referrals dropped to about one-fifth the previous level.

Standards for Professional Development

High-quality professional development is grounded in standards. Standards for professional development are based on three questions:

- What are all students expected to know and be able to do?
- What must teachers know and do to ensure student success?
- Where must staff development focus to meet both goals? (National Staff Development Council, 2004)

Standards for effective professional development include leadership that guides continuous instructional improvement, is based on student and teacher proficiency data, uses effective techniques to help teachers learn and change, helps staff collaborate, builds high expectations for student learning, involves families and the community, and continually evaluates the effectiveness of professional development (National Staff Development Council, 2004).

BOX 12.2

Data-Based Professional Development: Personal Perspective

On the basis of administering IRIs to their students, the staff at Urban Public noted that students were reading on varied levels. With the help of the school's coaches, they initiated additional guided reading groups. Later, noting that vocabulary scores were low, the staff discussed ways of building vocabulary and initiated a vocabulary building program. Instruction was based on students' performance on an informal vocabulary survey. Deficiencies on basal anthology end-of-theme tests resulted in an extensive program to build higher-level thinking and comprehension skills. Incomplete books logs led to a reexamination and restructuring of the school's voluntary reading program. All of these changes were accompanied by extensive professional development.

Steps for Creating a Professional Development Program

Steps for creating and implementing an effective program of professional development include adherence to National Staff Development Council (NSDC) standards
and implementation of the following steps, which are based on procedures followed by districts judged to have the most effective professional development
program (Hassel, 1999).

Step 1: Create a professional development committee.

Step 2: Decide on literacy goals or standards. These should be aligned with state
and district goals. A typical state goal might be that all students are reading on grade-level or achieve a certain score on a literacy test. Translate
school goals into individual or class goals.

Step 3: Create a needs assessment in terms of school goals. Include indicators of
whether students goals are being met and whether this is a gap or a
strength. Also create a needs assessment for teachers to show what teaching skills are needed to help students to reach their goals. Note whether
goals are being met. Determine student and teacher gaps.

Identifying student learning gaps helps define precisely the level and type of skill
that staff members need to help a particular set of students meet learning goals.
Likewise, identifying staff gaps helps schools focus professional development on
areas of teacher skill and competence most needing development to meet student
learning needs (Hassel, 1999).

You can also include parent skills needed to help students achieve goals.
Parents might need to read to their children every night or make sure that
they complete their homework assignments.

Step 4: Select standards or benchmarks to be met.

Step 5: Select sources of data to determine student and teacher competence. Possible sources for students include standardized tests, high-stakes tests, IRIs,
running records, observations, portfolios, checklists, questionnaires, and
learning logs. For teachers, data include surveys, questionnaires, discussions, observations, and portfolios.

Step 6: Set professional development goals based on the needs assessment. Typical goals include to improve all students' learning and to improve teacher
effectiveness. However, these goals need to be translated into specific
objectives. Professional development objectives are closely tied to student
objectives. The needs assessments might be used to create benchmarks for
continuous monitoring and final evaluation. When students fail to meet
objectives, this is taken as a sign that the professional development needs
to be improved (Hassel, 1999).

Step 7: Set content and activities for professional development. Instead of being
seen as a series of workshops, professional development should be viewed
as being an integrated part of the school's activities. Professional development is viewed as a continual quest to improve teacher competence so that
teachers can improve students' competence. Specify content and activities.

Content is the knowledge that you want teachers to learn. Content is what teachers need to know and be able to do to help their students close the gap. Activities are the means for conveying content. Content consists of instituting best practices not now being used or helping teachers optimize their practices. Content should be selected that best helps you meet your professional development objectives.

Possible professional development activities include the following.

- Workshops.
- Study groups. Study groups provide a forum for staff members to share ideas and attack a common problem or issue. Participants can develop collaborative units, share lesson plans, develop materials, adapt programs, or investigate areas of concern (Murphy, 1992). Based on her experience as an administrator, Murphy (1992) recommends that study groups meet once a week for an hour.

  Kits for study groups are available from the International Reading Association. The IRA Literacy Study Groups kits include a facilitator's guide, articles, books, and a reflection journal. Kits are available on beginning reading, adolescent literacy, reading comprehension, and vocabulary.

  Study groups that revolve around the reading of a text are sometimes known as "book clubs." Planning professional development around the reading of a text fosters collegiality. Instead of being the source of wisdom, the literacy facilitator becomes a learner along with the other members of the group (Walpole & McKenna, 2004).
- Grade-level meetings (see Chapter 11).
- Student progress meetings in which individual teachers meet with administrators and support staff to discuss students' progress and ways of helping those students not making adequate progress. Professional development can be geared to gaps in students' progress.
- Observations of other teachers or demonstrations.
- Observations by peer, support staff, or principal.
- Mentoring of a novice teacher by a more experienced teacher
- Action research, in which teachers design a study to assess how well a new technique or program works, judging effectiveness by noting whether students outperform a comparison group or whether the technique results in higher achievement than students typically make. At Urban Public, teachers sought effective ways to teach students the higher-level skills they need to pass today's more demanding assessments. A variety of techniques were tried out, including starting with brief, easy selections; using frames that would be gradually faded out; and providing prompts. To assess the effectiveness of these steps, students were given a pretest and then were assessed weekly to see if they were making progress. Based on results, the program was altered. A major finding is that fostering higher-level skills is possible but it takes time and carefully planned teaching. Action research was also used to assess the effectiveness of the school's intervention programs.
- Attendance at institutes or conferences.

- Professional reading.
- Online courses or professional discussion groups.
- University courses.
- Working with struggling readers. An extremely effective way to learn how to help struggling readers is to work with a struggling reader while being supervised. In Early Steps, a highly successful one-on-one program, classroom teachers are given released time from classroom duties to work with a student who is having difficulty with reading (Morris, 1999). Given the chance to work intensively with just one student, classroom teachers learn how to monitor progress, plan and adjust instruction, and deal with significant learning problems in a way that they wouldn't be able to do in a whole-class setting. Originally trained to work with average students, teachers gain new insights and competencies in working with struggling students.

Step 8: Implement professional development. Remember that Joyce and Showers warned that a new technique needs to be tried out 20 to 30 times before it becomes a part of the teacher's repertoire. Joyce and Showers (2002) also note, "Effective implementation is thorough. Teachers understand the theory behind the new element, understand how to implement it, are provided with support and feedback as they implement the element" (p. 57). The key to effective professional development is supporting implementation.

Step 9: Evaluate and improve professional development. Evaluation means figuring out whether you are meeting your goals, why or why not, and what you should do next to improve (Hassel, 1999). For workshops and similar activities, use a questionnaire to assess the quality and utility of the presentation. Evaluate implementation through observations and discussions. Most importantly, assess students' progress on those areas that have been highlighted as needing improvement. When assessing, go beyond test scores and look at the quality of teacher assignments and students' work. Are assignments challenging enough? Do they demand application and involve higher-level thinking skills? Assess on a continuous basis, so that you can make adjustments as needed. Evaluation should assess improvements in teaching and student performance and should also indicate whether the gap was being narrowed. The essence of successful professional development is monitoring. There is evidence that teachers and students are making progress toward reaching their learning goals.

Effective professional development requires a cultural change (Hassel, 1999). All staff members need to see that they are involved in a common undertaking: to improve their competence and that of all their students. Teachers need to view professional development as an essential part of the process. The school becomes a learning community. Set aside time daily or weekly to focus exclusively on professional development. Integrate professional development into other activities. Schools with successful professional development programs have found that it's easier to make small changes throughout the year and make major changes annually. Annual changes gave schools the time need to gather data and make preparations needed for larger changes.

Team Approach

A team approach to professional development is recommended. Commenting on the successful implementation of professional development in Australia, Hill and Crévola (2000) note:

> The team is the main vehicle for growing professionally. Team members take joint responsibility for all students supervised by all team members and also assume responsibility for each other's professional growth. The professional learning team is the key strategy for bringing all classes up to the level of the most effective class and for then moving on to become even more effective.

Results of an improved program can be immediate. In one school, promotion rates jumped from 30 percent to 70 percent in just one year as the rate of learning increased by 60 percent. Of course, time helps. In the second year, the passing rate hit 95 percent (Joyce & Showers, 2002). As the researchers noted,

BOX 12.3

Study Groups at Urban Public: Personal Perspective

Study groups are most effective when they deal with an area of genuine concern. At Urban Public, classroom observations indicated that students were having difficulty retelling stories. At the author's urging, the kindergartner teachers formed a study group in which they read, discussed, and implemented recommendations for teaching retellings provided by Benson and Cummins (2002) in their text, *The Power of Retelling: Developmental Steps for Building Comprehension.* After each meeting, the teachers agreed to try out at least one recommendation. At the next meeting, they discussed these tryouts. When third grade teachers discussed the need for higher-level thinking skills, the author recommended Oczkus's (2003) *Reciprocal Teaching at Work: Strategies for Improving Reading Comprehension.* This highly practical text provided an easy-to-follow guide for implementing reciprocal teaching along with a number of high-quality strategies not normally included in reciprocal teaching. Upper-grade teachers used Fountas and Pinnell's (2001) detailed recommendations in *Guiding Readers and Writers Grades 3–6* to help them learn about and set up an independent reading program. When instituting a vocabulary program, a cross-grade study group consulted Beck, McKeown, and Kucan's (2002) text, *Bringing Words to Life: Robust Vocabulary Instruction.*

Study groups that revolve around the reading of a text are sometimes known as "book clubs." Revolving professional development around the reading of a text fosters collegiality. Instead of being the fount of wisdom, the literacy facilitator becomes a learner along with the other members of the group (Walpole & McKenna, 2004).

Many educators believe that school improvement efforts will not have demonstrable effects on students for several years, but the evidence points toward quite a different conclusion. Students respond right away to changes in instruction and begin to accelerate their rates of learning provided that the educational environment is designed to do just that—teach the students to learn more effectively. (Joyce & Showers, 2002, p. 42)

Assessing the Professional Development Component of Your Program

Professional development is the life blood of a program designed to close the literacy gap. Closing the gap requires using the most effective techniques for assessment, instruction, and management and also the most appropriate materials. Professional development is a process of continuous learning. Use the checklist in Table 12.2 to determine strengths and weaknesses of the professional development component of your program.

TABLE 12.2 *Assessment Checklist for Professional Development*

Action	Fully	Partially	Limited	Suggestions
Professional development is data based.				
Professional development is based on the needs of the students.				
Professional development is intensive with follow-up support.				
Professional development is ongoing.				
Professional development includes all staff members.				
Professional development committee plans and monitors professional development.				
Professional development takes many forms.				
Professional development includes personal as well as schoolwide goals.				
Professional development is monitored in terms of improvement in student performance.				
Professional development is evaluated and revised as necessary.				

References

Adams, M. J. (1990). *Beginning to read: Thinking and learning about print: A summary.* Cambridge, MA: MIT Press.

Adams, M. J. (1994). Modeling the connections be-tween word recognition and reading. In R. B. Ruddell, M. R. Ruddell, & H. Singer (Eds.), *Theoretical models and processes of reading* (4th ed., (pp. 838–863). Newark, DE: International Reading Association.

Alexander, K., Entwisle, D., & Olson, L. S. (1997). *Early schooling and inequality: Socioeconomic disparities in children's learning.* London: Falmer Press.

Alleman, S. (2003). *The instructional role of the reading specialist: A view from the inside.* Paper presented at International Reading Association Convention, New Orleans.

Allington, R. (2001) *What really matters for struggling readers: Designing research-based programs.* New York: Addison Wesley Longman.

Allington, R. L., Johnston, P. H., & Day, J. P. (2002). Exemplary fourth-grade teachers. *Language Arts, 79,* 462–466.

Almasi, J. F., O'Flahavan, J. F., & Arya, P. (2001). A comparative analysis of student and teacher development in more and less proficient discussions of literature. *Reading Research Quarterly, 36,* 96–120.

Anderson, R. C. (1990, May). *Microanalysis of classroom reading instruction.* Paper presented at the annual conference on reading research, Atlanta.

Anderson, R. C., Wilson, P. T., & Fielding, L. G. (1988). Growth in reading and how children spend their time outside of school. *Reading Research Quarterly, 23,* 285–303.

Atwell, N. (1987). *In the middle.* Portsmouth, NH: Boynton/Cook.

Baumann, J. F., Edwards, E. C., Font, G., Tereshinski, C., Kame'enui, E. J., & Olejnik, S. F. (2002, April/May/June). Teaching morphemic and contextual analysis to fifth-grade students. *Reading Research Quarterly, 37,* 150–173.

Baumann, J. F., & Ivey, G. (1997). Delicate balances: Striving for curricular and instructional equilibrium in a second-grade, literature/strategy-based classroom. *Reading Research Quarterly, 32,* 244–275.

Bear, D. R., & Helman, L. (2004). Word study for vocabulary development in the early stages of literacy learning: Ecological perspectives and learning English. In J. Baumann & E. Kame'enui (Eds.), *Vocabulary instruction: Research to practice* (pp. 139–158). New York: Guilford.

Bear, D. R., Invernizzi, M., Templeton, S., & Johnston, F. (2004). *Words their way: Word study for phonics, vocabulary, and spelling instruction* (3rd ed.). Upper Saddle River, NJ: Pearson.

Beck, I. L., & McKeown, M. G. (2001). Text talk: Capturing the benefits of read-aloud experiences for young children. *The Reading Teacher, 55,* 10–20.

Beck, I. L., McKeown, M. G., Hamilton, R. L., & Kucan, L. (1997). *Questioning the author: An approach for enhancing student engagement with text.* Newark, DE: International Reading Association.

Beck, I. L., & McKeown, M. G., & Kucan, L. (2002). *Bringing words to life: Robust vocabulary instruction.* New York: York.

Beers, K. (2003). *When kids can't read, what teachers can do: A guide for teachers 6–12.* Portsmouth, NH: Heinemann.

Benard, B. (2003). Turnaround teachers and schools. In B. Williams (Ed.), *Closing the achievement gap: A vision for changing beliefs and practices* (2nd ed., pp. 115–137). Alexandria, VA: Association for Supervision and Curriculum Development.

Benson, J. (2003). *Survey shows preschool can have later benefits for kindergartners.* Hartford, CT: Connecticut Commission on Children. Available online at http://www.cga.state.ct.us/coc/Preschool%20Survey.htm

Benson, V., & Cummins, C. (2002). *The power of retelling: Developmental steps for building comprehension.* Bothell, WA: Wright Group/McGraw-Hill.

Betts, E. A. (1946). *Foundations of reading instruction.* New York: American Book.

Biemiller, A. (1999). *Language and reading success.* Cambridge, MA: Brookline.

Biemiller, A. (2001). Teaching vocabulary: Early, direct, and sequential. *American Educator, 25,* 25–28.

Biemiller, A. (2004). Teaching vocabulary in the primary grades: Vocabulary instruction needed. In J. Baumann & E. Kame'enui (Eds.), *Vocabulary Instruction: Research to practice* (pp. 28–40). New York: Guilford.

Biemiller, A., & Slonin, N. (2001). Estimating root word vocabulary growth in normative and advantaged populations: Evidence for a common sequence of vocabulary acquisition. *Journal of Educational Psychology, 93,* 498–520.

Bjorklund, B., Handler, N., Mitten, J., & Stockwell, G. (1998, October). *Literature circles: A tool for developing students as critical readers, writers, and thinkers.* Paper presented at the forty-seventh annual conference of the Connecticut Reading Association, Waterbury.

Blachman, B. A., Ball, E., Black, R., & Tangel, D. M., (2000). *Road to the code.* Baltimore: Brookes.

Black, P., & Williams, D. (1998). Inside the black box: Raising standards through classroom assessment. *Phi Delta Kappan, 80*(2), 139–148.

Bloom, B. S. (1984). The 2 sigma problem: The search for methods of group instruction as effective as one-to-one tutoring. *Educational Researcher, 13*(6), 4–16.

Bohrnstedt, G. W., & Stechter, B. M. (2000). Summary of class size reduction in California: The 1998–99 evaluation findings. In American Youth Policy Forum (Ed.), *Raising minority achievement: A compendium of educational programs and practices* (pp. 94–97). Available online at http://www.aypf.org/rmaa/pdfs/ClassSizeRed.pdf

Bonacci, F. L. (1993). The acquisition of word knowledge from expository context in skilled and less-skilled readers. *Dissertation Abstracts International, 54* (05A). (UMI No. AA193-26302)

Borman, G. D. (2000). The effects of summer school: Questions answered, questions raised [Commentary]. *Monographs of the Society for Research in Child Development, 65*(1), 119–127.

Bourassa, D., & Treiman, R. (2003). Spelling in children with dyslexia: Analyses from the Treiman-Bourassa early spelling test. *Scientific Studies of Reading, 7,* 308-333.

Boyd, C. D., Gay, G., Geiger, R., Kracht, J. B., Panf, V. O., Rinsinger, F. C., & Sanchez, S. M. (2003). *Scott Foresman social studies: The United States.* Glenview, IL: Scott Foresman.

Boyle, E. A., Rosenberg, M. S., Connelly, V. J., Washburn, S. G., Brinckerhoff, L. C., & Banerjee, M. (2002). Reading's SLICK with new audio texts and strategies. *Teaching Exceptional Children, 35,* 50–55.

Boyles, N. (2002). *Teaching written response to text: Constructing quality answers to open-ended comprehension questions.* Gainsville, FL: Maupin House.

Bruck, M. (1992). Persistence of dyslexics' phonological awareness deficits. *Developmental Psychology, 28,* 874–886.

Bus, A. G., & van Ijzendoorn, M. H. (1999). Phonological awareness and early reading: A meta-analysis of experiential training studies. *Journal of Educational Psychology, 91,* 403–414.

California State Department of Education. (2004). *Education Code Section 48070-48070.5.* Available online at http://www.cde.ca.gov/re/lr/pr/

Calkins, L. (2001). *The art of teaching reading.* Portsmouth, NH: Heinemann.

Calkins, L. (2003). *Units of study for primary writing: A yearlong program.* Portsmouth, NH: Heinemann.

Calkins, L. (2004). *Reading instruction and the classroom library: An introduction to workshop structures.* Available online at http://fieldguides.heinemann.com/how/workshop_structures.asp

Carbo, M. (1997). *What every principal should know about teaching reading: How to raise test scores and nurture a love of reading.* Syosset, NY: Reading Styles Institute.

Carey, K. (2004). The real value of teachers: Using the new information about teacher effectiveness to close the achievement gap. *Thinking, K–16, 8*(1), 3–42. Available online at http://www2.edtrust.org/edtrust/product+catalog/main

Carlo, M. S., August, D., McLaughlin, B., Snow, C. E., Dressler, C., Lippman, D. N., Lively, T. J., & White, C. E. (2004). Closing the gap: Addressing the vocabulary needs of English-language learners in bilingual, and mainstream classrooms. *Reading Research Quarterly, 39,* 188–215.

Carnine, D., Kame'enui, E. J., & Coyle, G. (1984). Utilization of contextual information *Reading Research Quarterly, 19,* 188–204.

Carver, R. P. (1975–1976). Measuring prose difficulty using the rauding scale. *Reading Research Quarterly,* 11, 660–685.

Carver, R. P. (1994). Percentage of unknown vocabulary words in text as a function of the relative difficulty of the text: Implications for instruction. *Journal of Reading Behavior, 26,* 413–437.

Case, R. (1992). *The mind's staircase.* Hillsdale, NJ: Erlbaum.

Center on Education Policy (2005). *From the capital to the classroom: Year 3 of the No Child Left Behind Act.* Available online at http://www.cep-dc.org/pubs/nclby3/

Chall, J. S., Bissex, G. L., Conard, S. S., & Harris-Sharples, S. H. (1996). *Qualitative assessment of text difficulty: A practical guide for teachers and writers.* Cambridge, MA: Brookline.

Chall, J. S., Jacobs, V. A., & Baldwin, L. E. (1990). *The reading crisis: Why poor children fall behind.* Cambridge, MA: Harvard University Press.

Charney, R. S. (2002). *Teaching children to care* (Rev. ed.). Greenfield, MA: Northeast Foundation for Children.

Clay, M. M. (1993a). *An observation survey of early literacy achievement.* Portsmouth, NH: Heinemann.

Clay, M. M. (1993b). *Reading Recovery: A guidebook for teachers in training.* Portsmouth, NH: Heinemann.

Clay, M. M. (2003, December). *Simply by sailing in a new direction.* Paper presented at the National Reading Conference, Scottsdale, AZ.

Closing the Achievement Gap Section, School Improvement Division, North Carolina Department of Public Instruction (2004). *Closing the gap.* Raleigh, NC: Author. Available online at http://www. ncpublicschools.org/schoolimprovement/ closingthegap/

Connecticut State Department of Education (2004). *Governor's summer reading challenge.* Available online at http://www.state.ct.us/sde/ctread/ ctread.htm

Cooper, H. (2003, May). *Summer learning loss: The problem and some solutions.* Eric Digest, EDO-PS-03-5. Available online at: http://ericeece.org/pubs/digests/ 2003/cooper03.pdf

Cooper, H., Charlton, K., Valentine, J. C., & Muhlenbruck, L. (2000). Making the most of summer school: A meta-analytic and narrative review. *Monographs of the Society for Research in Child Development, 65*(1), 1–117.

Cooper, H., Nye, B., Charlton, K., Lindsay, J., & Greathouse, S. (1996). The effects of summer vacation on achievement test scores: A narrative and meta-analytic review. *Review of Educational Research, 66,* 227–268.

Cooper, P. D., Boschenken, I., McWilliams, J., & Pistochini, L. (2000). A study of the effectiveness of an intervention program designed to accelerate reading for struggling readers in the upper grades. In T. Shanahan & F. V. Rodriquez-Brown (Eds.), *49th yearbook of the National Reading Conference* (pp. 477–486). Chicago: National Reading Conference.

Council of Chief State School Officers (2002). *Expecting success: A study of five high performing, high poverty elementary schools.* Washington, DC: Author. Available online at http://www2.edtrust.org/edtrust/

Coxhead, A.J. (1998). *An academic word list.* English Language Institute Occasional Publication Number 18. Wellington, New Zealand: Victoria University of Wellington

Crèvola, C., & Vineis, M. (2004). *Building essential literacy with bookshop.* New York: Mondo.

Cummins, C. (2004). *Internalization and transfer of comprehension processes: integrated strategies using the GO! Chart—Impact on learning and motivation.* Paper presented at the National Reading Conference, San Antonio.

Cunningham, A., & Stanovich, K. (1998, Spring/Summer). What reading does for the mind. *American Educator, 22,* 1–8.

Cunningham, J. W., Erickson, K., Spadorcia, S. A., Koppenhaver, D. A., Cunningham, P. M., Yoder, D. E., & McKenna, M. C. (1999). Assessing decoding from an onset-rime perspective. *Journal of Literacy Research, 31,* 391–414.

Currie, J. (2001, March). *A fresh start for Head Start?* Children's Roundtable Report. Washington, DC: Brookings Institution. Available online at http://www.brook.edu/comm/childrens roundtable/issue5.htm

Curtis, M. E., & Longo, A. M. (2001, November). Teaching vocabulary to adolescents to improve comprehension. *Reading Online, 5*(4). Available online at http://www.readingonline.org/articles/art_index .asp?HREF=curtis/index.html

Dale, E., & O'Rourke, J. (1971). *Techniques of teaching vocabulary.* Chicago: Field.

Daniels, H. (2002). *Literature circles: Voice and choice in the student-centered classroom.* Portland, ME: Stenhouse.

Donahue, P., Daane, M., & Grigg, W. (2003). *The nation's report card: Reading highlights 2003.* Washington, DC: National Center for Educational Statistics. Available online at http://nces.ed.gov/ pubsearch/pubsinfo.asp?pubid=2004452

Duffy, G. G, & Hoffman, J. V. (2002). Beating the odds in literacy education: Not the "betting on" but the bettering of schools and teachers? In B. Taylor & P. D. Pearson (Eds.), *Teaching reading, effective schools, accomplished teachers* (pp. 375–387). Mahwah, NJ: Erlbaum.

Duke, N. K. (2000). 3.6 minutes per day: The scarcity of informational texts in first grade. *Reading Research Quarterly, 35,* 202–224.

Duke, N. (2003, December). *Informational text in the primary grades.* Paper presented at the National Reading Conference, Scottsdale, AZ.

Duke, N. K., Bennett-Armistead, V. S., & Roberts, E. M. (2003). Filling the great void: Why we should bring nonfiction into the early-grade classroom. *American Educator, 27*(1), 30–35.

Duke, N. K., & Kays, J. (1998) "Can I say 'once upon a time?'": Kindergarten children developing knowledge of information book language. *Early Childhood Research Quarterly, 13,* 295–318.

Early Childhood-Head Start Task Force (2002). *Teaching our youngest: Guide for preschool teachers and child care and family providers.* Washington, DC: U.S. Department of Education, U.S. Department of Health and Human Services. Available online at http://www.ed.gov/teachers/how/early/ teachingouryoungest/index.html

Educational Research Service (2004). *What can schools do to reduce the achievement gap?* Arlington, VA: Author. Available online at http://www.ers.org/ otsp/otsp3.htm

Education Trust (2004). *Standards in practice.* Available online at http://www2.edtrust.org/EdTrust/ SIP+Professional+Development/ Standards+in+practice.htm

Education Trust and the Council of Chief State School Officers (1999). *Dispelling the myth: High poverty schools exceeding expectations.* Washington, DC: Education Trust.

Edwards, E. C., Font, G., Baumann, J. F., & Boland, E. (2004). Strategies for unlocking word meanings: Teaching morphemic and contextual analysis. In J. F. Baumann and E. Kame'enui (Eds.), *Vocabulary instruction: Research to practice* (pp. 159–176). New York: Guilford.

Elkonin, D. B. (1973). Reading in the USSR. In J. Downing (Ed.), *Comparative reading* (pp. 551–579). New York: Macmillan.

Entwisle, D. R., Alexander, K. L., & Olson, L. S. (2001). Keep the faucet flowing: Summer learning and home environment. *American Educator, 25*(3), 10–15, 47.

Enz, B. (1989). *The 90 per cent success solution.* Paper presented at the International Reading Association convention, New Orleans.

Farr, W. (2004). *Putting it all together: A reading anthology, guided reading, and reader's workshop.* Paper presented at the annual meeting of the Connecticut Reading Association.

Fernald, G. (1943). *Remedial techniques in basic school subjects.* New York: McGraw-Hill. [Reprinted in 1988 by Pro-Ed, Austin, TX.]

Fielding, L. G., Wilson, P. T., & Anderson, R. C. (1986). A new focus on free reading: The role of trade books in reading instruction. In T. E. Raphael (Ed.), *The contexts of school-based literacy* (pp. 149–160). New York: Random House.

Finn, J. D., Gerber, S. B., Achilles, C. M, & Boyd-Zaharias, J. (2001). The enduring effects of small classes. *Teachers College Record, 103,* 145–183.

Fletcher, R., & Portalupi, J. (2001). *Writer's workshop.* Portsmouth, NH: Heinemann.

Foorman, B. & Torgesen, J. K. (2001). Critical elements of classroom and small-group instruction to promote reading success in all children. *Learning Disabilities Research and Practice, 16,* 203–212.

FOSS. (2004a). *Frequently asked questions about the FOSS program: How is reading integrated into the FOSS program?* Available online at http://lhsfoss.org/faq.html#b2

FOSS. (2004b). *Science and literacy.* Available online at http://lhsfoss.org/sciencelit.html#scistories

Fountas, I. C., & Pinnell, G. S. (1996). *Guided reading: Good first teaching for all children.* Portsmouth, NH: Heinemann.

Fountas, I. C., & Pinnell, G. S. (2001). *Guiding readers and writers grades 3–6.* Portsmouth, NH: Heinemann.

Fountas, I. C., & Pinnell. G. S. (2005). *Leveled books for readers grades 3–6.* Portsmouth, NH: Heinemann.

Fredette, L. (2003, May). *Kindergarten extended education program (KEEP).* Paper presented at the International Reading Association Convention, Reno.

Fry, E. (1977). *Elementary reading instruction.* New York: McGraw-Hill.

Funkhouser, J., Fiester, L., O'Brien, E., & Weiner, L. (1995). *Extending learning time for disadvantaged students: An idea book. Vol. 2: Profiles of promising practices.* Washington, DC: U.S. Department of Education. Available online at http://www.ed.gov/pubs/Extending/vol2/index.html

Gambone, M. A., Klem, A. M., Moore, W. P., & Summers, J. A. (n.d.). *First things first: Creating the conditions & capacity for community-wide reform in an urban school district.* Available online at http://www.irre.org/publications

Gaskins, I. W. (2003). Taking charge of reader, text, activity, and context variables. In A. Sweet & C. Snow (Eds.), *Rethinking reading comprehension* (pp. 141–165). New York: Guilford.

Gaskins, I. (2004, December 3). *Benchmark School: Teaching struggling readers to read is just the beginning of recovery.* Paper presented at the National Reading Conference, San Antonio.

Gaskins, I. W., & Baron, J. (1985). Teaching poor readers to cope with maladaptive cognitive styles: A training program. *Journal of Learning Disabilities, 18,* 390–394.

Gaskins, R. W., Gaskins, I. W., Anderson, R. C., & Schommer, M. (1995). The reciprocal relationship between research and development: An example involving a decoding strand for poor readers. *Journal of Reading Behavior, 27,* 337–377.

Gill, T. (2004, May). *Grade-level expectations vs. instructional-level needs: What matters, what doesn't, what gets in the way.* Paper presented at the International Reading Association Convention, Reno.

Gill, C. H., & Scharer, P. L. (1996). "Why do they get it on Friday and misspell it on Monday?" Teachers inquiring about their students as spellers. *Language Arts, 73,* 89–96.

Good, R. H., Simmons, D., Kame'enui, E., Kaminski, R. A., & Wallin, J. (2002). *Summary of decision rules for intensive, strategic, and benchmark instructional recommendations in kindergarten through third grade* (Technical Report No. 11). Eugene: University of Oregon.

Gordon, C. J. (1985). Modeling inference awareness across the curriculum. *Journal of Reading, 28,* 444–447.

Gottlieb, J. (2004, March 9). North End's school success studied. *The Hartford Courant,* pp. B1, B 7.

Grabe, W., & Stoller, F. (2001). Reading for academic purposes: Guidelines for the ESL/EFL teacher. In M. Celce-Murcia (Ed.), *Teaching English as a second or foreign language* (3rd ed., pp. 187–203). New York: Heinle & Heinle.

Greaney, K., Tunmer, W., & Chapman, J. W. (1997). Effects of rime-based orthographic analogy training as an intervention strategy for reading disabled children. In B. Blachman (Ed.), *Foundations of reading acquisition and dyslexia: Implications for early intervention* (pp. 327–345). Hillsdale, NJ: Erlbaum.

Gu, Y., & Johnson, R. K. (1996). Vocabulary learning strategies and language learning outcomes. *Language Learning, 46,* 643–679.

Gunning, T. (1990). *How useful is context?* Unpublished study, Southern Connecticut State University, New Haven.

Gunning, T. (1995). Word building: A strategic approach to the teaching of phonics. *The Reading Teacher, 48,* 484–488.

Gunning, T. (2000). *Assessing the difficulty level of material in the primary grades: A study in progress.* Paper presented at the annual meeting of the National Reading Conference, Scottsdale, AZ.

Gunning, T. (2001). *Building Words.* Boston: Alyn & Bacon.

Gunning, T. (2002). *Assessing and correcting reading and writing difficulties* (2nd ed.). Boston: Allyn & Bacon.

Gunning, T. G. (2003). The role of readability in today's classrooms. *Topics in Language Disorders, 23,* 175–189.

Gunning, T. (2005). *Creating literacy instruction for all students* (5th ed.). Boston: Allyn & Bacon.

Gunning, T. (2006). *Assessing and correcting reading and writing difficulties* (3rd ed.). Boston: Allyn & Bacon.

Guthrie, J. (2003). *Concept-oriented reading instruction.* Available online at http://www.cori.umd.edu/Research/Papers/Classroom.htm

Guthrie, J. (2004, May 1). *Classroom practices promoting engagement and achievement in comprehension.* Paper presented at the International Reading Association Convention, Reno.

Harris, T. L., & Hodges, R. E. (1995). *The literacy dictionary, the vocabulary of reading and writing.* Newark, DE: International Reading Association.

Harris-Rolls, J. (2004, May). *Critical components of a nonfiction reading workshop.* Paper presented at the International Reading Association Convention, Reno.

Hart, B., & Risley, T. (1995). *Meaningful differences in the everyday experiences of young American children.* Baltimore: Brookes.

Hart, B., & Risley, T. R. (2002). Revised Preface to *Meaningful differences in the everyday experience of young American children.* Baltimore, MD: Brookes.

Hassel, E. (1999). *Professional development: learning from the best: A toolkit for schools and districts based on the National Awards Program for Model Professional Development.* Oak Brook, IL: North Central Regional Educational Laboratory. Available online at http://www.ncrel.org/pd/toolkit.htm

Haycock, K. (2001). Helping all students achieve: Closing the achievement gap. *Educational Leadership, 58*(6), 6–11.

Heyns, B. (1978). *Summer learning and the effects of schooling: A national study of school effectiveness for language minority students' long-term academic achievement.* New York: Academic.

Hiebert, E. H., Martin, L. A., & Menon, S. (2005). Are there alternatives in reading textbooks? An examination of three beginning reading programs. *Reading and Writing Quarterly: Overcoming Learning Difficulties, 21*(1), 7–32.

Hill, P. W., & Crévola, C. A. (2000). *Initial evaluation of multi-site replications of a whole-school, design approach to improving early literacy.* Paper presented at International Congress for School Effectiveness and Improvement, Hong Kong.

Hirsch, E. D. (2003). Reading comprehension requires knowledge—of words and the world. *American Educator, 27,* 10–31.

Hoffman, L. (1993, October). *Using readers theater in the general English classroom: Motivating reluctant readers and writers.* Paper presented at the annual meeting of the Connecticut Reading Association, Waterbury.

Hyman, R. T. (1978). *Strategic questioning.* Englewood Cliffs, NJ: Prentice Hall.

International Reading Association & National Association for the Education of Young Children. (1998). Learning to read and write: Developmentally appropriate practices for young children. *The Reading Teacher, 52,* 193–216.

Invernizzi, M., & Hayes, L. (2004). Developmental spelling research: A systematic imperative. *Reading Research Quarterly, 39,* 216–228.

Jencks, C., Steele, C. M., Ceci, S. J., Williams, W. M., Kornhaber, M., Bernstein, J., Rothstein, R., Loury, G. C., & Phillips, M. (1998). America's next achievement test: Closing the black-white test score gap. *The American Prospect, 9*(4). Available online at http://www.prospect.org/print/V9/41/jencks-c.html

Jenkins, J. R., Payton, J. A., Sanders, E. A., & Vadasay, P. F. (2004). Effects of reading decodable text in supplemental first-grade tutoring. *Scientific Studies in Reading, 8,* 53–85.

Jenkins, J. R., Stein, M. L., & Wysocki, K. (1984). Learning vocabulary through reading. *American Educational Research Journal, 21,* 767–777.

Jetton, T. L., & Dole, J. A. (2004). Improving literacy through professional development: Success and sustainability in a middle school. In D. S. Strickland & D. E. Alvermann (Eds.), *Bridging the literacy achievement gap grades 4–12* (pp. 164–182). New York: Teachers College Press.

Jiménez, R. T. (2003, December). *Theoretical promise, perennial problems, and empirical progress, concerning Latino students and literacy.* Paper presented at the National Reading Conference, Scottsdale, AZ.

Johannessen, L. R. (2004). Helping "struggling" students achieve success. *Journal of Adolescent Literacy, 47,* 638–647.

Johns, J. L. (2001). *Basic reading inventory* (8th ed.). Dubuque, IA: Kendall/Hunt.

Johns, J. L., & Lenski, S. D. (2002). *Improving reading strategies & resources* (3rd ed.). Dubuque, IA: Kendall/Hunt.

Johnson, J. F. (2002). High-performing, high-poverty, urban elementary schools. In B. M. Taylor & P. D. Pearson (Eds.), *Teaching reading: Effective schools, accomplished teachers* (pp. 89–114). Mahwah, NJ: Erlbaum.

Johnson, M. S., Kress, R. A., & Pikulski, J. J. (1987). *Informal reading inventories* (2nd ed.). Newark, DE: International Reading Association.

Johnston, F., Invernizzi, M., & Juel, C. (1998). *Book buddies: Guidelines for volunteer tutors of emergent and early readers.* New York: Guilford.

Joyce, B., & Calhoun, E. (1996). School renewal: An inquiry, not a prescription. In B. Joyce & E. Calhoun (Eds.), *Learning experiences in school renewal: An exploration of five successful programs* (pp. 175–190). Eugene, OR: ERIC Clearinghouse on Educational Management.

Joyce, B., & Showers, B. (2002). *Student achievement through staff development* (3rd ed.). Alexandria, VA: Association for Supervision and Curriculum Development.

Juel, C., & Minden-Cupp, C. (2000). Learning to read words: Linguistic units and instructional strategies. *Reading Research Quarterly, 35,* 458–492.

Juel, C., & Roper-Schneider, D. (1985). The influence of basal readers on first-grade reading. *Reading Research Quarterly, 20,* 134–152.

Juniper Gardens Children's Project (2004). *Classwide peer tutoring.* Kansas City, KS: University of Kansas, Author. Available online at http://www.jgcp.ku.edu/index.htm

Karweit, N. (1985, June/July). Should we lengthen the school term? *Educational Researcher, 14*(6), 9–15.

Keene, E. O., & Zimmermann, S. (1997). *Mosaic of thought: Teaching reading comprehension in a reader's workshop.* Portsmouth, NH: Heinemann.

Kibby, M. W, & Wieland, K. (2004). *How readers think during vocabulary acquisition: Findings from the verbal protocols of good readers when encountering unknown words in context with applications to instruction.* Paper presented at the International Reading Association Convention, Reno.

Killgallon, P. A. (1942). *A study of relationships among certain pupil adjustments in language situations.* Doctoral dissertation. State College: Pennsylvanai State College (Doctoral Dissertations, 1943, Vol. 10, p. 75).

King, R., & Torgesen, J. (2000). *Improving the effectiveness of reading instruction in one elementary school: A description of the process.* Tallahassee: Florida State University and Florida Center for Reading Research. Available online at http://www.fcrr.org/science/technicalreports.htm

Kletzien, S. B., & Szabo, R. J. (1998, December). Information text or narrative text? *Children's preferences revisited.* Paper presented at the National Reading Conference, Austin.

Knapp, M. S., Shields, P. M., & Turnbull, B. J. (1992). *Academic challenge for the children of poverty. Summary report.* Washington, DC: U.S. Department of Education.

Laberge, D., & Samuels, S. J. (1974). Toward a theory of automatic information processing in reading. *Cognitive Psychology, 6,* 293–323.

Lake, J. H. (1973). *The influence of wait time on the verbal dimensions of student inquiry behavior. Dissertation Abstracts International, 34,* 6476A. (UMI No. 74-08866)

Lance, K. C. (1994). The impact of school library media centers on academic achievement. *SLMQ, 22*(3). Available online at http://www.ala.org/ala/aasl/aaslpubsandjournals/slmrb/editorschoiceb/infopower/selectlancehtml.htm

Langer, J. A. (2004). Beating the odds: Teaching middle and high school students to read and write well. In R. B. Ruddell & N. J. Unrau (Eds.), *Theoretical models and processes of reading* (5th ed., pp. 1040-1082). Newark, DE: International Reading Association.

Langer, J. A., & Applebee, A. N. (1987). *How writing shapes thinking.* Urbana, IL: National Council of Teachers of English.

Lapp, D., Flood, J., Frey, N., Begley, M., & Moore, K. (2004, May). Enduring success for all K–1 students: Differentiating instruction within a literacy workshop. Paper presented at the International Reading Association Convention, Reno.

Lewis, M., & Samuels, S. J. (2003). *Read more—read better? A meta-analysis of the literature on the relationship between exposure to reading and reading achievement.* Minneapolis: University of Minnesota.

Lindamood, C. H., & Lindamood, P. C. (1975). *The A.D.D. Program: Auditory discrimination in depth.* Allen, TX: DLM Teaching Resources.

Lindamood, P., & Lindamood, P. (1998). *The Lindamood phoneme sequencing program for reading, spelling, and speech: LIPS.* Austin, TX: Pro-Ed.

Lipson, M. Y., Mosenthal, J. H., Mekkelsen, J., & Russ, B. (2004). Building knowledge and fashioning success one school at a time. *The Reading Teacher, 57,* 534–542.

Livingston, N., Kurkijan, C., Young, T., & Pringle, L. (2004). Nonfiction as literature: An untapped goldmine. *The Reading Teacher, 57,* 582–591.

Lyons, C. A., & Pinnell, G. S. (2001). *Systems for change in literacy education: A guide to professional development.* Portsmouth, NH: Heinemann.

MacIver, D. J. (1991). *Enhancing students' motivation to learn by altering assessment, reward, and recognition structures: Year 1 of the incentives for improvement program.* Baltimore: Johns Hopkins University, Center for Research on Effective Schooling for Disadvantaged Students.

Mallette, M. (2003, December). *Accelerated kindergarten: Helping early literacy learners succeed.* Paper presented at the National Reading Conference, Scottsdale, AZ.

Manning, G. L., & Manning, M. (1984). What models of

recreational reading make a difference? *Reading World, 23,* 375–380.

Manzo, A. V. (1969). The ReQuest procedure. *Journal of Reading, 13,* 123–126.

Manzo, A. V., Manzo, V. C., & Albee, J. J. (2004). *Reading assessment for diagnostic-prescriptive teaching* (2nd ed.). Belmont, CA: Wadsworth.

Marshall, S. C. (2002). *Are they really reading? Expanding SSR in the middle grades.* Portland, ME: Stenhouse.

Marzano, R. J. (2004). The developing vision of vocabulary instruction. In J. Baumann & E. Kame'enui (Eds.), *Vocabulary instruction: Research to practice* (pp. 118–138). New York: Guilford.

Marzano, R. J., Gaddy, B. B., & Dean, C. (2000). *What works in classroom instruction.* Aurora, CO: Mid-Continent Research for Education and Learning.

Maslin, P. (2003). *Comparing basal programs.* University of Virginia. Available online at http://readingfirst. virginia.edu/pdfs/Maslin_whitepaper.pdf

May, F. B. (1986). *Reading as communication: An interactive approach.* Columbus, OH: Merrill.

McCormick, S. (1992). Disabled readers' erroneous responses to inferential comprehension questions: Description and analysis. *Reading Research Quarterly, 27,* 55–77.

McDermott, R., & Varenne, H. (1995). Culture as disability. *Anthropology & Education Quarterly, 26,* 324–348.

McHugh, B., & Stringfield, S. (1998). *Implementing a highly specified curricular, instructional, and organizational school design in a high-poverty, urban elementary school: Three year results* (Tech. Rep. No. 20). Baltimore: Johns Hopkins University, Center for Research on the Education of Students Placed At Risk. Available online at http://www.aypf.org/rmaa/pdfs/Calvert.pdf

McIntyre, C. W., & Pickering, J. S. (1995). *Multisensory structured language programs: Content & principles of instruction.* Available online at http://www.ldonline.org/ld_indepth/reading/mssl_methods.html

McKenna, M. C., Kear, D. J., & Ellsworth, R. A. (1995). Children's attitudes toward reading: A national survey. *Reading Research Quarterly, 30,* 934–956.

McKeown, M. G. (1985). The acquisition of word meaning from context by children of high and low ability. *Reading Research Quarterly, 20,* 522–535.

McKeown, M. G., &, Beck, I. L. (2004). Direct and rich vocabulary instruction. In J. Baumann & E. Kame'enui (Eds.), *Vocabulary instruction: Research to practice* (pp. 13–27). New York: Guilford.

McKeown, M. G., Beck, I. L., & Sandora, C. A. (1996). Questioning the author: An approach to developing meaningful classroom discourse. In M. F. Graves, P. Van den Broek, & B. M. Taylor, (Eds.), *The first R, every child's right to read* (pp. 97–119). New York: Teachers College Press.

Means, B., & Knapp, M.S. (1991). Rethinking teaching for disadvantaged students. In B. Means, C. Chelemer, & M. S. Knapp (Eds.), *Teaching advanced skills to at-risk students* (pp. 282–289). San Francisco: Jossey-Bass.

Menon, S., & Hiebert, E. H. (2005). A comparison of first-graders' reading acquisition with little books or literature anthologies. *Reading Research Quarterly, 40,* 12–38.

Mesmer, H. A. (1999). Scaffolding a crucial transition using text with some decodability. *The Reading Teacher, 53,* 130–142.

Meyer, R. J. (2002). Captives of the script: Killing us softly with phonics. *Language Arts, 79,* 452–461.

Minneapolis Public Library (2004). *2004 Summer reading program summary report.* Available online at http://www.mplib.org/minutes/lba111704a.pdf

Minneapolis Public Schools. (2002). *Master basics and learn more in summer session 2002.* Minneapolis: Author. Retrieved August 19, 2002, from www.mpls.k12.mn.us/schools/summer_school_enrichment/index2.shtml

Morris, D. (1999). *The Howard Street tutoring manual: Teaching at-risk readers in the primary grades.* New York: Guilford.

Mosenthal, J., Lipson, M., Sortino, S., Russ, B., & Mekkelsen, J. (2002). Literacy in rural Vermont: Lessons from schools where children succeed. In B. Taylor, B & P. D. Pearson (Eds.), *Teaching reading: Effective schools, accomplished teachers* (pp. 115–140). Mahwah, NJ: Erlbaum.

Moss, B. (1997) A qualitative assessment of first graders' retelling of expository text. *Reading Research and Instruction, 37,* 1–13.

Moustafa, M. (1995). Children's productive phonological recoding. *Reading Research Quarterly, 30,* 464–476.

Murphy, C. (1992). Study groups foster schoolwide learning. *Educational Leadership, 50*(3), 71–74.

Murphy, J. M. (1996). *A follow-up study of delayed readers and an investigation of factors related to their success in young adulthood.* Unpublished doctoral dissertation, University of Pennsylvania, Philadelphia.

Nagy, W. E., & Anderson, R. C. (1984). How many words are there in printed English? *Reading Research Quarterly, 19,* 304–330.

Nash, R. (1993). *NTC's dictionary of Spanish cognates thematically organized.* New York: McGraw-Hill.

Nation, P. (2001). *Learning vocabulary in another language.* Cambridge, England: Oxford University Press.

National Assessment Governing Board. (2004). *Reading framework for the 2005 National Assessment of Educational Progress.* Washington, DC: U.S. Government Printing Office.

National Association for the Education of Young Children (NAEYC) and The National Association of Early Childhood Specialists in State Departments of Education (NAECS/SDE) (2002, 2005). *Early learning standards: Creating the conditions for suc-*

cess. Available online at http://www.naeyc.org/about/positions/early_learning_standards.asp

National Association of School Psychologists (2003). *Position statement on student grade retention and social promotion.* Available online at http://www.nasponline.org/information/pospaper_graderetent.html

National Center on Education and the Economy and the University of Pittsburgh. (1997). *Performance standards. Volume 1, Elementary school.* Washington, DC: Author.

National Commission on Writing (2003). *The neglected "R": The need for a writing revolution.* College Entrance Examination Board. Available online at http://www.writingcommission.org/

National Reading Panel. (2000). *Report of the National Reading Panel. Teaching children to read: An evidence-based assessment of the scientific research literature on reading and its implications for reading instruction* (NIH Publication No. 00-4769). Washington, DC: U.S. Government Printing Office.

National Staff Development Council. (2004). *Standards for staff development.* Available online at http://www.nsdc.org/standards/about/index.cfm

Nessel, D. (1987). The new face of comprehension instruction: A closer look at questions. *The Reading Teacher, 40,* 604–606.

New Standards Speaking and Listening Committee. (2001). *Reading and writing grade by grade: Primary literacy standards through third grade.* Washington, DC: National Center on Education and the Economy & The University of Pittsburgh.

Northwest Regional Educational Laboratory. (2002, May). *Working together for successful paraeducator services.* Portland, OR: Author. Available online at http://www.nwrel.org/request/may2002/foreword.html

Oczkus, L. D. (2003). *Reciprocal teaching at work: Strategies for improving reading comprehension.* Newark, DE: International Reading Association.

Olson, R. K. (1985). Disabled reading processes and cognitive profiles. In D. Gray & J. Kavanaugh (Eds.), *Biobehavioral measures of dyslexia* (pp. 215–234). Timonium, MD: York.

Palincsar, A. S., & Brown, A. L. (1986). Interactive teaching to promote independent learning from text. *The Reading Teacher, 39,* 771–777.

PALS (2004). *Peer-assisted learning strategies.* Nashville: Vanderbilt University. Available online at http://kc.vanderbilt.edu/kennedy/pals/about.html

Pane, N., Mulligan, I., Ginsburg, A., & Lauland, A. (1999). *A guide to continuous improvement management (CIM): For 21st century community learning centers.* Washington, DC: U.S. Department of Education.

Paris, S. G., Paris, A. H., & Carpenter, R. D. (2002). Effective practices for assessing young readers. In B. Taylor & P. D. Pearson (Eds.), *Teaching reading: Effective schools, accomplished teachers* (pp. 141–160). Mahwah, NJ: Erlbaum.

Parsons, L. (1990). *Response journals.* Portsmouth, NH: Heinemann.

Paul, T. D. (2003). *Guided independent reading an examination of the reading practice database and the scientific research supporting guided independent reading as implemented in reading renaissance.* Wisconsin Rapids, WI: Renaissance Learning. Available online at http://www.renlearn. com/girp. htm

PEBC Staff Developers. (2001). *Thinking strategies for learners.* Available online at http://www.pebc. org/publications/strategies.html

Pickett, A., Vasa, S., & Steckelberg, A. (1993). *Using paraeducators effectively in the classroom.* Fastback # 358. Bloomington, IN: Phi Delta Kappa Foundation.

Picucci, A., Brownson, A., Kahlert, R., & Sobel, A. (2002). *Driven to succeed: High-performing, high-poverty, turnaround middle schools Volume I: Cross-case analysis of high-performing, high-poverty, turnaround middle schools.* Austin: Charles A. Dana Center, University of Texas. Available online at http://www. utdanacenter.org/

Pinnell. G. S., & Fountas, I. C., (2002). *The Fountas and Pinnell leveled book list, K–8.* Portsmouth, NH: Heinemann.

Portalupi, J., & Fletcher, R. (2004). *Teaching the qualities of writing.* Portsmouth, NH: Heinemann.

Postman, N. (1979). *Teaching as a conserving activity.* New York: Delacorte.

Powell, G. (1980, December). *A meta-analysis of the effects of "imposed" and "induced" imagery upon word recall.* Paper presented at the National Reading Conference, San Diego (ERIC Document Reproduction Service No. ED 199644.)

Pressley, M., Wharton-McDonald, R., Raphael, L. M., Bogner, K., & Roehrig, A. (2002). Exemplary first-grade teaching. In B. Taylor & P. D. Pearson (Eds.), *Teaching reading: Effective schools, accomplished teachers* (pp. 73–88). Mahwah, NJ: Erlbaum.

Purcell-Gates, V. (1988). Lexical and syntactic knowledge of written narrative held by well-read-to kindergarten and second graders. *Research in the Teaching of English, 22,* 128–160.

Purcell-Gates, V., McIntyre, E., & Freppon, P. (1995). Learning written storybook language in school: A comparison of low-SES children in skills-based and whole language classrooms. *American Educational Research Journal, 32,* 659–685.

RAND Reading Study Group (2004). A research agenda for improving reading comprehension. In R. B. Ruddell & N. J. Unrau (Eds.), *Theoretical models and processes of reading* (5th ed., pp. 720–754). Newark, DE: International Reading Association.

Rapaport, W. J. (2004, May). *What is "context" in contextual vocabulary acquisition? Lessons learned from artificial intelligence and verbal protocol of good readers when they encounter unknown words in context.* Paper presented at the International Reading Association Convention, Reno.

Raphael, T. E. (1986). Teaching question/answer relationships, revisited. *The Reading Teacher, 39,* 516–522.

Raphael, T., & Boyd, F. B. (1997). Writing in the book club program. In S. I. McMahon, T. E. Raphael, V. J. Goatley, & L. S. Parson (Eds.), *The book club connection: Exploring literature-based reading instruction.* New York: Teachers College Press.

Raphael, T. E., Florio-Ruane, S., George, M., Hasty, N. L., & Highfield, K. (2004). *Book club plus: A literacy framework for the primary grades.* Lawrence, MA: Small Planet.

Reading Today (February/ March, 2004). Libraries called key. Available online at http://www. reading.org/publications/reading_today/ samples/RTY-0402-libraries.html

Reeves, D. (2000). The 90/90/90 schools: A case study. In D. Reeves, *Accountability in action* (pp. 185–196). Denver: Center for Resource Assessment.

Reeves, D. (2003). *High performance in high poverty schools: 90/90/90 and beyond.* Denver: Center for Resource Assessment. Available online at http://www. makingstandardswork.com/ResourceCtr/ fullindex.htm

Resnick, L. B. (1999, June 16). Making America smarter. *Education Week on the Web, 18.* Available online at http://www.edweek.org/ew/vol-18/40resnick. h18

Resnick, L. B., & Hall, M. W. (2001). *The principles of Learning: Study tools for educators.* [CD-ROM, version 2.0]. Pittsburgh, PA: University of Pittsburgh, Learning Research and Development Center, Institute for Learning. www. instituteforlearning.org

Reynolds, A. J., & Temple, J. A. (1998). Extended early childhood intervention and school achievement: Age 13 findings from the Chicago Longitudinal Study. *Child Development, 69,* 231–246.

Rivkin, S. G., Hanushek, E. A., & Kain, J. F. (1998). *Teachers, schools and academic achievement, University of Texas-Dallas Texas Schools Project.* Dallas: University of Texas.

Rosenshine, B., & Meister, C. (1994). Reciprocal teaching: A review of the research. *Review of Educational Research, 64,* 479–531.

Rowe, M. B. (1969). Science, silence, and sanctions. *Science for Children, 6*(6), 11–13.

Ruddell, M. R. (1992). Integrated content and long-term vocabulary learning with the vocabulary self-collection strategy. In E. K. Dishner, T. W. Bean, J. E. Readence, & D. W. Moore (Eds.), *Reading in the content areas: Improving classroom instruction* (3rd ed., pp. 190–196). Dubuque, IA: Kendall/Hunt.

Ryder, R. J., & Graves, M. F. (1994). Vocabulary instruction presented prior to reading in two basal readers. *The Elementary School Journal, 95,* 139–153.

Sanders, W. L., & Rivers, J. C. (1996). *Cumulative and residual effects of teachers on future student academic achievement.* Knoxville: University of Tennessee.

Santa, C. M., & Høien, T. (1999). An assessment of Early Steps: A program for early intervention. *Reading Research Quarterly, 34,* 54–79.

Schefelebein, C. A. (2004, May). *The staff developer's role in implementation: Creating a successful environment.* Paper presented at the International Reading Association Convention, Reno.

Schlagal, R. C. (1982). *A qualitative inventory of word knowledge: A developmental study of spelling in grades one through six.* (Doctoral dissertation, University of Virginia). *Dissertation Abstracts International, 47* (03), 915.

Schweinhart, L. J. (2004). *The High/Scope Perry Preschool study through age 40: Summary, conclusions, and frequently asked questions.* Available online at http://www.highscope.org/Research/ PerryProject/perrymain.htm

Seifert, K. L. (2004). *Cognitive development and the education of young children.* Available online at http://home.cc.umanitoba.ca/~seifert/ cogchapweb.html

Share, D. (1995). Phonological recoding and self-teaching: Sina qua non of reading acquisition. *Cognition, 55,* 151–218.

Shearer, B. (1999). *The vocabulary self-collection strategy (VSS) in a middle school.* Paper presented at the forty-ninth annual meeting of the National Reading Conference, Orlando.

Shefelbine, J. (1990). A syllabic-unit approach to teaching decoding of polysyllabic words to fourth- and sixth-grade disabled readers. In J. Zutell & S. McCormick (Eds.), *Literacy theory and research: Analyses from multiple paradigms (thirty-ninth yearbook of the National Reading Conference)* (pp. 223–229). Chicago: National Reading Conference.

Showers, B., Murphy, C., & Joyce, B. (1996). The River City program: Staff development becomes school improvement. In B. Joyce & E. Calhoun (Eds.), *Learning experiences in school renewal: An exploration of five successful programs* (pp. 13–51). Eugene, OR: ERIC Clearinghouse on Educational Management. (ED 401 600).

Singer, H. (1975). The seer technique: A non-computational procedure for quickly estimating readability levels. *Journal of Reading Behavior, 3,* 255–267.

Smith, E. G. (2001). *Texas school libraries: Standards, resources, services, and students' performance.* Austin:

Texas State Library and Archives Commission. Available online at http://www.tsl.state.tx.us/ld/pubs/schlibsurvey/survey.pdf.

Smith, E. J., Pellin, B., J., & Agruso, S. A. (2003). *Bright Beginnings: An effective literacy-focused PreK program for educationally disadvantaged four-year-old children.* Arlington, VA: Educational Research Service.

Stahl, S. A., & Fairbanks, M. M. (1986). The effects of vocabulary instruction: A model-based meta-analysis. *Review of Educational Research, 56,* 72–110.

Stahl, S. A., & McKenna, C. (2002). The concurrent development of phonological awareness , word recognition , and spelling. CIERA Archive #01-07. Atlanta: University of Georgia, Center for the Improvement of Early Reading Achievement. Available online at http://www.ciera.org/library/archive/index.html

Stahl, S. A., Osborne, J., & Lehr, F. (1990). *Beginning to read: Thinking and learning about print: A summary.* Urbana: Center for the Study of Reading, University of Illinois at Urbana-Champaign.

Stallman, A. C., Commeyras, M., Hartman, D. K., Jimenez, R., Kerr, B. M., & Meyer-Reimer, K. (1987, December). *Vocabulary control in basal materials.* Paper presented at the National Reading Conference, St. Petersburg, FL.

Steiner, K. (1986). *Grade retention and promotion.* ERIC Clearinghouse on Elementary and Early Childhood Education No. ED267899. Available online at http://www.ericdigests.org/pre-923/grade.htm

Swanborn, M. S. L., & de Glopper, K. (1999). Incidental word learning while reading: A meta-analysis. *Review of Educational Research, 69,* 261–285.

Taylor, B., Pearson, P. D., Clark, K., & Walpole, S. (2002). Effective schools and accomplished teachers: Lessons about primary-grade reading instruction in low-income schools. In B. Taylor & P. D. Pearson (Eds.), *Teaching reading: Effective schools, accomplished teachers* (pp. 3–72). Mahwah, NJ: Erlbaum.

Taylor, B., Peterson, D., Rodriguez, M. C., Pearson, & P. D., (2002). *The CIERA school change project: Supporting schools as they implement home-grown reading reform.* CIERA Report #2-016. Ann Arbor: University of Michigan, Center for the Improvement of Early Reading Instruction.

Taylor, H. H. (2001). Curriculum in head start. *Head Start Bulletin 67.* Available online at http://www.headstartinfo.org/publications/hsbulletin67/hsb67_00.htm

Templeton, S. (2004). The vocabulary-spelling connection: Orthographic development and morphological knowledge at the intermediate grade level. In J. Baumann & E. Kame'enui (Eds.), *Vocabulary instruction: Research to practice* (pp. 118–138). New York: Guilford.

Thomas, W. P., & Collier, V. P. (2002). *A national study of school effectiveness for language minority students' long-term academic achievement final report: Project 1.1.* Center for Research on Education, Diversity, and Excellence. Available online at http://crede.ucsc.edu/research/llaa/1.1_final.html#top

Thompson, C., & Cunningham, E. (2000). *Retention and social promotion: Research and implications for policy.* ERIC Digest. New York: ERIC Clearinghouse on Urban Education. (ERIC Document Reproduction Service No. ED 449241)

Tierney, R. J., & Readence, J. E. (2005). *Reading strategies and practices: A compendium* (6th ed.). Boston: Allyn & Bacon.

Torgesen, J. K., Morgan, S. T., & Davis, C. (1992). Effects of two types of phonological awareness training on word learning in kindergarten children. *Journal of Educational Psychology, 84,* 364–370.

Traub, N., & Bloom, F. (2000). *Recipe for reading* (New century ed.). Cambridge, MA: Educators Publishing Service.

Tunmer, W. E., & Chapman, J. W. (1999). Teaching strategies for word identification. In G. B. Thompson & T. Nicholson (Eds.), *Learning to read: Beyond phonics and whole language* (pp. 74–102). New York: Teachers College Press, Columbia University.

Uhry, J. K., & Ehri, L. (1999). Ease of segmenting two- and three-phoneme words in kindergarten: Rime cohesion or vowel salience? *Journal of Educational Psychology, 91,* 594–603.

U.S. Department of Education. (1993). *Summer challenge. Model summer programs for disadvantaged students.* Washington, DC: Author.

Valadez, J. D., & Freve, Y. (2002). *A preliminary summary of findings from a study of the effects of hands-on/inquiry-based instruction on SAT 9 reading scores.* Fresno, CA: Fresno Unified School District. Available online at http://sustainability2002.terc.edu/invoke.cfm/page/143

van Bon, W. H., Boksebeld, L. M., Font-Freide, T. A., & van den Hurk, A. J. (1991). A comparison of three methods of reading-while-listening. *Journal of Learning Disabilities, 24,* 471–476.

Vandervelden, M. C., & Siegel, L. S. (1997). Teaching phonological processing skills in early literacy: A developmental approach. *Learning Disabilities Quarterly, 20,* 63–81.

Vandivere, S., Gallagher, M., & Moore, K. A. (2004). *Changes in children's well-being and family environments.* Available online at http://www.urban.org/url.cfm?ID=310912

Wade, S. (1983). A synthesis of the research for improving reading in the social studies. *Review of Educational Research, 53,* 461–497.

Walker-James, D., Jurich, S., & Estes, S. (2001). *Raising minority academic achievement: A compendium of education programs and practices.* Washington, DC: American Youth Policy Forum.

Walmsley, S. A. (1978–1979). The criterion referenced measurement of an early reading behavior. *Reading Research Quarterly, 14,* 574–604.

Walpole, S., & McKenna, M. C. (2004). *The literacy coach's handbook: A guide to research-based practice.* New York: Guilford.

Walsh, K. (2003). Basal readers: The lost opportunity to build the knowledge that propels comprehension. *American Educator, 27,* 24–27. Available online at http://www.aft.org/pubs-reports/american_educator/spring2003/Basal_readers.pdf

Wang, J. H., & Guthrie, J. T. (2004). Modeling the effects of intrinsic motivation, extrinsic motivation, amount of reading, and past reading achievement on text comprehension between U.S. students and Chinese students. *Reading Research Quarterly, 39,* 162–186.

Wasik, B. A. (1998). Volunteer tutoring programs in reading: A review. *Reading Research Quarterly, 33,* 266–292.

Wasik, B. A., & Slavin, R. E. (1993). Preventing early reading failure with one-to-one tutoring: A review of five programs. *Reading Research Quarterly, 28*(2), 178–200.

West, J., Denton, K., & Germino-Hausken, E. (2000). *Early childhood longitudinal study: Kindergarten class of 1998–99.* Washington, DC: National Center for Educational Statistics. Available online at http://nces.ed.gov/pubsearch/pubsinfo.asp?pubid=2000070

Westby, C. E. (1999). Assessing and facilitating text comprehension problems. In H. W. Catts & A. G. Kamhi (Eds.), *Language and reading disabilities* (pp. 154–223). Boston: Allyn & Bacon.

White, T. G., Power, M. A., & White, S. (1989). Morphological analysis: Implications for teaching and understanding vocabulary growth. *Reading Research Quarterly, 24,* 283–304.

Wigfield, A. (1997). Children's motivations for reading and writing engagement. In J. Guthrie & A. Wigfield (Eds.), *Motivating readers through integrated instruction* (pp. 14–33). Newark, DE: International Reading Association.

Wilson, B. (1997). *Wilson reading system.* Millbury, MA: Wilson Learning Center.

Wilson, B., & Corbett, H. (2001). *Listening to urban kids: School reform and the teachers they want.* New York: State University of New York Press.

Wilson, P. (1986). *Voluntary reading.* Paper presented at the annual convention of the International Reading Association, Philadelphia.

Wilson, P. (1992). Among nonreaders: Voluntary reading, reading achievement, and the development of reading habits. In C. Temple & P. Collins (Eds.), *Stories and readers: New perspectives on literature in the elementary classroom* (pp. 157–169). Norwood, MA: Christopher-Gordon.

Winne, R. H., Graham L., & Prock, L. (1993). A model of poor readers' text-based inferencing: Effects of explanatory feedback. *Reading Research Quarterly, 28,* 536–566.

Wirt, J., Choy, S., Rooney, P., Provasnik, S., Sen, A., & Tobin, R. (2004). *The condition of education 2004* (NCES 2004-077). U.S. Department of Education, National Center for Education Statistics. Washington, DC: U.S. Government Printing Office.

Wolf, M., & Katzir-Cohen, T. (2001). Reading fluency and its intervention. *Scientific Studies of Reading, 5,* 211–238.

Zeno, S. M., Ivens, S. H., Millard, R. T., & Duvvuri, R. (1995). *The educator's word frequency guide.* Brewster, NY: Touchstone Applied Science Associates.

Children's Books

Aliki. (1979). *The two of them.* New York: Greenwillow.

Byars, B. C. (1977). *The pinballs.* New York: Harper & Row.

Freeman, D. (1978). *A pocket for Corduroy.* New York: Puffin.

Geisel, T. (1957). *The cat in the hat.* New York: Random House.

Geisel, T. (1974). *There's a wocket in my pocket.* New York: Random House.

George, J. C. (1988). *My side of the mountain.* New York: Dutton.

Greenfield, E. (1988). *Grandpa's face.* New York: Philomel.

Kelly, I. (2003). *It's a hummingbird's life.* New York: Holiday House.

Morris, A. (1993). *Hats, hats, hats.* New York: HarperCollins.

Paulsen, G. (1987). *Hatchet.* New York: Viking.

Pringle, L. (1997). *An extraordinary life: The story of a Monarch butterfly.* New York: Orchard.

Spinelli, E. (2004). *Do you have a hat?* New York: Simon & Schuster.

Wolf, J. (1996). *Daddy, could I have an elephant?* New York: Greewillow.

Yee, W. H. (1996). *Mrs. Brown went to town.* Boston: Houghton Mifflin.

Zion, G. (1956) *Harry the dirty dog.* New York: HarperCollins.

Index